First Principles of the Essay

First Principles of the Essay

ROBERT MILES

Harper & Row, Publishers

New York
Evanston
San Francisco
London

First Principles of the Essay
Copyright © 1971 by Robert Miles

Standard Book Number: 06-044442-8

LIBRARY OF CONGRESS CATALOG CARD NUMBER: 70-137816

Acknowledgments

Grateful acknowledgment is made for permission to quote from the following works:

FREDERICK LEWIS ALLEN, *The Great Pierpont Morgan*. Harper & Row, 1949. Reprinted by permission of Harper & Row, Publishers, Inc.

FREDERICK LEWIS ALLEN, *Since Yesterday*. Harper & Row, 1940. Reprinted by permission of Harper & Row, Publishers, Inc.

STUART CHASE, *For This We Fought*. Twentieth Century Fund, New York, N.Y., 1946.

W. MACNEILE DIXON, *The Human Situation*. Reprinted by permission of St. Martin's Press, Inc. and Edward Arnold (Publishers) Ltd., London.

CHARLES W. FERGUSON, "A Sane Approach to Style," from *Say It with Words*, by Charles W. Ferguson. Copyright © 1959 by Charles W. Ferguson. Reprinted by permission of Alfred A. Knopf, Inc.

ERIC GOLDMAN, *Rendezvous with Destiny*. Copyright 1952, © 1956 by Alfred A. Knopf, Inc. Reprinted by permission.

DONALD HALL, "A Hundred Thousand Straightened Nails," adapted from *String Too Short to be Saved* by Donald Hall. Copyright © 1960, 1961 by Donald Hall. All rights reserved. Reprinted by permission of The Viking Press, Inc.

MICHAEL HARRINGTON, *The Other America*. Copyright © Michael Harrington 1962. Reprinted by permission of The Macmillan Company.

GILBERT HIGHET, *Poets in a Landscape*. Copyright © 1957 by Gilbert Highet. Reprinted by permission of Alfred A. Knopf, Inc.

ROBERT MAYNARD HUTCHINS, "Gate Receipts and Glory." Copyright 1938, Curtis Publishing Company. Reprinted by permission of *The Saturday Evening Post*.

ROBERT MAYNARD HUTCHINS, "Why Go to College?" Copyright 1938, Curtis Publishing Company. Reprinted by permission of *The Saturday Evening Post*.

X. J. KENNEDY, "Who Killed King Kong?" Reprinted by permission of the author and the editors of *Dissent*.

LEO KIRSCHBAUM, an exercise derived from *Clear Writing*. Reprinted by permission of the Estate of Leo Kirschbaum.

ROBERT LYND, *The Pleasures of Ignorance*. Reprinted by permission of Methuen & Co. Ltd., London.

DWIGHT MACDONALD, "Too Big," from *Memoirs of a Revolutionist*. Reprinted from *Politics*, December, 1946.

MARYA MANNES, "Park Avenue," from *The New York I Know* by Marya Mannes. Copyright, ©, 1961, 1960, 1959 by Marya Mannes. Reprinted by permission of J. B. Lippincott Company.

F. O. MATTHIESSEN, THEODORE DREISER. Published by William Sloane Associates. Copyright, 1951, by William Sloane Associates, Inc. Reprinted by permission of William Morrow and Company, Inc.

W. SOMERSET MAUGHAM, *The Summing Up*. Copyright 1938 by W. Somerset Maugham. Reprinted by permission of Doubleday & Company, Inc.

H. L. MENCKEN, "The Genealogy of Etiquette." Copyright 1919 by Alfred A. Knopf, Inc. and renewed 1947 by H. L. Mencken. Reprinted from *Prejudices: First Series* by H. L. Mencken, by permission of the publisher.

H. L. MENCKEN, "The Libido for the Ugly." Copyright 1927 by Alfred A. Knopf, Inc. and renewed 1955 by H. L. Mencken. Reprinted from *A Mencken Chrestomathy* by permission of the publisher.

H. L. MENCKEN, "Professor Veblen." Copyright 1919 by Alfred A. Knopf, Inc. and renewed 1947 by H. L. Mencken. Reprinted from *A Mencken Chrestomathy* by permission of the publisher.

JOSEPH MITCHELL, "The Cave Dwellers," from *McSorley's Wonderful Saloon.* Reprinted by permission of Meredith Press.

JOSEPH MITCHELL, "The Rats on the Waterfront," from *The Bottom of the Harbor.* Copyright 1944, by Joseph Mitchell. Reprinted by permission of Harold Ober Associates Incorporated.

THOMAS B. MORGAN, "The Heroes of Teen-Agers," from *Self-Creations: 13 Impersonalities* by Thomas B. Morgan. Reprinted by permission of Holt, Rinehart and Winston, Inc.

FREDERIC MORTON, "The Art of Courtship." Copyright © 1957, Curtis Publishing Company. Reprinted by permission of *Holiday.*

The New American Roget's College Thesaurus in Dictionary Form by arrangement with The New American Library, Inc., New York.

GEORGE ORWELL, *Down and Out in Paris and London,* from *The Orwell Reader,* edited by Richard Rovere. Reprinted by permission of Brandt & Brandt, Miss Sonia Brownell, and Secker & Warburg, Ltd.

GEORGE ORWELL, "Such, Such Were the Joys," from *Such, Such Were the Joys and Other Essays* by George Orwell. Copyright, 1945, 1952, 1953, by Sonia Brownell Orwell. Reprinted by permission of Harcourt Brace Jovanovich, Inc., Miss Sonia Brownell, and Secker & Warburg, Ltd.

GEORGE ORWELL, "A Hanging," from *Collected Essays, Journalism and Letters,* I. Reprinted by permission of Harcourt Brace Jovanovich, Inc., Miss Sonia Brownell, and Secker & Warburg, Ltd.

GEORGE ORWELL, "Marrakech," from *Collected Essays, Journalism and Letters,* I. Reprinted by permission of Harcourt Brace Jovanovich, Inc., Miss Sonia Brownell, and Secker & Warburg, Ltd.

GEORGE ORWELL, *Homage to Catalonia,* from *The Orwell Reader,* edited by Richard Rovere. Reprinted by permission of Harcourt Brace Jovanovich, Inc., Miss Sonia Brownell, and Secker & Warburg, Ltd.

GEORGE ORWELL, *The Road to Wigan Pier.* Reprinted by permission of Harcourt Brace Jovanovich, Inc., Miss Sonia Brownell, and Secker & Warburg, Ltd.

GEORGE ORWELL, "Inside the Whale," from *Collected Essays, Journalism and Letters,* I. Reprinted by permission of Harcourt Brace Jovanovich, Inc., Miss Sonia Brownell, and Secker & Warburg, Ltd.

VANCE PACKARD, "The Ad and the Id." First published in *Harper's Bazaar,* August, 1957.

VANCE PACKARD, "America the Beautiful—and Its Desecraters." Copyright © 1961, by The Atlantic Monthly Company, Boston, Mass. Reprinted by permission.

HORTENSE POWDERMAKER, *Hollywood, The Dream Factory.* Little, Brown and Co., 1950.

FRITZ REDLICH AND JUNE BINGHAM, *The Inside Story.* Copyright 1953 · by June R. Bingham. Reprinted by permission of Alfred A. Knopf, Inc.

PAUL ROBERTS, *Understanding English.* Reprinted by permission of Harper & Row, Publishers, Inc.

RICHARD ROVERE, "Wallace." Copyright 1950 The New Yorker Magazine, Inc. Reprinted by permission.

ARTHUR M. SCHLESINGER, JR., *The Age of Jackson.* Copyright 1945, by Arthur M. Schlesinger, Jr. Reprinted by permission of Little, Brown and Co.

GEORGE STEINER, "Close-Up of Britain's Censor." Copyright © 1956 by The New York Times Company. Reprinted by permission.

JOHN D. STEWART, "Vulture Country." Copyright © 1959, by The Atlantic Monthly Company, Boston, Mass. Reprinted by permission.

WILLIAM STRUNK, JR., AND E. B. WHITE, *The Elements of Style.* Copyright © 1959 by The Macmillan Company. Reprinted by permission.

ALLEN TATE, *Stonewall Jackson.* Copyright 1928 by Minton Balch & Co. Reprinted by permission of G. P. Putnam's Sons.

EDWIN WAY TEALE, "Winged Bullets," from *Adventures in Nature* by Edwin Way Teale. Copyright 1937, 1959 by Dodd, Mead & Company, Inc. Reprinted by permission.

JAMES THURBER, "Soapland." Copyright 1948 by James Thurber. *From The Beast in Me—and Other Animals,* published by Harcourt Brace Jovanovich, Inc. Originally printed in *The New Yorker.*

JAMES THURBER, "University Days." Copyright 1933, © 1961 James Thurber. From *My Life and Hard Times,* published by Harper & Row. Originally printed in *The New Yorker.*

JAMES THURBER, "Courtship Through the Ages." Copyright 1942 James Thurber. From *My World—and Welcome to It,* published by Harcourt Brace Jovanovich, Inc. Originally printed in *The New Yorker.*

Time, "The Numbers Game." Copyright Time Inc. 1960. Courtesy *Time.*

MARK TWAIN, "Fenimore Cooper's Literary Offenses." Reprinted by permission of Harper & Row, Publishers, Inc.

MARK TWAIN, *Life on the Mississippi.* Reprinted by permission of Harper & Row, Publishers, Inc.

ROBERT PENN WARREN, Introduction to Ernest Hemingway's *A Farewell to Arms.* Copyright 1949 Charles Scribner's Sons. Reprinted by permission.

ROBERT PENN WARREN, "A Lesson Read in American Books." Copyright © 1955 by The New York Times Company. Reprinted by permission.

Webster's New World Dictionary of the American Language, College Edition. Copyright 1968 by The World Publishing Company, Cleveland, Ohio.

E. B. WHITE, "Progress and Change," from *One Man's Meat* by E. B. White. Copyright 1939 by E. B. White. Reprinted by permission of Harper & Row, Publishers, Inc.

RUPERT WILKINSON, "The Slave Trade." Copyright © 1962, Harrison-Blaine of New Jersey, Inc. Reprinted by permission of *The New Republic.*

EDMUND WILSON, "A Great Magician," from *The Shores of Light.* Reprinted by permission of the author.

Contents

Preface

The purpose of this text is to present basic rules that will enable the student to write clear, persuasive essays.

The student is not asked to cover difficult material of doubtful utility. The apprentice writer for whom the book is intended is not ready for such subjects as classical rhetoric, formal logic, or stylistics; nor is he ready to emulate the subtle strategies employed by sophisticated essayists. Instead, he needs clear guidance: definite, dependable "first principles."

These principles are of course not to be regarded as ultimate truths. "Seek simplicity," said Whitehead, "and distrust it." The textbook simplifies; but even though the student may benefit from the simplicity, he must learn to distrust it—must see that the rules presented here are provisional and open to exception and that once he has mastered the rules he may frequently have excellent reasons for violating them.

Each chapter explains one basic principle, or several related principles, and provides illustrative passages and an abundance of exercises. There are more exercises than any student is likely to need. The teacher, after gauging his students' ability as writers, can assign as many exercises as will be helpful but not so many that the exercises will become tedious busy-work. Many of the exercises might be termed "composition substitutes": without requiring entire compositions, these exercises engage the student in activities necessary to the writing of paragraphs and essays. Obviously such exercises, instructive though they may be, cannot truly substitute for the student's writing of compositions, cannot teach him all he may learn by writing paragraphs and essays of his own; nevertheless, the text offers few assignments in the writing of paragraphs and essays, on the grounds that the topics for a student's compositions are best chosen by the student and his teacher, not by a textbook.

The four major sections of the book treat (1) the paragraph, (2) the short essay, (3) the long or "complex" essay, and (4) prose style. The sections need not be taught in the order in which they are presented; but it is recommended that the section on the paragraph be taught first (since it introduces ideas basic to the other three sections) and, of course, that the short essay be dealt with before the long. (My own preference is to teach the paragraph first, then prose style, then the essay. Thus the student can concentrate on prose style while still writing single paragraphs, before he tries to handle the essay and its more difficult problems of reasoning and organization. And for my part, I can comment on style more thoroughly if I am reading a single paragraph rather than an essay.)

A list of all the people who have helped with this book would be very long indeed. I am indebted to many authors whose books offer valuable instruction in essay-writing. Some of the authors are mentioned in the text, particularly in the section entitled "The Writer's Library"; to the others I address a general thank-you. I am grateful also to the friends who have offered encouragement, to the colleagues who have offered advice, and to the hundreds of students who have used, and have helped me develop, the lessons now contained in this book.

I wish to name the people who have been most helpful. Among them are Byrd and Macaulay Bruton, Grant Bruton, Charles Church, Alex Hirschberg, Muriel Ladenburg, Garry Meyers, Wyatt Teubert, and Professors Reginald Archambault, Ronald Freeman, Lee Jacobus, Richard Lehan, Geraldine Murphy, and Robert Tisdale. I am indebted to several students— Barbara Cohen, Mark Halliday, and Jennifer Reed—for allowing me to adapt their compositions for use in the text. The people at Harper & Row have all been remarkably helpful, particularly Leslie Carola. And I owe special thanks to my wife, whose work as editor and typist has been indispensable.

This book is dedicated, with love and gratitude, to my wife and to my mother.

ROBERT MILES

Introduction

It is a popular belief that skill in essay-writing is a mysterious gift granted to a few lucky people; although these inspired few produce superior essays as easily as pen can move across paper, the uninspired many will never write good prose.

The premise of this text, however, is that the would-be writer should not yearn for some occult power over words but should consider himself an apprentice learning a craft. The writer of essays has a definite job to do —the effective expression of ideas and information—and there are basic principles he can learn in order to do the job well. Marianne Moore has compared writing to carpentry and has spoken of writing as "a trade embodying principles attested by experience." And the author William Morris went so far as to insist that "talk of inspiration is sheer nonsense; there is no such thing. It is a mere matter of craftsmanship."

The Paragraph

II

The paragraph is a fairly new invention, still ignored by many writers as recently as 1600. Montaigne's *Essays* (1588) used no paragraphing whatever, although one essay occupied 150 pages. (Imagine reading 150 pages of complex argument about the limits of knowledge without a single indentation to mark a stopping-place.) Modern editors divide that essay into paragraphs; the modern reader expects an occasional pause that will let him straighten out his thoughts before he reads on.

Today's great diversity of paragraphs ranges from the one-sentence sputter of the gossip columnist to the elaborate creations of such master essayists as Edmund Wilson and James

Baldwin. But you need not learn all varieties. The following chapters present one kind of paragraph that will serve you well in your essays.

Terms referring to this sort of paragraph are widely known—*topic sentence, development, transition,* and so on—but many people who mouth the terms understand them so inadequately that they cannot write a competent paragraph and do not realize what a demanding task it is. To produce a successful paragraph, the writer must conceive an idea, state it, clarify it, and defend it; he must arrange his thoughts logically and link them for easy reading. In short, he must apply all the essential skills of thought and expression. And once he has mastered the paragraph, he can easily learn to write an essay.

1

The Paragraph - Idea

Each paragraph should be based on one central idea. We can call it the *paragraph-idea*.

Only a certain kind of idea can serve as a paragraph-idea. This idea could serve: "That book makes several questionable charges against American women." But this one could not: "That book contains 257 pages and has a green cover." Why the first but not the second? Because the first contains *abstract* and *general* wording that needs to be explained and defended in a paragraph, while the second is *specific* and needs no discussion.

Specific wording refers to particular things or people. *The checkered shirt Sam is wearing* is specific because it refers to a particular thing; *Bertrand Russell* is specific because it refers to a particular person. *William Faulkner, Senator Robert Taft, the mechanical pencil Barbara is using, the tarantula perched on that mound of sand*—these are all specific wordings.

General wording, however, refers to *groups* of things or people. *Shirt* refers to any shirt at all and is therefore more general than *the checkered shirt Sam is wearing*. And wording becomes more general as it refers to larger groups. *Shirt* is less general than *clothing; Bertrand Russell* is less general than *English philosopher*, which is less general than *Englishman*. Here is a longer sequence that moves from specific to general:

William Faulkner's novel *The Sound and the Fury*
a novel by William Faulkner
a work of literature by William Faulkner
a work of literature by a writer of the modern American South
a work of modern American literature
a work of American literature
a work of literature
a piece of written material
a means of communication

And so on, until we reach an all-encompassing term such as *thing* or *entity*.

Abstract wording is not quite the same as general wording. Abstract words refer to intangibles: *love, beauty, pain, injustice, heat, ugliness, democracy*. We can touch voters, politicians, people on a jury, but not the abstraction *democracy*. We can see specific instances of *ugliness*—a dog crushed on the highway, a leech sucking blood—but not the idea of ugliness. If someone uses the abstract word *hot*, we may ask him to be more definite. To some people *hot* means 70 degrees; to others, 110; it means one thing to an Alaskan, another to a Californian. The speaker, in order to be more specific, could give concrete evidence of the heat: the dampness of his shirt, the swelling of his feet, the glaring sidewalk, the melting asphalt in the roadway. And if he wants to be quite specific, he can give us a temperature reading: 107 degrees Fahrenheit.

Now it can be seen why only a certain kind of idea may serve as a paragraph-idea. A specific statement needs no paragraph: "That book contains 257 pages and has a green cover" requires no elaboration. A paragraph-idea, however, rises above concrete particulars and enters the dubious region of abstractions and generalities. It ventures an opinion; it raises questions and doubts. If a writer says, "That book makes several questionable charges against American women," the reader may demand that so abstract and general a statement be explained, then defended with evidence. ("What are the charges?" he may ask. "And why are they questionable?") Such a statement can serve as a paragraph-idea. The paragraph will supply the necessary explanation and evidence.

How it accomplishes this task is the subject of the next chapter.

Practice

I. Find the most general term in each list.

1. a. blotter
    b. wastebasket
    c. office equipment
    d. desk
    e. filing cabinet
2. a. ruby
    b. diamond
    c. pearl
    d. jewel
    e. sapphire
3. a. tree
    b. oak
    c. elm
    d. pine
    e. maple
4. a. tree
    b. flower
    c. weed
    d. shrub
    e. plant
5. a. elm
    b. mountain laurel
    c. dandelion
    d. gorse
    e. plant

II. Find the abstraction in each list.

1. a. town meeting
    b. democracy
    c. senator
    d. voting machine
    e. Gettysburg Address

2. a. sunset
    b. lovely girl
    c. Van Gogh's "Sunflowers"
    d. beauty
    e. a lake in Maine

3. a. steel
    b. Jack Dempsey
    c. diamonds
    d. strength
    e. United States Air Force

4. a. squirrel
    b. hummingbird
    c. fox
    d. Red Grange
    e. quickness

5. a. student
    b. learning
    c. book
    d. pen
    e. classroom

III. Give a specific instance for each general term. If the general term were *man,* you might give *Alexander the Great, Socrates, Bela Bartok, Sidney Hook, Albert Jay Nock,* or any other man.

1. person
2. woman
3. student
4. actress
5. playwright
6. novelist
7. novel by Dickens
8. room
9. piece of furniture
10. seat

IV. For each of the following abstractions, give a concrete word or phrase that could serve as an illustration. For the abstract word *hot,* the concrete illustration could be *melting asphalt.* For the abstraction *fear,* the illustration could be *a rabbit chased by dogs.*

1. excitement
2. danger
3. dignified
4. efficient
5. artistry
6. courageous
7. speedy
8. education
9. intelligent
10. cold

V. Arrange the terms in each of the following lists in a specific-to-general order.

1. a. red
    b. color
    c. primary color
    d. Chinese red

2. a. inanimate object
    b. precious stone
    c. thing
    d. Hope Diamond
    e. mineral
    f. diamond
    e. college football game
    f. event involving competition
    g. Army-Navy football game

3. a. actor
    b. mammal
    c. actor who often appeared in motion-picture Westerns
    d. Gary Cooper
    e. actor in motion pictures
    f. man
    g. actor who appeared in the motion-picture Western *High Noon*
    h. human being

5. a. to move quickly
    b. to sprint
    c. to sprint one hundred yards in 9.8 seconds
    d. to run
    e. to move

6. a. British work of literature
    b. *Man and Superman*
    c. work of literature by George Bernard Shaw
    d. play by George Bernard Shaw
    e. work of literature
    f. British work of literature written after 1875

4. a. athletic event
    b. football game
    c. event
    d. Army-Navy football game of 1965

VI. Not only single terms but whole statements can be compared for their relative generality. This statement is fairly specific and concrete: "Sam dropped his chemistry text on the sidewalk." But here is a much more general and abstract statement about the same event: "Most students are careless with their textbooks." A statement even more general and abstract would be: "Young people neglect their belongings."

In each of the following exercises, arrange the statements in a sequence beginning with the most specific and concrete, and ending with the most general and abstract.

1. a. John felt a sharp pain in his arm.
    b. John felt pain.
    c. John felt a sharp pain.

2. a. The postal service is a mess.
    b. Our mailman often makes mistakes.

    c. Mailmen are inefficient.

    d. Last Thursday our mailman neglected to pick up our outgoing mail.

3. a. Senator Stentorian always opposes measures for the protection of migratory birds.

    b. Yesterday Senator Stentorian, a member of the Federalist party, voted against the bill for the protection of the yellow-headed griping-bird.

    c. The Federalists hate all American wildlife.

    d. The Federalist party believes that all wildlife should be destroyed.

    e. The Federalist party believes that the federal government should not assume any responsibility for protecting American wildlife.

4. a. Stanley has a violent temper.

    b. Stanley habitually becomes so angry that he hits things.

    c. Young people have violent tempers.

    d. This afternoon, in a moment of rage, Stanley banged his fist on his desk top.

    e. Boys have violent tempers.

    f. Stanley often shows anger.

    g. The human being is a violent, raging animal.

5. a. Salinger's fiction shows that people today are restless and discontented.

    b. Modern literature shows that mankind has become hopelessly unhappy.

    c. In *The Catcher in the Rye*, by J. D. Salinger, Holden Caulfield is dissatisfied with the schools he has attended.

    d. Modern American fiction reflects the anxiety and despair felt today by most Americans.

    e. Many of Salinger's characters are dissatisfied with the life they have been living.

VII. Answer this question in a few sentences: Why must a writer be cautious in using abstractions and generalities?

2

Clarifying and Defending the Paragraph=Idea

A statement with abstract and general wording may leave a reader skeptical. After proposing such a statement, the writer must take measures to make it convincing. He must *clarify the statement* if it is vague. He must *defend it with evidence.* And to do these jobs well, he must *keep his wording specific.*

To illustrate these points, let us say that a person distrustful of vague language attends a political meeting at which one speaker finishes with these words:

> . . . The network of the Communist conspiracy has thrown its tentacles around our federal government. But we should not be surprised at this new progress on the devil's part. For

in the history of mankind, whenever an unsuspecting nation has adopted welfare-state policies, the people have soon afterward given up their rights to a dictatorial central government.

To challenge these windy abstractions and generalities, our skeptical person asks questions pointing out the speaker's lack of clarification and evidence. (Questions 1, 3, and 5 ask for clarification; 2, 4, and 6, for evidence.)

1. Do you mean that some members of our federal government are members of the Communist party and are actively supporting Communism?
2. If so, which people? And exactly how are they helping Communism?
3. What do you mean by the term "welfare state"? Exactly how does a welfare state operate?
4. In the past, what nation has become a welfare state and then a dictatorship?
5. Do you mean that our central government is becoming dictatorial?
6. In what particular actions has it shown itself to be dictatorial? Can you give examples?

Pressed to abandon his verbal smoke screen and talk in specific terms, the speaker will probably retreat into silence.

All this applies to the writing of paragraphs because every paragraph-idea contains abstract, general wording. After stating the idea, the writer may have to clear up obscurities by restating it in more specific terms. Then he must defend it with specific evidence.

Suppose his paragraph-idea is this: "Mark Twain held a low opinion of mankind." The abstract, general phrase *low opinion of mankind* seems vague. Does the writer mean that Twain thought people cruel, crazy for power, or what? Did the opinion apply to all mankind without exception? Though some paragraph-ideas need no clarification, certainly this one does. It must be restated in more specific terms: "Twain insisted that most people give little thought to their beliefs and accept whatever they are told, no matter how ludicrous it may be." ("Mankind" has become "most people," and Twain's "low opinion" is said to be based not on men's cruelty or lust for power but on their gullibility.) Next the statement must be defended with specific evidence: anecdotes, examples, details, statistics, direct quotations—anything that will help convince a skeptical reader. (Incidentally, these specifics will add further clarification and dispel any lingering doubts about the meaning of the paragraph-idea.)

Now the paragraph is complete:

Mark Twain held a low opinion of mankind.   *Paragraph-idea*

He insisted that most people give little thought to   *Clarification*
their beliefs and accept whatever they are told, no   *with specific*
matter how ludicrous it may be.   *wording*

Sometimes Twain used half-humorous aphorisms to   *Defense*
insult man's foolishness: "April 1. This is the day   *with specific*
upon which we are reminded of what we are on the   *evidence*
other three hundred and sixty-four." And, "The
asylums can hold the sane people, but if we tried to
shut up the insane we should run out of building
materials." These aphorisms pinch, but in his essay
Corn-Pone Opinions Twain slashes deep. The essay
argues that few people think their ideas through:

> I am persuaded that a coldly-thought-out and
> independent verdict upon a fashion in clothes, or
> manners, or literature, or politics, or religion, or
> any other matter that is projected into the field of
> our notice and interest is a most rare thing if it
> has indeed ever existed ... We are creatures of
> outside influences: as a rule we do not think, we
> only imitate.

"We only imitate." The essay states that since we
wish to seem admirable in the eyes of other people,
we accept their beliefs and convince ourselves that
whatever ideas are popular must also be true. Our
credulity is further satirized in Twain's fiction. In
Huckleberry Finn, for instance, Twain shows two
charlatans, the King and the Duke, bamboozling one
crowd of people after another. Finally it seems that
Twain must agree with the King when he has the
King say, "Hain't we got all the fools in town on our
side? And ain't that a big enough majority in any
town?"

This might convince even the reader who has cherished the popular stereotype of Mark Twain—that jovial, cigar-smoking humorist who wrote pleasant anecdotes about the good old days.

For another example of effective paragraph development we can turn to the writings of George Orwell. Because he dealt with subjects about which most readers had done little thinking, Orwell was especially thorough in clarifying and defending his ideas. His *Down and Out in Paris and London* depicts the hardships of poverty, and the following paragraph from that book tells something he learned while living on six francs a day in a Paris boardinghouse.

You discover . . . the secrecy attaching to poverty.	*Paragraph-idea*
At a sudden stroke you have been reduced to an income of six francs a day. But of course you dare not admit it—you have got to pretend that you are living quite as usual. From the start it tangles you in a net of lies, and even with the lies you can hardly manage it.	*Clarification with specific wording*
You stop sending clothes to the laundry, and the laundress catches you in the street and asks you why; you mumble something, and she, thinking you are sending the clothes elsewhere, is your enemy for life. The tobacconist keeps asking why you have cut down your smoking. There are letters you want to answer, and cannot, because stamps are too expensive. And then there are your meals—meals are the worst difficulty of all. Every day at meal times you go out, ostensibly to a restaurant, and loaf an hour in the Luxembourg Gardens, watching the pigeons. Afterward you smuggle your food home in your pockets. Your food is bread and margarine, or bread and wine, and even the nature of the food is governed by lies. You have to buy rye bread instead of household bread, because the rye loaves, though dearer, are round and can be smuggled in your pockets. This wastes you a franc a day. Sometimes, to keep up appearances, you have to spend sixty centimes on a drink, and go correspondingly short of food. Your linen gets filthy, and you run out of	*Defense with specific evidence*

soap and razor blades. Your hair wants cutting, and
you try to cut it yourself, with such fearful results
that you have to go to the barber after all, and spend
the equivalent of a day's food. All day you are
telling lies, and expensive lies.

Orwell begins by stating his paragraph-idea. But because the
phrase *secrecy attaching to poverty* is vague, he restates the idea
in more specific terms. Then he defends the idea with ample evidence from his own experience.

Thus a single paragraph can advance an idea, explain it,
and convince the reader of its truth.

Practice

I. The following statements might serve as paragraph-ideas, but the
statements are somewhat vague. Clarify each idea by adding a
sentence or two restating the idea in more specific terms.

1. She is a changeable person.
2. He is actually quite different from the sort of person he at
first appears to be.
3. This essay is not convincing.
4. Though his methods were unorthodox, he was an effective
teacher.
5. This motion picture tries to be up-to-date.
6. This book is not worth reading.
7. Charles Darwin's writings caused a furor.
8. This book has aroused the public's indignation.
9. He thought the theories of Sigmund Freud to be obnoxious.

II. Each of the following paragraphs contains an initial statement of
the paragraph-idea, then a clarification of the idea, then supporting evidence. Determine where the paragraph-idea ends and
clarification begins, and where clarification ends and supporting
evidence begins.

1. Cooper's word-sense was singularly dull. When a person has a poor ear for music he will flat and sharp right
along without knowing it. He keeps near the tune, but it is
not the tune. When a person has a poor ear for words, the

result is a literary flatting and sharping; you perceive what he is intending to say but you also perceive that he doesn't *say* it. This is Cooper. He was not a word-musician. His ear was satisfied with the *approximate* word. I will furnish some circumstantial evidence in support of this charge. My instances are gathered from half a dozen pages of the tale called *Deerslayer*. He uses "verbal" for "oral"; "precision" for "facility"; "phenomena" for "marvels"; "necessary" for "predetermined"; "unsophisticated" for "primitive"; "preparation" for "expectancy"; "rebuked" for "subdued"; "dependent on" for "resulting from"; "fact" for "conjecture"; "precaution" for "caution"; "explain" for "determine"; "mortified" for "disappointed"; "meretricious" for "factitious"; "materially" for "considerably"; "decreasing" for "deepening"; "increasing" for "disappearing"; "embedded" for "inclosed"; "treacherous" for "hostile"; "stood" for "stooped"; "softened" for "replaced"; "rejoined" for "remarked"; "situation" for "condition"; "different" for "differing"; "insensible" for "unsentient"; "brevity" for "celerity"; "distrusted" for "suspicious"; "mental imbecility" for "imbecility"; "eyes" for "sight"; "counteracting" for "opposing"; "funeral obsequies" for "obsequies."

MARK TWAIN, "Fenimore Cooper's Literary Offenses"

2. Such a memory as [Mr. Brown's] . . . is a great misfortune. To it, all occurrences are of the same size. Its possessor cannot distinguish an interesting circumstance from an uninteresting one. As a talker, he is bound to clog his narrative with tiresome details and make himself an insufferable bore. Moreover, he cannot stick to his subject. He picks up every little grain of memory he discerns in his way, and so is led aside. Mr. Brown would start out with the honest intention of telling you a vastly funny anecdote about a dog. He would be "so full of laugh" that he could hardly begin; then his memory would start with the dog's breed and personal appearance; drift into a history of his owner; of his owner's family, with descriptions of weddings and burials that had occurred in it, together with recitals of congratulatory verses and obituary poetry provoked by the same; then this memory would recollect that one of these

events occurred during the celebrated "hard winter" of such-and-such a year, and a minute description of that winter would follow, along with the names of people who were frozen to death, and statistics showing the high figures which pork and hay went up to. Pork and hay would suggest corn and fodder; corn and fodder would suggest cows and horses; cows and horses would suggest the circus and certain celebrated bare-back riders; the transition from the circus to the menagerie was easy and natural; from the elephant to equatorial Africa was but a step; then of course the heathen savages would suggest religion, and at the end of three or four hours' tedious jaw, the watch would change, and Brown would go out of the pilot-house muttering extracts from sermons he had heard years before about the efficacy of prayer as a means of grace. And the original first mention would be all you had learned about that dog, after all this waiting and hungering.

MARK TWAIN, *Life on the Mississippi*

3. If nature gave us logic, she appears to be singularly lacking in what she bestows. For she herself drives no straight furrow, and exhibits an inconsistency which in a man would be accounted madness. Her habit is to turn upon herself, wound and inflict herself, undoing with her left hand what she has done with her right. What more inharmonious than that she should send hailstones to the destruction of her own blossoms and fruits, tempests upon the crops she has herself ripened to the harvest? The meteorite that, in 1908, fell in Siberia, about 100 tons in weight, destroyed the forest in which it fell for a radius of about forty miles. The lightning splits the tree, and sets the forest aflame. The sand of the desert or the encroaching sea turns fertile fields into barren wastes, and reduces whole populations to distress or starvation. It is her own features which nature thus rends and mangles. Wild beasts destroy 3000 persons every year in India, and 20,000 die of snake-bite. There are 700 million sufferers from malaria in the world. Forty percent of the children born in Central China perish from cold or famine before they are a year old.

W. MACNEILE DIXON, *The Human Situation*

euphemism / polite language

taking / beating around the bush

4.   Linguistic diffidence can take various forms. One is what we call *euphemism*. This is the tendency to call a spade "a certain garden implement" or women's underwear "unmentionables." It is stronger in some eras than others and in some people than others but it always operates more or less in subjects that are touchy or taboo: death, sex, madness, and so on. Thus we shrink from saying "He died last night" but say instead "passed away," "left us," "joined his Maker," "went to his reward." Or we try to take off the tension with a lighter cliché: "kicked the bucket," "cashed in his chips," "handed in his dinner pail." We have found all sorts of ways to avoid saying *mad:* "mentally ill," "touched," "not quite right upstairs," "feeble-minded," "innocent," "simple," "off his trolley," "not in his right mind." Even such a now plain word as *insane* began as a euphemism with the meaning "not healthy."

PAUL ROBERTS, *Understanding English*

3

Building a Solid Defense

The writer's attempt to defend a paragraph-idea will be defeated before it starts if the idea is too broad and complex. Here is a presumptuous writer's defense of an inflated paragraph-idea. (The paragraph-idea is underlined twice, the clarification once.)

Grading systems are harmful to students. A to F, zero to 100, one to four—it makes no difference which system is used. Any grading system will hurt students in one important way. It will make them care more about grades than about what they learn. Consider my roommate, who strains at his

English compositions every night. He yearns to get good grades but cares little about what he is writing. Now, it might be argued that he is simply following the dictates of human nature, and that most people are inherently indifferent to intellectual studies. But no one could say this who has watched children at their studies. They enjoy them thoroughly. Then they begin to worry about grades, and their enjoyment ends. They are told repeatedly that grades are important, that grades in the present determine careers in the future. And the students become so anxious about grades that they can find little pleasure in their studies, with the ultimate result that they regard studies as a necessary evil and think grades to be the real end of education.

Though the paragraph-idea is provocative, the defense is weak. The writer says that children enjoy their studies but gives no evidence to support the contention. He charges that older students care more about grades than about learning, but his evidence is an isolated example, his roommate. (Nor does he establish that the roommate is indifferent to learning; since the writer offers no evidence to the contrary, the roommate's hard work every night may indicate a deep concern for his studies.) But if we grant the writer both points—children enjoy learning, older students do not—there is still an enormous hole in his argument. Grading, he says, is the one cause of this growing indifference towards learning. But why place the full blame on grading? Perhaps other factors are responsible—teachers, textbooks, overcrowded classes, parents, television, easy access to automobiles, and so on.

The more holes we poke in this defense, the more obvious it becomes that the writer's so-called paragraph-idea, though it might be handled in a long essay, cannot be defended in a paragraph. It must be narrowed down. Even the following revision would be too broad and problematic: "Grading systems have been harmful to most of the students on our campus." But this next revision could serve as a paragraph-idea: "Many students on our campus care more about grades than about learning."

But a properly limited paragraph-idea is no guarantee

that the writer will build a strong defense. He might erect a flimsy barricade that would fall at the first attack:

> Many students on our campus care more about grades than about learning. They are more concerned about the grades on their school record than about the skills and knowledge those grades are meant to reflect. My roommate, for instance, openly admits that he works for grades rather than for anything he might learn. He chose to major in English because in his opinion the English department offers mostly "snap" courses, courses that give high grades for little work. He complains incessantly about the "sludgy stuff" he has to read for English courses, and he never reads an unassigned book. Though he works several hours each night on his papers for English, he doesn't really care about what he is writing. When his papers come back he ignores the instructor's written comments, searches anxiously for the grade-mark, sighs with satisfaction to find a B, then tosses the paper in the wastebasket.

Though the roommate is convicted of caring "more about grades than about learning," the paragraph has not kept its promise to prove "many students" guilty of the charge. One cynical, grade-grubbing student is not "many" grade-grubbers.

Upon recognizing the weakness in his paragraph, the writer could keep his portrait of the roommate, but then strengthen the argument by speaking of "many students on our campus." He could continue—

> . . . then tosses the paper in the wastebasket. Nor is my roommate unusual. Snap courses is a favorite topic of conversation on the campus. One has only to overhear the casual talk at the Student Union building and the fraternity houses to know how eager the typical student is to find easy courses, whether he will learn anything from them or not. Or consider the annual issue the campus newspaper devotes to its "evaluation" of courses. More than two-thirds of each "evaluation" is concerned with how difficult the textbooks tend to be, how rigid the instructor is about absenteeism, and how many A's and F's he gives. And after the courses are

over for the term, many of the students still care more about grades than about what they have or have not learned. Listen to them as they emerge from the final exams. When they ask each other "How did you do?" they are asking about the grades they'll probably get, not about whether anybody has learned anything. Finally, listen to a group of students discussing their grade-cards, complacently bragging about getting a B or C "without knowing a thing."

A thorough defense can have an extra benefit. Besides convincing the reader to accept the paragraph-idea as valid, the defense can catch the reader's interest with a vivid portrayal of people and things and events. Consider the sort of defense that might develop from this paragraph-idea: "The car has obviously been involved in an accident." Perhaps the car has run under the rear end of a truck, so that the windshield is splintered and the roof has been mashed in as if by a huge sledgehammer. Looking inside, one sees the things left behind: a man's crushed hat, a copy of *Playboy*, a child's doll. . . . Or consider a less sensational example, the paragraph about grade-grubbers. Though the paragraph-idea is mildly interesting, the development contains the details that give the paragraph some life and drama: the students eager for snap courses, the students who boast of getting a B or a C without learning anything, and the unhappy roommate, hating his studies but anxious about grades.

Practice

I. Which of these statements might serve as paragraph-ideas? Which are too broad and questionable to be defended in a single paragraph?

1. The third edition of *Webster's New International Dictionary* is based on a mistaken conception of the purposes a dictionary should serve.

2. Joe Gould looked like a bum and lived like a bum.

3. The *New English Bible* has changed a good many of the respected, often-quoted phrases that appear in the *King James Version*.

4. In the Spanish Civil War the Communists showed themselves to be more concerned with power politics than with the welfare of the proletariat.
5. The smoking of cigarettes is harmful to health.
6. Though Sacco and Vanzetti were judged guilty in a court of law, the evidence did not justify that verdict.
7. In *By Love Possessed* James Gould Cozzens makes much use of clumsy, roundabout wording.
8. In some of the popular stories told about him, Davy Crockett was given superhuman powers.
9. The new proliferation of expert "city planners" and "city managers" will in the end be the solution to the problems of our cities.

II. Evaluate the following paragraphs for the thoroughness with which they defend their central ideas. In evaluating each paragraph, answer these questions:

A. What is the paragraph-idea?
B. Does the paragraph support its main idea with convincing evidence?
C. If the evidence is inadequate, could the paragraph be improved by the addition of further evidence? Or is its main idea too general and abstract to be defended in a single paragraph?

1. The people of Soapland are subject to a set of special ills. In the world of radio soap opera, people seem to suffer from illnesses and diseases that rarely strike people who belong to the real world. One such affliction is forgetfulness in its extreme form—amnesia. This is a difficulty rarely encountered in real life, but in Soapland it is the cause of many a dramatic situation. Whenever the story-line slows down a bit, you can depend on amnesia to enter in and thicken the plot. The hero of one soap opera wandered around in a forgetful daze for several months last year. When he finally regained his memory, he found that his affairs had worked out just as well as if he had had his brain fully at work all that time. Notice how convenient amnesia can be. This is fortunate for the people of Soapland, because amnesia strikes almost as often there as the common cold in our world. And so it is with a whole set of ailments

and afflictions. They are rare in our real world. But in Soapland they become scourges threatening vast numbers.

2. In the year 1950 the total number of paperbacks sold was no less than 214 million; in 1951 the figure jumped to 231 million. Two-thirds or more of these paper-bound books, to be sure, were novels or mysteries—thus falling into classifications too inclusive to be reassuring to the public taste—and some were rubbish by any tolerable standard. But consider these sales figures (as of January, 1952) for a few paper-bound books: Tennessee Williams's *A Streetcar Named Desire*, in play form, over half a million; George Orwell's *Nineteen Eighty-four*, over three-quarters of a million; Norman Mailer's *The Naked and the Dead*, over a million and a quarter; Ruth Benedict's *Patterns of Culture*, 400,000; and—to cite an incontrovertibly classical example—a translation of *The Odyssey* (with an abstract cover design), 350,000. And remember that these sales, which are above and beyond book-club sales and regular bookstore sales, have been achieved in a nation of avid magazine readers. There is an interesting phenomenon here. There is a big American market for good writing if it and the price are within easy reach.

3. In every field during the thirties, well-known reformers gave evidence of the trend toward acceptance of Communist ideology. A leading liberal journalist carried on an open flirtation with the Communists in the writers' union of which he was a part. A noted historian reinterpreted periods of American history according to Communist dogma. Famous magazines published highly sympathetic reports on Communist activities. An important religious leader apologized for the actions and policies of Communism. Standards of "proletarian literature" rose to importance in many leading magazines. One of the most prominent of the guilds for American writers was no more than an offshoot of a Communist guild, and yet it could command for its manifestos liberal names of great renown. More than any other book, Lincoln Steffens's *Autobiography* brought the first jabs of political excitement to college students in the thirties, and the *Autobiography* was quite revealing in its attitude toward Soviet Russia.

4. The nation's aquatic wildlife has been finding our inland waters increasingly unbearable. Some months ago, ten thousand scarce canvasback and redhead ducks were destroyed on the Detroit River by the release of untreated sewage. Thousands of dead fish have turned up in the Passaic River, from which several northern New Jersey communities have been drawing their drinking water. Fish can no longer survive in parts of New Hampshire's Merrimack, once famed for its fishing. Many of the salmon runs of the Northwest are being disrupted by the fact that the fish, in their relentless migrations up to the headwaters of streams, perish in badly polluted stretches of these streams. The Public Health Service reports finding in many parts of the country that fish taken alive from waters downstream from sewer outfalls have been sickly or dwarfed. And it reports finding hundreds of cases of complete fish kills. By "complete," it means that every fish, in stretches of water up to nineteen miles long, has perished.

5. If you knew where to look, you were able to find evidence that a major economic depression was upon us. First, the lack of food in some districts. This provided plain evidence of the country's economic plight. Second, there were those settlements ironically known as "Hoovervilles" in various places around the country. Anyone seeing the conditions in these villages could hardly doubt that hard times had come. Third, there were the people who could be seen in any empty places they could find, struggling just to keep the fires of life burning. The sight of these people was another reminder of economic hardship. Fourth, there was the vastly increased number of transients, drifters ever on the move, searching half-aimlessly. Within a brief period the number of migrants had grown enormously, and many of them were quite young. The number of migrants had become so large in some sections of the country that the efforts of police to restrain them had proved ineffectual. Here was still further evidence, obvious to all who dared to look, that the nation was in the midst of an economic catastrophe.

6. In learning to sell to our subconscious, the persuaders soon discovered unsuspected areas of tension and guilt.

Self-indulgent and easy-does-it products are a significant sector of the total American market, yet Americans, it seems, have in them a larger streak of Puritanism than is generally recognized. For instance, the hidden attitude of women toward labor-saving devices is decidedly surprising. Working wives can accept them, but the full-time housewife is liable to feel that they threaten her importance and creativity. The research director of an ad agency sadly explained the situation as follows: "If you tell the housewife that by using your washing machine, drier or dishwasher she can be free to play bridge, you're dead!—the housewife today already feels guilty about the fact that she is not working as hard as her mother. Instead, you should emphasize that appliances free her to have more time with her children." Makers of ready-mixes and foods with "built-in maid service" ran into the same sort of problem. In the early days, the packages promised to take over all the work, but wives were not grateful for this boon. A leading motivational analyst, James Vicary, has stated the reason. Cake-making, he finds, is steeped in creative symbolism for women—it is, in fact, "a traditional acting out of the birth of a child." This feeling shows up in our folklore in such jokes as the one which says that brides whose cakes fall obviously can't produce a baby yet.

7.   Television has had several damaging effects on American society. This palpable truth is vigorously denied by the purveyors of television, since most of them stand to gain additional thousands from it, as well as what they have already taken from the American public under false pretenses. But the much-maligned Newton Minow, then chairman of the FCC, was understating the case when he charged television with being a "vast wasteland." It is worse than a wasteland; it is an infested bog in which disease flourishes. Consider just one affliction it has brought upon us—the national crime-rate, which, according to J. Edgar Hoover and other authorities, is steadily rising. The number of murders in our country each year is one of the highest among civilized nations—even after differences in population are accounted for. For instance, "the United States homicide rate is ten times that of Denmark," according to scholar Herbert

Hendin. Surely the prevalence of television in our society has had a bearing on our crime-rate. If an American family watches television for an evening, as many families do, it can be sure of seeing at least two or three deaths by violence. Thus our people, including the young, become habituated to violence and accept it as "just one of those things." All the worse when the violence is caused by the "good guys"—the police or private detective or heroic marshal. For then the youngster learns not only that violence is an inevitable part of society but also that it is an *approved* part. When a man thinks he is in the right, the message is, then he may resort to violence. Indeed, he may well be viewed as a coward if he does *not* resort to violence. And this is only one of the vile attitudes spread among us by the infection of television.

H idea

~~And~~ sub topic sentences

first

2nd

3rd

Specific illustration

4

Topic and Subtopic Sentences

Up to this point we have discussed the paragraph's content. Now we must discuss how the content can best be arranged. Ideally the writer devises so clear an arrangement for each paragraph that the reader can follow the line of reasoning from start to finish with no difficulty whatever.

PLACEMENT OF THE PARAGRAPH-IDEA AND ITS CLARIFICATION

Generally speaking, the writer should state his paragraph-idea in a sentence or two (the *topic sentence*) somewhere in the paragraph. Usually it is advisable to put the topic sentence near the beginning of the paragraph and to supply clarification, if any is needed, directly afterward. Thus the reader can get a firm hold on the paragraph-idea before he tries to trace its development. The longer and more complicated the paragraph is, the more grateful he will be for an opening statement to guide him. For an example of this form, look again at the paragraph about Mark Twain's "low opinion of mankind" (see p. 15) or George Orwell's paragraph about "the secrecy attaching to poverty" (pp. 16–17) or the paragraph about students preoccupied with grades (pp. 23–24).

Even if a paragraph is not particularly long or complicated, the writer does well to supply the topic sentence at the beginning:

> Many . . . experts in home selling have recently cited "snob appeal" as one of the great secret weapons. One strategy . . . is to drop some French phrases . . . Newspaper advertisements of housing developers [have been] drenched in French. One, penned by a developer in Manetto Hills, Long Island, exclaimed: *"C'est Magnifique! Une maison Ranch très originale avec 8 rooms, 2½ baths . . . 2-Cadillac garage . . . $21,990 . . . No cash for veterans."* And a builder in Bel Air, Florida, unveiled his $42,000 chateaus by proclaiming his prototype *"une autre maison contemporaine de Floride."* His entire ad, except for the price, was in French. Some builders began referring to their 15′ x 18′ living room as "The Living Forum" or the "Reception Galleria," and to their 9′ x 14′ bedroom as "The Sleeping Chamber." A split-level house on Long Island became "a Georgian split, with a bi-level brunch bar in a maitre d' kitchen." And tiny parcels of ground became "Huge ½-acre Estate Sites." According to one rule-of-thumb, cited by a building consultant, any lot larger than one-fourth acre can reasonably be described as an "estate," and anything larger than half an acre can be labeled as a "farm."
>
> VANCE PACKARD, *The Status Seekers*

The opening sentence states the main point of the paragraph so that as the reader makes his way through the development he will know what all the French phrases and fancy labels are meant to convey: real-estate salesmen rely on snob appeal.

To be doubly sure of giving the reader safe passage, the writer can state the main idea twice: at the beginning of the paragraph and again at the end. This strategy, though appropriate in some short paragraphs, is especially valuable in a long paragraph whose accumulation of detail could otherwise make the reader forget the point of it all. A word-for-word reiteration, however, would be tiresome, and in the following paragraph Frederic Morton rewords his second statement of the paragraph-idea almost entirely.

> Romance has become as large a component of the American dream as success. Road signs shout romance, transmitters croon it, juke-boxes yowl it. Romance bulges on Cinemascope screens, flickers from TV sets, gleams on magazine covers. Laboratories hum from coast to coast making cheeks more kissable, hands more touchable, legs more lookable. Factories whir to resculpt waistlines, bosomize bosoms, cleopatrize eyes. A whole galaxy of industries labors to lure him to her with perfumes, parasols, pendants; her to him with the checks on his shirt, the monogram on his belt, the shaving lotion on his jaws. Under all this pressure, how pitiful the American who cannot command the smile of a sexpot.
>
> "The Art of Courtship," *Holiday*, March, 1957

Occasionally the writer may wish to save the topic sentence for the middle of the paragraph or the end. When he does this, however, he must be careful to give the reader clear guidance through the earlier sections of the paragraph. In the following paragraph—George Orwell's description of the foolish way he was taught history—the topic sentence is held back until the middle. Orwell begins by explaining that his teacher, nicknamed "Bingo," asked no questions but those found on past examinations for the Harrow History Prize. Orwell tells what the questions were like, provides examples of them, and only then reaches his main idea. But notice how skillfully he guides the reader through the first part of the paragraph: he offers several intimations of what the main idea will be. Notice, too, that after the idea has been stated Orwell echoes it again toward the end of the paragraph, still intent that the reader not lose track. (Those helpful references to the main idea are italicized; the topic sentence itself is underlined.)

There was in those days *a piece of nonsense* called the Harrow *History* Prize, an annual competition for which many preparatory schools entered. At Crossgates we mugged up every paper that had been set since the competition started. They were *the kind of stupid question that is answered by rapping out a name or a quotation*. Who plundered the Begams? Who was beheaded in an open boat? Who caught the Whigs bathing and ran away with their clothes? Almost all our *historical teaching* was on this level. <u>History was a series of unrelated, unintelligible but—in some way that was never explained to us—important facts with resounding phrases tied to them.</u> Disraeli brought peace with honour. Clive was astonished at his moderation. Pitt called in the New World to redress the balance of the Old.... Bingo ... revelled in this kind of thing. I recall positive orgies of dates, with the keener boys leaping up and down in their places in their eagerness to shout out the right answers, and *at the same time not feeling the faintest interest in the meaning of the mysterious events they were naming.*

"1587?"
"Massacre of St. Bartholomew!"
"1707?"
"Death of Aurangzeeb!"
"1713?"
"Treaty of Utrecht!"
"1773?"
"The Boston Tea Party!"
"1520?"
"Oh, Mum, please, Mum—"
"Please, Mum, please, Mum! Let me tell him, Mum!"
"Well; 1520?"
"Field of the Cloth of Gold!"
And so on.

"Such, Such Were the Joys," *Collected Essays, Journalism and Letters,* IV

There are other ways to handle the topic sentence. Sometimes a writer can split it in two, letting one half come early in the paragraph, the other half later; or he may dispense with the topic sentence altogether and merely suggest his paragraph-idea without stating it. But if an experiment with such techniques might cause difficulties for the reader, then the writer should employ one of the more conservative policies discussed above.

SUBTOPIC SENTENCES

In a complicated paragraph the writer can supply *sub-topic sentences* to keep his reader heading in the right direction.

Suppose the writer is planning a paragraph with this as its main idea: "Though most of the time Mr. Griff is obnoxious, every year at Christmastime he is almost likable." Because this is vague, the writer adds clarification: "During most of the year Mr. Griff affects a noisy cheerfulness and amiability, but in the rush of the Christmas season he reveals his true meanness and anxiety, so that one begins to feel some sympathy for the man." But now, as the writer reviews the mass of notes he has compiled, he finds that his development of this idea could become a sprawling confusion. How can he keep the paragraph clear? First, he can put his topic sentence at the head of the paragraph instead of burying it in the middle. Second, he can divide the paragraph into several sections, each dealing with a single subject. (The paragraph can be divided into two sections—one dealing with Mr. Griff's usual demeanor, the other with the Christmastime revelation of the true Mr. Griff.) Third, at the beginning of each subordinate section, the writer can supply a *subtopic sentence:* he can *begin each section by stating its main point.*

Ready to write the paragraph, he opens with the topic sentence: "Though most of the time Mr. Griff is obnoxious, every year at Christmastime he is almost likable." The writer would ordinarily provide clarification next, but the subtopic sentences can act as substitutes. Here is the first: "During most of the year Mr. Griff affects a noisy cheerfulness and amiability."

Now come specifics about Mr. Griff's customary phoniness. Then the second subtopic sentence: "But in the rush of the Christmas season he reveals his true meanness and anxiety, so that one begins to feel some sympathy for the man." Then come specifics about Mr. Griff's Christmastime desperation. The paragraph would look like this:

Though most of the time Mr. Griff is obnoxious, every year at Christmastime he is almost likable. During most of the year Mr. Griff affects a noisy cheerfulness and amiability. _____

_____
_____. _____
_____
_____
_____. _____

_____. But in the rush of the Christmas season he reveals his true meanness and anxiety, so that one begins to feel some sympathy for the man. _____

_____
_____. _____
_____
_____. _____

For added clarity the writer may announce in advance the number of subtopic sentences his paragraph will contain. Topic sentences like these can serve the purpose:

There are two sides to Mr. Griff's personality—one obnoxious, the other almost likable.

There were three basic reasons for the failure of Jackson's raid.

Mrs. O'Donnell's deterioration began with two agonizing events: the death of her husband and a vicious argument with her best friend.

Joseph Mitchell uses this technique in the following paragraph. (The main idea is underlined twice; the subtopic sentences, once.)

Many aged people reconcile themselves to the certainty of death and become tranquil; Mr. Flood is unreconcilable. There are three reasons for this. First, he deeply enjoys living. Second, he comes of a long line of Baptists and has a nagging fear of the hereafter, complicated by the fact that the descriptions of heaven in the Bible are as forbidding to him as those of hell. "I don't really want to go to either one of those places," he says. He broods about religion and reads a chapter of the Bible practically every day. Even so, he goes to church only on Easter. On that day he has several drinks of Scotch for breakfast and then gets in a cab and goes to a Baptist church in Chelsea. For at least a week thereafter he is gloomy and silent. "I'm a God-fearing man," he says, "and I believe in Jesus Christ crucified, risen, and coming again, but one sermon a year is all I can stand." Third, he is a diet theorist—he calls himself a seafoodetarian—and feels obliged to reach a spectacular age in order to prove his theory. He is convinced that the eating of meat and vegetables shortens life and he maintains that the only sensible food for man, particularly for a man who wants to hit a hundred and fifteen, is fish.

Old Mr. Flood

(The reason the first subtopic sentence is not developed is that Mr. Mitchell develops the idea at great length elsewhere in *Old Mr. Flood*. Anyone who reads the book is convinced that Mr. Flood "deeply enjoys living.")

If subtopic sentences appear in all paragraphs, even the shortest and simplest, the reader will feel that he is being led by the hand like a child. But he will welcome these extra signposts in the more elaborate paragraphs that might otherwise cause him to be puzzled and frustrated.

Practice

I. Find the topic sentences in the following paragraphs. Some of the paragraphs may state the main idea more than once.

1. In every field [during the thirties], well-known reformers gave evidence of the trend [toward acceptance of Communist

ideology]. The liberal's most beloved journalist, Heywood Broun, carried on an open flirtation with the Communists in his Newspaper Guild, while W. E. B. DuBois published *Black Reconstruction*, an interpretation of that pivotal period in American history which could have been written in Moscow. The *New Republic* and the *Nation* published highly sympathetic reports on Soviet activities, and John Haynes Holmes, the revered leader of liberal Protestantism, adopted an attitude he later described as one that "defended, or at least apologized for, evils in the case of Russia which horrified us wherever else they appeared." While standards of "proletarian literature" rose to importance in many of the leading critical reviews, the League of American Writers, an offshoot of the International Union of Revolutionary Writers, could command for its manifestos liberal names of the prominence of Van Wyck Brooks, Erskine Caldwell, John Dos Passos, Theodore Dreiser, Clifton Fadiman, Waldo Frank, Granville Hicks, Langston Hughes, Robert Morss Lovett, Lewis Mumford, Lincoln Steffens, Edmund Wilson, and Richard Wright. More than any other book, Lincoln Steffens's *Autobiography* brought the first jabs of political excitement to college students in the thirties, and the *Autobiography* was a description of Steffens's transition from muckraking to his growing enthusiasm over Soviet Russia.

ERIC GOLDMAN, *Rendezvous with Destiny;*
A History of Modern American Reform

2.   The young J. Pierpont Morgan went to New Orleans to make a several weeks' first-hand study of the cotton and shipping business. He spent a good deal of time exploring the waterfront, ranging from dock to dock and boarding the vessels tied up there to find out how their imports and exports were handled. One day, boarding a ship, he found it loaded with coffee in bags and learned that its captain was in a quandary: the man to whom the shipment had been consigned could not be found, and the captain, consulting his Brazilian headquarters, had been instructed to dispose of the cargo of coffee as best he could. Pierpont saw an opportunity. He went off with samples of the coffee in his pockets, made the rounds of the local merchants, collected orders, returned to the ship, and bought *the entire cargo* with a sight draft on

Duncan, Sherman and Co. The next day, within a few hours of the time when his superiors in New York began spluttering with rage at his temerity, he was able to telegraph them that he had sold every bag of coffee in the cargo to various merchants at a neat profit, and was forwarding to Duncan, Sherman and Co. the checks made out in payment. What the men in New York had supposed to be a foolhardy operation had been a methodically prudent one; he had collected orders for every bag before he bought the shipload. But in addition to being a prudent transaction, it had been a bold one for a neophyte.

Beginner

                FREDERICK LEWIS ALLEN, *The Great Pierpont Morgan*
                (The wording has been changed slightly.)

Contrast

3.   Another phase of life here which has lost something through refinement is the game of croquet. We used to have an old croquet set whose wooden balls, having been chewed by dogs, were no rounder than eggs. Paint had faded, wickets were askew. The course had been laid out haphazardly and eagerly by a child, and we all used to go out there on summer nights and play good-naturedly, with the dogs romping on the lawn in the beautiful light, and the mosquitoes sniping at us, and everyone in good spirits, racing after balls and making split shots for the sheer love of battle. Last spring we decided the croquet set was beyond use, and invested in a rather fancy new one with hoops set in small wooden sockets, and mallets with rubber faces. The course is now exactly seventy-two feet long and we lined the wickets up with a string; but the little boy is less fond of it now, for we make him keep still while we are shooting. A dog isn't even allowed to cast his shadow across the line of play. There are frequent quarrels of a minor nature, and it seems to me we return from the field of honor tense and out of sorts.

           E. B. WHITE, "Progress and Change," *One Man's Meat*

4.   Not one style, but an awareness of many, so that the one best suited to the subject can be chosen—this should be the controlling principle of one who seeks to improve self-expression. The best craftsmen will be found to follow this principle. In the heyday of *The American Mercury* and in his "Prejudices," H. L. Mencken showed himself a master of protest, dealing with Dr. Coolidge, the Bible Belt, the Sahara

of the Bozart, mountebanks, and charlatans, and lashing out against hocus-pocus. In "The American Language" he showed an occasional flash of humor, but for the most part he wrote with smooth regard for reader and subject, and he respected the dignity of both. He was not the same Mencken. And in his reminiscent book, "Happy Days," being the recounting of his Baltimore childhood, his prose was properly benign, his mood mellow, and his style quiet. There was no need to whambang. In "The American Language" he was a scholar and he wrote in an appropriate manner. In his "Prejudices" he was the Bad Boy of Baltimore, in "Happy Days" an old man recalling. In each case he adapted his writing to the requirements of the job.

CHARLES W. FERGUSON, "A Sane Approach to Style,"
Say It with Words

5. Let us visit George and Amy Lansing. . . . George is an investment banker with a Wall Street firm, Amy is the daughter of a prominent corporation lawyer, lately deceased. . . . George is on many boards, Amy on many charities. Their large rooms are carpeted wall-to-wall in a neutral shade, the sofas and chairs are covered either in flowered muted chintz or in beige brocade, and the curtains drawn across the windows are of matching chintz. The furniture is mostly English antique. Over the fireplace is a portrait, thinly painted, of Amy's mother—the kind of woman with the long sloping undivided bust mysteriously achieved in her day, and an expression of mild reproof. The other pictures are mostly etchings of ducks in flight or English hunting prints, and the tops of tables are crowded with family photographs in silver frames. There is nothing in the rooms that could possibly offend anyone and nothing that could possibly delight. The Lansings have comfort for their money but no fun, and the observant guest cannot help but pity such spiritual constipation. What is more, two sets of curtains and a half-lowered shade cut out in daytime the luxury of light that their fifteenth-floor apartment could provide them, and this perpetual muffling and diffusion and carpeting and covering gives these rooms the feeling of large and elaborate padded cells in which one could die of anoxia. Physically and mentally, the Lansings are sealed in their own amber.

MARYA MANNES, "Park Avenue," *The New York I Know*

II. Find the topic and subtopic sentences in the following paragraphs.

1. The people of Soapland [the world of radio soap operas] are subject to a set of special ills. Temporary blindness, preceded by dizzy spells and headaches, is a common affliction of Soapland people. The condition usually clears up in six or eight weeks, but once in a while develops into [a] brain tumor and the patient dies. One script writer, apparently forgetting that General Mills was the sponsor of his serial, had one of his women characters go temporarily blind because of an allergy to chocolate cake. There was hell to pay, and the writer had to make the doctor in charge of the patient hastily change his diagnosis. Amnesia strikes almost as often in Soapland as the common cold in our world. There have been as many as eight or nine amnesia cases on the air at one time. The hero of "Rosemary" stumbled around in a daze for months last year. When he regained his memory, he found that in his wanderings he had been lucky enough to marry a true-blue sweetie. The third major disease is paralysis of the legs. This scourge usually attacks the good males. Like mysterious blindness, loss of the use of the legs may be either temporary or permanent. The hero of "Life Can Be Beautiful" was confined to a wheel chair until his death last March, but young Dr. Malone, who was stricken with paralysis a year ago, is up and around again. I came upon only one crippled villain in 1947: Spencer Hart rolled through a three-month sequence of "Just Plain Bill" in a wheel chair. . . .

JAMES THURBER, "Soapland," *The Beast in Me—
and Other Animals*

2. Maine's chief distinction is . . . not size but character. One element in this is intrepidity. The state is largely marked by fingers of land poking out into the sea; in the most literal sense its lobstermen and other fishermen make their living by combat with the elements. Another factor is the complete simplicity and financial integrity of almost all old Maine citizens. Money doesn't count for everything in their scale of values; people will spend their last cent on a coat of pale yellow paint for their houses; drop a pocketbook in the streets of Augusta, and a dozen passersby will return it.

Another element is humor. This is not as wry and bitter as is humor in Vermont, say; it has a glow; it has been softened by the Atlantic fogs. Still, it can be sharp. For instance, Bert Sinnett, an old retired lobsterman and a member of one of the ancient families of Maine, was once called as a witness in a lawsuit.

Q. Your name is Bert Sinnett?

A. Yes.

Q. You live in Bayley Island?

A. Yes.

Q. Lived there all your life?

A. Not yet.

JOHN GUNTHER, *Inside U.S.A.*

3.   The two most impressive things about . . . [Wallace] were his mouth and the pockets of his jacket. By looking at his mouth, one could tell whether he was plotting evil or had recently accomplished it. If he was bent upon malevolence, his lips were all puckered up, like those of a billiard player about to make a difficult shot. After the deed was done, the pucker was replaced by a delicate, unearthly smile. How a teacher who knew anything about boys could miss the fact that both expressions were masks of Satan I'm sure I don't know. Wallace's pockets were less interesting than his mouth, perhaps, but more spectacular in a way. The side pockets of his jacket bulged out over his pudgy haunches like burro hampers. They were filled with tools—screwdrivers, pliers, files, wrenches, wire cutters, nail sets, and I don't know what else. In addition to all this, one pocket always contained a rolled-up copy of *Popular Mechanics*, while from the top of the other protruded *Scientific American* or some other such magazine. His breast pocket contained, besides a large collection of fountain pens and mechanical pencils, a picket fence of drill bits, gimlets, kitchen knives, and other pointed instruments. When he walked, he clinked and jangled and pealed.

RICHARD ROVERE, "Wallace," *The New Yorker*, Feb. 4, 1950

Topic sentence

5

Arranging the Evidence

The most difficult problems of arrangement occur when the writer tries to find a clear order for his supporting evidence. But if he ignores these problems, his paragraph may become monstrously confused. The following paragraph parodies the reckless writer who pours his words out and assumes that inspiration will give shape to his blathering. (The parody mutilates a splendid paragraph by Joseph Mitchell.)

> The winter of 1933 was a painful one. I was sent out to stand on a busy corner with a Salvation Army woman, and I caught a head cold. I spent a harried half-hour (on the day before) in the anteroom of a magistrate's court talking with

a stony-faced woman. The Salvation Army woman's job was to ring a bell and attract attention to a kettle in the hope that passers-by would drop money into it for the Army's Christmas fund. "Just stand there three or four hours," I was told, "and see what happens; there ought to be a story in it." I was a reporter on a newspaper in those days. It seems like a hundred and thirty-three years ago, but I remember it distinctly. I was sent up to the big "Hoover Village" on the Hudson at Seventy-fourth Street to ask about the plans the people there were making for Christmas. In the three weeks preceding Christmas there was, of course, an abundance of stories about human suffering, and for one reason or another I was picked to handle most of them. If the squatters at the Hoover Village had turned on me and pitched me into the river I wouldn't have blamed them. The husband of the stony-faced woman had taken a dollar and eighty cents she had saved for Christmas presents for their children and spent it in one of the new repeal gin mills. That was the winter of repeal and the fifth winter of the depression. "I sure fixed his wagon," she said. She had stabbed her husband to death with a knife. She began to moan. My editors believed that nothing brightened up a front page so much as a story about human suffering. The gaunt squatters stood and looked at me with a look I probably never will get over. The bellringer was elderly and hollow-eyed and she had a head cold. "The man on the street is so gloomy nowadays," one of the editors used to say, "that a story about somebody else's bad luck cheers him up."

Several principles of arrangement can help the writer avoid such incoherence.

The first is that descriptive details should be arranged in a clear *spatial order.* One possibility is to start the description at a definite point in space and then move point by point to the opposite extreme; the writer might start with extreme left, for example, then describe things from left to right until he reaches extreme right, or he might start with things close to him and then move to things farther away. Another possibility is to describe things in the order in which they catch the writer's atten-

Temporal order
time sequence

tion; in describing a room he could tell about the stuffed lion's head on the opposite wall, then the zebra skin stretched across the left-hand wall, the luxurious furniture all around the room, and finally the leather-bound books shelved on the right-hand wall. The writer can try a variety of other kinds of spatial arrangements too, so long as the reader will have no trouble following the description.

Chronological order, arrangement in a time sequence, can be applied to so many different kinds of material that the writer will probably find it useful in most of his paragraphs. In the following example, chronological order conveys details from biography and history. The passage is concerned with Ulysses S. Grant's *Personal Memoirs.*

> . . . He [Grant] set out to write the memoirs under handicaps as serious as any that he had faced in the Civil War. Grant was ill: he was suffering from cancer of the throat. But he dictated the first part of the manuscript, and when it became impossible to use his voice . . . he wrote out the rest of the story. He finished it in eleven months, and died about a week later, July 23, 1885. The book sold three hundred thousand copies in the first two years after publication . . . and made $450,000 for Grant's impoverished family. The thick pair of volumes of the *Personal Memoirs* used to stand, like a solid attestation of the victory of the Union forces, on the shelves of every pro-Union home. . . .
>
> EDMUND WILSON, *Patriotic Gore*

As another example of chronological arrangement, here is the original version of the paragraph that was mutilated on pp. 42–43. In contrast with the roundabout ramblings of the parody, the skillfulness of Joseph Mitchell's arrangement is all the more striking:

> The winter of 1933 was a painful one. It seems like a hundred and thirty-three years ago, but I remember it distinctly. That winter, the fifth winter of the depression and the winter of repeal, I was a reporter on a newspaper whose editors believed that nothing brightened up a front page so much as

a story about human suffering. "The man on the street is so gloomy nowadays," one of the editors used to say, "that a story about somebody else's bad luck cheers him up." In the three weeks preceding Christmas there was, of course, an abundance of such stories, and for one reason or another I was picked to handle most of them. One morning I spent a harried half-hour in the anteroom of a magistrate's court talking with a stony-faced woman who had stabbed her husband to death because he took a dollar and eighty cents she had saved for Christmas presents for their children and spent it in one of the new repeal gin mills. "I sure fixed his wagon," she said. Then she began to moan. That afternoon I was sent up to the big "Hoover Village" on the Hudson at Seventy-fourth Street to ask about the plans the people there were making for Christmas. The gaunt squatters stood and looked at me with a look I probably never will get over; if they had turned on me and pitched me into the river I wouldn't have blamed them. Next day I was sent out to stand on a busy corner with a Salvation Army woman whose job was to ring a bell and attract attention to a kettle in the hope that passers-by would drop money into it for the Army's Christmas Fund. "Just stand there three or four hours," I was told, "and see what happens; there ought to be a story in it." The bellringer was elderly and hollow-eyed and she had a head cold, which I caught.

"The Cave Dwellers," *McSorley's Wonderful Saloon*

At the start Mr. Mitchell supplies background information about conditions in 1933 and his job as a reporter. Then he tells three anecdotes in clear chronological sequence: they happened "one morning," "that afternoon," and the "next day." And within each anecdote the order is chronological.

Mr. Mitchell's paragraph suggests a third principle of clear arrangement: the writer should deal with *one subject at a time*. The paragraph has four sections for four subjects: first comes the background information; then come the three anecdotes presented one at a time.

If a writer wishes to draw comparisons between two or three subjects, the practice of staying with one subject at a time can prevent confusion. Thus the following passage, which compares Presidential candidates John F. Kennedy and Richard Nixon as they looked in their first television debate, describes first one man, then the other.

> ... Normally and in private, Kennedy under tension flutters his hands—he adjusts his necktie, slaps his knee, strokes his face. Tonight he was calm and nerveless in appearance. The Vice-President, by contrast, was tense, almost frightened, at turns glowering and, occasionally, haggard-looking to the point of sickness. Probably no picture in American politics tells a better story of crisis and episode than that famous shot of the camera on the Vice-President as he half slouched, his "Lazy Shave" powder faintly streaked with sweat, his eyes exaggerated hollows of blackness, his jaw, jowls, and face drooping with strain.
>
> THEODORE H. WHITE, *The Making of the President 1960*

Sometimes the writer may wish to compare his subjects point by point, one feature at a time. Mr. White might have compared Kennedy's and Nixon's facial expressions, then their gestures, their postures, and so forth. But the material was not suited to that kind of organization. Mr. White wished to mention Kennedy's gestures but not Nixon's, Nixon's face but not Kennedy's. The problem with a point-by-point comparison is that it forces the writer to say something about each subject on every point. He can use this framework if his material fits it, but more often he will find it convenient to discuss each subject fully by itself, as Mr. White does in the paragraph above.

These few principles of arrangement will be useful in most paragraphs. And when the writer hits a problem not solved by these principles, he can refer to the master principle underlying them: *Always be considerate of the reader*. The writer can evaluate his arrangement from the point of view of a reader and watch for passages that might be difficult to follow. "Will the reader hit a dead end after that sentence? Maybe I should put it elsewhere in the paragraph. ... Will he find this section difficult so near the beginning? I'll put it towards the end so I can prepare him for it. ... How about these important details? I'd better mention them earlier in the paragraph to help the reader understand what comes later."

Another point that should be mentioned here is not concerned with clarity but with forcefulness. The writer should *end the paragraph with something important* and thus leave the reader with a strong final impression. In the following two-paragraph illustration Edmund Wilson ends his first paragraph with a striking detail, his second with a paragraph-idea. The passage deals with Hemingway's *In Our Time*, a book of stories mostly about a young man named Nick Adams. The first paragraph, which tells that Nick discovered life in the Michigan woods to be brutal and ugly, ends with an emphatically ugly detail. The second paragraph ends with Mr. Wilson's main idea: life sometimes seems enjoyable in the Hemingway stories, but beneath appearances the ugliness and suffering persist.

> ... Was not life in the Michigan woods ... destructive and cruel? Nick had gone once with his father, the doctor, when he had performed a Caesarean operation on an Indian squaw with a jackknife and no anaesthetic and had sewed her up with fishing leaders, while the Indian hadn't been able to bear it and had cut his throat in his bunk. Another time, when the doctor had saved the life of a squaw, her Indian had picked a quarrel with him rather than pay him in work. And Nick himself had sent his girl about her business when he had found out how terrible her mother was. Even fishing in Big Two-Hearted River—away and free in the woods—he had been conscious in a curious way of the cruelty inflicted on the fish, even of the silent agonies endured by the live bait, the grasshoppers kicking on the hook.
>
> Not that life isn't enjoyable. Talking and drinking with one's friends is great fun; fishing in Big Two-Hearted River is a tranquil exhilaration. But the brutality of life is always there. And it is somehow bound up with the enjoyment. Bullfights are especially enjoyable. It is even exhilarating to build a simply priceless barricade [in World War I, and shoot] the enemy as they are trying to get over it. The condition of life is pain; and the joys of the most innocent surface are somehow tied to its stifled pangs.
>
> "Hemingway: Gauge of Morale," *The Wound and the Bow*

Not every paragraph can end as forcefully as these do. But a writer can resolve that none of his paragraphs will fade away at the end with trivia.

Practice

I. What principles of clear arrangement are at work in each of the following paragraphs? Does the paragraph employ spatial order? Chronological order? Does it proceed topic by topic? Most of the paragraphs employ several of these techniques.

Ask one other question concerning each paragraph: Does it have a forceful ending?

1. ... The very person and appearance [of Sherlock Holmes] were such as to strike the attention of the most casual observer. In height he was rather over six feet, and so excessively lean that he seemed to be considerably taller. His eyes were sharp and piercing, save during those intervals of torpor to which I have alluded; and his thin, hawk-like nose gave his whole expression an air of alertness and decision. His chin, too, had the prominence and squareness which mark the man of determination. His hands were invariably blotted with ink and stained with chemicals, yet he was possessed of extraordinary delicacy of touch, as I frequently had occasion to observe when I watched him manipulating his fragile philosophical instruments.

SIR ARTHUR CONAN DOYLE, *A Study in Scarlet*

2. ... If you knew where to look, some of the major phenomena of the Depression ... would begin to appear. First, the breadlines in the poorer districts. Second, those bleak settlements ironically known as "Hoovervilles" in the outskirts of the cities and on vacant lots—groups of makeshift shacks constructed out of packing boxes, scrap iron, anything that could be picked up free in a diligent combing of the city dumps: shacks in which men and sometimes whole families of evicted people were sleeping on automobile seats carried from auto-graveyards, warming themselves before fires of rubbish in grease drums. Third, the homeless people sleeping in doorways or on park benches, and going the rounds of the restaurants for left-over half-eaten biscuits,

piecrusts, anything to keep the fires of life burning. Fourth, the vastly increased number of thumbers on the highways, and particularly of freight-car transients on the railroads: a huge army of drifters ever on the move, searching half-aimlessly for a place where there might be a job. According to Jonathan Norton Leonard, the Missouri Pacific Railroad in 1929 had "taken official cognizance" of 13,745 migrants; by 1931 the figure had already jumped to 186,028. It was estimated that by the beginning of 1933, the country over, there were a million of these transients on the move. Forty-five thousand had passed through El Paso in the space of six months; 1,500 were passing through Kansas City every day. Among them were large numbers of young boys, and girls disguised as boys. According to the Children's Bureau, there were 200,000 children thus drifting about the United States. So huge was the number of freight-car hoppers in the South-west that in a number of places the railroad police simply had to give up trying to remove them from the trains: there were far too many of them.

FREDERICK LEWIS ALLEN, *Since Yesterday*

3. But Juvenal never set his foot on the ladder [of social and political advancement]. For some reason—we can never know why—he received no appointment, however insignificant. Possibly a bitter censorious nature was apparent in his manner even then. Lieutenants and assistant undersecretaries are expected to look bright and cooperative, not coldly critical; to smile and say "Certainly, sir," not to maintain a morose and dubious silence. The months passed. The years passed. Juvenal was still unemployed. He had enough to live on, but he felt his talents were being wasted. Year after year, he stood in the corridors of the emperor's palace, and visited influential noblemen, hoping to be noticed, perhaps to be called in to fill a sudden vacancy. But he was always passed over. And gradually he saw that the posts of greatest value were allotted, not to the men who best deserved them, but to those who had the right friends at court, who knew how to flatter, who could share a dirty secret with a powerful minister, or toady to a ballet-dancer who had caught the emperor's fancy. For some time he brooded on this. He had been dabbling in literature as a pastime. Now he tried his

hand at verse, and produced a short lampoon on the corruption of the court and the government. A few lines of it have survived.

Actors have far more power than gentlemen. Do you
    still haunt the homes of old and noble families?
Now ballet-dancers hand out rank, and make promotions.
              GILBERT HIGHET, Poets in a Landscape

4. ... [Marcucci] has the ability to analyze precisely the demands of the teen-age public and to know what to do about it. He has found a career in exporting his talent to Teen-Land. First, he selects promising raw material. Then he molds it. He indoctrinates it for three months. Then he lets it make a few test records. Since it cannot sing too well without an orchestra and the electronic facilities (echo chambers, bass and treble modulators, tape splicers and the works) of a recording studio, he teaches it to pantomime while its records play over the loud-speaker during its first public appearance before an audience of two hundred. He dresses it first in sweaters and white bucks, then in open-Belafonte shirts and big belt buckles. He coifs it by modifying the duck-tail and getting more of the Ricky Nelson bob. He postures it, taking advantage of good shoulders, which should bunch forward, and narrow hips, which should always be off-keel. He takes it on the road, shows it to the disk-jockeys, and advertises it in the trade papers. He decides (brilliantly) to use only its first name instead of its last. He interests Dick Clark in it, and after one shot on TV, it breaks up an audience of 24,000 in Albany, New York. It sells 300,000 copies of a record called I'm a Man, then 750,000 of Turn Me Loose. It records Tiger.... [Then] it is known not only as Fabian, but as Tiger, too. It is a hero.

              THOMAS B. MORGAN, "The Heroes of Teen-Agers,"
              Self-Creations: 13 Impersonalities

5. ... No human beings could have seemed more different than Hugh Johnson and Rexford Tugwell. Johnson learned to spell to the whinnying of cavalry horses and the bawling of top sergeants at Fort Scott, Kansas, yelling to anyone who would listen to him: "Everybody in the world is a rink-stink but Hughie Johnson and he's all right!" Tugwell, the son of a prosperous farmer and cannery-owner in Sinclairville,

New York, was raised to a genteel tradition of concern with community problems, almost to a Rooseveltian *noblesse oblige*. West Point remembered Johnson as the most talented hazer and the possessor of the biggest nose in the history of the school. The University of Pennsylvania recalled Tugwell as a handsome, smartly dressed ideologue, a gourmet with a special pride in his elaborate salads, who was given to practicing his sharp wit on bourgeois America and was more than likely to steer his date to a reform soiree. While Johnson was doing a hell-roaring border patrol along the Rio Grande, Tugwell was showing intimates a poem that included the lines:

> *I am sick of a Nation's stenches*
> *I am sick of propertied Czars. . . .*
> *I shall roll up my sleeves—make America over!*
>
> ERIC GOLDMAN, *Rendezvous with Destiny;*
> *A History of Modern American Reform*

II. This exercise is based on three paragraphs whose original arrangement of sentences is quite clear. But here the sentences have been shuffled. Restore the sentences to their original order so that each paragraph will again be clear.

1. (Based on a paragraph by Frederick Lewis Allen.)

    a. He spent a good deal of time exploring the waterfront, ranging from dock to dock and boarding the vessels tied up there to find out how their imports and exports were handled.

    b. He went off with samples of the coffee in his pockets, made the rounds of the local merchants, collected orders, returned to the ship, and bought *the entire cargo* with a sight draft on Duncan, Sherman and Co.

    c. What the men in New York had supposed to be a foolhardy operation had been a methodically prudent one; he had collected orders for every bag before he bought the shipload.

    d. The young J. Pierpont Morgan went to New Orleans to make a several weeks' first-hand study of the cotton and shipping business.

    e. The next day, within a few hours of the time when his superiors in New York began spluttering with rage at his temerity, he was able to telegraph them that he had sold every bag of coffee in the cargo to various merchants at a neat profit, and was forwarding to Duncan, Sherman and Co. the checks made out in payment.

f. One day, boarding a ship, he found it loaded with coffee in bags and learned that its captain was in a quandary: the man to whom the shipment had been consigned could not be found, and the captain, consulting his Brazilian headquarters, had been instructed to dispose of the cargo of coffee as best he could.

g. But in addition to being a prudent transaction, it had been a bold one for a neophyte.

h. Pierpont saw an opportunity.

2. (Based on a paragraph by E. B. White.)

a. Last spring we decided the croquet set was beyond use, and invested in a rather fancy new one with hoops set in small wooden sockets, and mallets with rubber faces.

b. The course had been laid out haphazardly and eagerly by a child, and we all used to go out there on summer nights and play good-naturedly, with the dogs romping on the lawn in the beautiful light, and the mosquitoes sniping at us, and everyone in good spirits, racing after balls and making split shots for the sheer love of battle.

c. A dog isn't even allowed to cast his shadow across the line of play.

d. Paint had faded, wickets were askew.

e. Another phase of life here which has lost something through refinement is the game of croquet.

f. There are frequent quarrels of a minor nature, and it seems to me we return from the field of honor tense and out of sorts.

g. We used to have an old croquet set whose wooden balls, having been chewed by dogs, were no rounder than eggs.

h. The course is now exactly seventy-two feet long and we lined the wickets up with a string; but the little boy is less fond of it now, for we make him keep still while we are shooting.

3. (Based on a paragraph by Paul Roberts.)

a. We have found all sorts of ways to avoid saying *mad*: "mentally ill," "touched," "not quite right upstairs,"

"feeble-minded," "innocent," "simple," "off his trolley,"
"not in his right mind."

b. This is the tendency to call a spade "a certain garden
implement" or women's underwear "unmentionables."

c. Thus we shrink from saying "He died last night" but say
instead "passed away," "left us," "joined his Maker,"
"went to his reward."

d. Linguistic diffidence can take various forms.

e. It is stronger in some eras than others and in some people
than others but it always operates more or less in subjects that are touchy or taboo: death, sex, madness, and
so on.

f. Even such a now plain word as *insane* began as a
euphemism with the meaning "not healthy."

g. Or we try to take off the tension with a lighter cliché:
"kicked the bucket," "cashed in his chips," "handed in
his dinner pail."

h. One is what we call *euphemism*.

III. Suppose that you are planning a paragraph about the daily life
of a typical family on the American prairies in 1850. The paragraph-idea is: "The prairie farmer and his wife had a difficult
existence." You have jotted down the following sentences as
notes for the paragraph.

a. The nearest house was probably at least three or four
miles away.

b. The woman's cooking was laborious and time-consuming,
since she had no ready-made foods and only a wood fire
for cooking.

c. There were no newspapers available, and no other source
of news except an occasional passerby.

d. The farmer worked in the fields all the daylight hours.

e. During most of the day the woman would have no adult
to chat with or to call in an emergency.

f. Although a number of her children would die early, the
woman ordinarily still had at least five youngsters to
care for.

g. The farmer would probably have to do even his heaviest
work alone, since there would be no neighboring men
to help.

\ h. At first the family would have to live in a "dugout," a big hole dug in the side of a hill and walled in with squares of sod.

i. The woman had to make the family's clothes and keep them mended.

j. There was almost certainly no doctor within a day's ride, so that roughly half the family's children would die at birth or during infancy.

k. The man had only rude equipment for his work—a shovel, an ax, and a plow, which, if he had no horse, he would have to pull or push by himself.

2 l. After they had a house their walls would still be squares of sod, and the floor of the one and only room would be the bare ground.

m. The woman worked late into the evening—putting away preserved foods for the winter, mending clothes, or doing one of her many other jobs.

n. In the early morning the woman would milk the cow and tend to the other livestock.

Now follow these steps:

1. Divide the notes by subject, so that each group of note-sentences can become one section of the paragraph.
2. Within each section, arrange the sentences in a clear order.
3. Place the sections in a clear order.
4. Write a subtopic sentence for each section.
5. Write the paragraph, revising the note-sentences, if necessary, for the sake of continuity or clarity.

6

Transitions

Once a writer has placed his sentences in a clear order, he must link them with *transitions*. Otherwise his prose will resemble the following mutilated version of a paragraph by Edmund Wilson. With almost all its transitions removed, the paragraph seems to be a collection of disconnected thoughts.

> Houdini was by no means content with even the undisputed title of Handcuff King. There was much occupation with researches: many books had been collected and read with a characteristically tireless voracity. A good deal of trouble had been taken to talk to retired magicians and think about all kinds of wonder-workers. Some writing was done. Few

55

escapes were done. He appeared to the public in something like true character and at something like full stature. An exhaustive study had been made of spiritualism such as had been made of prisons and locks. Any person was challenged to show phenomena which could not be exposed and reproduced. In the demonstrations and lectures there was perhaps even more ardent enthusiasm than in the escapes: there was a certain intellectual and moral interest, and the campaign was a veritable crusade.

One kind of transition is the *marker*, which explicitly points the reader in the right direction. In passages with a spatial arrangement the reader may be helped by such markers as *here, there, on the left wall, over the bookshelves, under the window.* Other markers can guide the reader through a chronological arrangement: *then, immediately, later, after several weeks.* Markers may also indicate a logical relationship. To present a new point, the writer may use *moreover, furthermore,* and the like. To introduce an illustration: *for instance, for example.* To lead into a contrasting statement: *but, however, on the contrary.* And the markers listed here are only a fraction of those available.

Markers are so helpful that the writer may be lured into using them too often and too conspicuously:

> Hart Crane's father derided the boy for writing poetry. *Therefore* Hart found a job that would make him independent of his father. His new job, *however,* was the writing of advertising copy. *Consequently,* each day's work would dull his sensitivity to words. In the evenings, *therefore,* he drank heavily and played loud music. *Thus* he could write poetry. *However,* he began to depend on the drinking. *Finally* he had to do a good deal of drinking before he could do any writing. *Ultimately* the drinking became habitual.

Some of these markers can be omitted. Others can be replaced with less obtrusive ones that are just as effective:

> Because Hart Crane's father derided the boy's writing of poetry, Hart found a job that would make him independent of his father. *But* his new job, writing advertising copy,

Conjective adverbs — moreover
Furthermore
consequently,

and — conjuctions
But

would each day dull his sensitivity to words. In the evenings he drank heavily and played loud music so that he could write his poetry. He began to depend on the drinking. *Soon* he had to do a good deal of drinking before he could do any writing, *and eventually* the drinking became habitual.

Now, by restoring the original markers, we can improve the mutilated version of Edmund Wilson's paragraph about Houdini.

Houdini was by no means content with even the undisputed title of Handcuff King. *During all this period,* there was *also* much occupation with researches: many books had been collected and read with a characteristically tireless voracity, *and* a good deal of trouble had been taken to talk to retired magicians and think about all kinds of wonder-workers. Some writing was done. Few escapes were done. *And in his last years,* he *for the first time* appeared to the public in something like true character and at something like full stature. An exhaustive study had been made of spiritualism such as had been made of prisons and locks. *And now* any person was challenged to show phenomena which could not be exposed and reproduced. In the demonstrations and lectures *of this period* there was perhaps even more ardent enthusiasm than in the *earlier* escapes: there was a certain intellectual and moral interest, and the campaign *turned into* a veritable crusade.

Obviously this is still not Mr. Wilson's original. The paragraph is still not so fluent as it should be, because markers, by themselves, cannot secure continuity. The writer must employ a second kind of transition: *the repetition of words or ideas.* For example:

The comedian's *jokes* were so stale and obvious that they drew only polite *laughter.* As the *jokes* became less funny, the *laughter* turned to silence.

The italicized words appear in both sentences and thus link the sentences in the reader's mind.

If repetition of the same words threatens to grow tiresome, the writer can vary his words and still achieve repetition.

One means of doing this is the pronoun:

> The comedian's jokes were so stale and obvious that they drew only polite laughter. As *they* became less funny, the laughter turned to silence.

> One morning the attendant at the city dump got a surprise. *He* saw a pickup truck come in loaded with books. *Its* driver, a well-dressed man wearing horn-rimmed glasses, stopped by a pile of garbage. Then *he* threw the books onto the garbage. After heaving the last of *them, he* drove out of the dump with a contented look on *his* face. Perhaps *he* was a college professor grown weary of reading.

In the second illustration the pronouns are particularly helpful in securing continuity.

Synonyms can accomplish the same end. In one sentence from the passage above, the man "*threw* the books"; although the next sentence could have started "After *throwing* the last of them," the writer switched to "After *heaving* the last of them." Here is another example:

> The *student* insisted that he needed only an hour to *write* his *essay*. But the *composition* the *boy produced* was vague in its wording, disorganized, and illogical.

Student becomes *boy, write* becomes *produce, essay* becomes *composition,* and thus the passage has both repetition and variety. The writer can achieve the same effect without confining himself to close synonyms. Any clear rewording will serve:

> The landslide piled earth and boulders onto the mountain highway. It was several days before *this obstruction* could be cleared away.

> Marx believed that people's desires for material goods determine history, that economic forces shape human events. *This doctrine* has influenced most subsequent historians, including those who would not call themselves Marxists.

Now we can examine Edmund Wilson's paragraph about Houdini with all its transitions restored. Note that the paragraph uses more repetitions than markers. (The markers are underlined; the words used for repetition are italicized. The numbers beneath repeated words or ideas are intended to show exactly how the repetitions occur; all words referring to Houdini, for instance, are labeled (1).)

... *Houdini* was *by no means content* with even *his* un-
(1)   (2)   (1)

disputed title of *Handcuff King*. *He* had also, during all this
(3)   (1)

period, been occupied with *scholarly researches: he* had been
(4)   (1)

collecting and reading books on *magic* with a characteris-
(4)   (5)

tically *tireless voracity,* and had taken *a good deal of trouble*
(2)   (2)

to *interview* retired *magicians* and *investigate* all kinds of
(4)   (5)   (4)

wonder-workers. He began *himself to write* on *the subject.*
(5)   (1)   (1)   (4)   (5)

And in *his* last years, *he* did few *escapes* and for the first
(1)   (1)   (3)

time *appeared to the public* in something like *his* true
(6)   (1)

character and at something like *his* full stature. *He* had been
(1)   (1)

making of *spiritualism and mediums* the same kind of *ex-*
(5)

haustive study that *he* had made of *prisons and locks.* And
(2)   (4)   (1)   (3)

he now *challenged* any *medium* to show *him supernatural*
(1)   (7)   (5)   (1)   (5)

phenomena which *he* could not *expose and reproduce.* To the
(1)   (8)

demonstrations and lectures of this period, *he* brought a
(4, 6)   (1)

perhaps even more *ardent enthusiasm* than *he* had to *his*
(2)   (1)   (1)

earlier *escapes:* the *deflation* of *this higher fakery* had a
(3)   (8)   (5)

certain *intellectual* and moral *interest,* and *Houdini's*
(4)   (2)   (1)

campaign against the *mediums* turned into a veritable *cru-*
(7)   (5)

sade.
(7)

      EDMUND WILSON, "A Great Magician," *The Shores of Light*

Mr. Wilson's markers are helpful without being obtrusive. And his repetitions, though abundant, are not allowed to grow tiresome. Houdini figures in every sentence, but often in the form of a pronoun. Magic, especially magic connected with spiritualism, is referred to with a variety of terms (*magicians, wonder-workers, the subject, spiritualism, mediums, supernatural phenomena,* and *higher fakery*). Mr. Wilson's skill with transitions—both markers and repetitions—results in an easy, natural continuity.

Practice

I. The following passage, which recounts the last events in the life of President Harding, uses many transitional markers. Write down the number of each sentence, then list its markers.

> (1). . . In time rumors began to spread around Washington. (2)Then a member of the Ohio gang committed suicide just before Harding left on a trip to Alaska in the summer of 1923. (3)The President himself began perhaps to have a sense of impending disaster. (4)He suddenly invited his Secretary of Commerce, Herbert Hoover, to join the trip. . . . (5)Harding had never seemed more restless. . . . (6)One day he finally took Hoover aside and asked him vaguely what he should do if, say, there were scandals in the administration. (7)The apprehensions were indefinite but obsessive. (8)By now the party was back in the Pacific Northwest, where the President, worn and haggard, resumed his speaking schedule. (9)Soon he was sick, laid low, it was stated, by bad crabmeat (though no crabmeat was to be found on the official menu). (10)For a day or so he seemed to rally. (11)Then, on August 3, while his wife was reading him an article about himself from the *Saturday Evening Post,* he turned pale and gave a shudder. (12)In a few moments he was dead.
>
> ARTHUR M. SCHLESINGER, JR., *The Crisis of the Old Order*

II. The next paragraph uses few markers. It secures continuity through the repetition of key terms or of pronouns, synonyms, or near-synonyms in place of the terms. Write down the number of each sentence (except the first); then list the words in that sentence that achieve continuity through repetition.

(1)Gould looked like a bum and lived like a bum. (2)He wore castoff clothes, and he slept in flophouses or in the cheapest rooms in cheap hotels. (3)Sometimes he slept in doorways. (4)He spent most of his time hanging out in diners and cafeterias and barrooms in the Village or wandering around the streets or looking up friends and acquaintances all over town or sitting in public libraries scribbling in dime-store composition books. (5)He was generally pretty dirty. (6)He would often go for days without washing his face and hands, and he rarely had a shirt washed or a suit cleaned. (7)As a rule, he wore a garment continuously until someone gave him a new one, whereupon he threw the old one away. (8)He had his hair cut infrequently ("Every other Easter," he would say), and then in a barber college on the Bowery. (9)He was a chronic sufferer from the highly contagious kind of conjunctivitis that is known as pinkeye. (10)His voice was distractingly nasal. (11)On occasion, he stole. (12)He usually stole books from bookstores and sold them to second-hand bookstores, but if he was sufficiently hard pressed he stole from friends. (13)(One terribly cold night, he knocked on the door of the studio of a sculptor who was almost as poor as he was, and the sculptor let him spend the night rolled up like a mummy in layers of newspapers and sculpture shrouds on the floor of the studio, and next morning he got up early and stole some of the sculptor's tools and pawned them.) (14)In addition, he was nonsensical and bumptious and inquisitive and gossipy and mocking and sarcastic and scurrilous. . . .

JOSEPH MITCHELL, *Joe Gould's Secret*

III. Here is a summary of the early life of the Russian novelist Dostoevsky. The passage contains many markers and also achieves continuity through repetition. Make two lists—one for the markers, the other for words used to achieve repetition.

(1). . . Dostoevsky detested his school and had but one passion: literature. (2)Shortly after graduation he resigned his position as a military draughtsman and devoted himself to writing. (3)After years of poverty and privation, he published his first novel, *Poor Folk*, which met with a certain success. (4)He published other novelettes and tales and wrote fever-ishly, brimming with projects and ideas. (5)Then a catastrophe befell him: he was arrested as a member of a clandestine group of young idealists who discussed Utopian socialism and dreamed of freedom. (6)In 1849 Dostoevsky, together with his friends, was sentenced to death and brought to the execution place in a public square before the firing squad. (7)At the very last moment an official came forward and announced the Czar's clemency, and the death sentence was commuted into one of penal servitude. . . .

MARK SLONIM, An Outline of Russian Literature

IV. The ill-written paragraph below is derived from a well-written paragraph by Gilbert Highet. The version below lacks almost all transitional markers and transitional uses of repetition. Add markers, add words to secure repetition, and turn this discontinuous passage into fluent prose. The measure of success will not be whether you reproduce Mr. Highet's original but whether you produce a fluent piece of writing.

The passage is concerned with Juvenal, the Roman satirist, who as a young man was unable to gain employment in Rome, though he waited for years.

. . . Juvenal never set his foot on the ladder of social and political advancement. For some reason—we can never know why—there was no appointment, however insignificant. Possibly a bitter censorious nature was apparent. There was no employment to be found. There was enough to live on. There was the hope of being noticed, perhaps to be called in to fill a sudden vacancy. He was passed over. The posts of greatest value were allotted, not to the men who best deserved them, but to those who had the right friends at court, and who knew how to flatter, who could share a dirty secret with a powerful minister, or toady to an entertainer who had caught the emperor's fancy. He brooded. Literature had been dabbled in as a pastime. Some verse was tried. A short lampoon on corruption was produced. A few lines have survived.

Actors have far more power than gentlemen. Do you still
haunt the homes of old and noble families?
Now ballet-dancers hand out rank, and make promotions.

V. Here is another paragraph that has been made discontinuous by the removal of transitions. (The original was by Paul Roberts.) Turn the passage back into fluent prose.

Linguistic diffidence can take various forms. There is what we call *euphemism*. People tend to call a spade "a certain garden implement" or woman's underwear "unmentionables." A tendency may be stronger in some eras than others and in some people than others, but the phenomenon always operates more or less in subjects that are touchy or taboo: death, sex, madness, and so on. We do not say "He died last night." We say "passed away," "left us," "joined his Maker," "went to his reward." Perhaps a light cliché may be used: "kicked the bucket," "cashed in his chips," "handed in his dinner pail." Many substitutes have been found for the word *mad*: "mentally ill," "touched," "not quite right upstairs," "feeble-minded," "innocent," "simple," "off his trolley," "not in his right mind." The word *insane* began as a word meaning "not healthy."

Further Practice on the Paragraph

I. Evaluate these two paragraphs, two samples of student writing. Do they follow the principles set forth in the previous chapters? If the paragraphs are not satisfactory, what revisions should be made?

1. William March's story "The Little Wife" illustrates a weakness in human nature. The characterization of Joe Hinckley, the main figure in the story, shows that when reality is painful, we will sometimes simply refuse to
5 accept reality. At the outset of the story Joe received two telegrams concerning his wife's ill health, but he refused to take them seriously. The first telegram stated that his wife, Bessie, was on the verge of death. But Joe refused to admit to himself that Bessie might die. Instead, he
10 assured himself that her ailments were minor and that by the time he reached her she would be completely recovered. But then, while Joe was heading home by train, he received a second telegram. His mind was in a turmoil: "It must be from Mrs. Thompkins [Bessie's mother] all
15 right. . . . She said she'd wire again if . . ." For a moment Joe let himself suspect the truth. But then: "No! It may not be from Mrs. Thompkins at all; it may be from somebody else. . . ." Trying to rid his mind entirely of his suspicions, he savagely ripped up the unopened telegram

20 and threw the torn remnants off the train. As a further attempt to ward off the suspected truth, Joe adopted a facade of gaiety and joviality, and he began talking excitedly to the other people on the train as if from an excess of cheerfulness. By talking gaily he could guard 25 against the suspicions nagging at him. And he brought up the subject of his wife, talking about her at great length as if she were alive and well. "He talked on and on, rapidly—feverishly. . . . He had a feeling that as long as he talked about her she would remain safe." Joe soon 30 became so caught up in his pretended cheerfulness that he ignored not only his own problems but also the problems of the people around him. The woman seated across the aisle from him had a large goiter on her neck, but Joe ignored her pain. As he left the train he ignored her 35 response:

"Goodbye, lady; I hope you have a nice trip." The woman answered: "The doctors said it wasn't no use operating on me. I waited too long." "Well that's fine!—That sure is fine!" said Joe.

40 But Joe's world of make-believe could not last. It shattered when he met reality head-on: Mrs. Thompkins in mourning. "A feeling of terror swept over him. He knew that he could no longer lie to himself." And he finally admitted what he had been doing: "I didn't want to 45 know that she was dead. I wanted to keep her alive a little longer."

2. It was hard to believe that Anna was nineteen. She seemed like an old maid. Her skin was not wrinkled or saggy, but her round horn-rimmed glasses and her lacklustre white face made her seem old. Her hair was a 5 healthy brown, but unkempt. It had the color of tree bark, but it was very thin, particularly on the top of her head, where she was getting bald. She wore it short, with bangs like curtains separating over her eyes, just brushing the tops of her glasses. Anna always claimed the hair 10 needed little attention. "With just a little coaxing," she would say, "it curls up and looks pretty good." She would rather spend her time preparing for excursions. She liked to visit old churches, to peer into the dark

abysses at vibrant stained-glass. For these excursions she
15 wore her favorite blouse. It was white, dirty-gray white,
with tiny pearl buttons and parallel flat ruffles down the
front. Her skirt would be a faded paisley or a plaid print.
It would be a full skirt but worn with a petticoat, so that
it would cling to her hips and emphasize her angular
20 thinness. In one hand she would clutch her carpetbag,
stuffed with her camera, her Michelin guide, and assorted
oddities. The other hand would grasp a stubby plaid umbrella. She carried it in all weather "in case of rain—it
always seems to rain if I leave the umbrella at home."
25 Even her shoes were those of a middle-aged woman. Instead of the loafers a teenager would wear, Anna wore
what she called her "sensible shoes"—plain brown ox-
fords, laced-up tightly and double-knotted. She had obviously worn these for years. Their threads had come loose
30 in back, and the heels were worn down by time and
tramping.

II. Now write a paragraph of your own. In choosing a topic you may
wish to follow the example of one of the paragraphs in exercise
I: you could write about a person you know or about a theme or
character from a work of fiction.

The Short Essay

II

introductory paragraph.
Essay idea
thesis

I

II

III

IV

Conclusion

The problems of writing an essay are almost identical to those of writing a paragraph. In both cases you must formulate a central idea, clarify it, provide supporting evidence, arrange the evidence, insert transitions, and so forth. When you write a long paragraph, you are only a few steps away from writing a short essay.

Consider the make-up of a typical long paragraph. The paragraph-idea, expressed in a topic sentence, is probably supported by several subtopic sentences; and each subtopic sentence is followed by supporting details. Here are the central and subordinate ideas from one such paragraph.

Topic sentence: Our Presidents have run in sequences, and since the middle of the nineteenth century, they have tended to be classifiable under three main types.

First subtopic sentence: You have, first, the public-spirited idealist who may or may not be a good politician, but who knows American history, understands the importance and the meaning of the United States in the larger world and assumes the responsibility of maintaining our unique role.

Second subtopic sentence: An administration on this high level is likely, however, to be followed by a slump, with an inferior type of man in office: the small party politician—Warren G. Harding or Harry S. Truman.

Third subtopic sentence: A third type, clearly defined, is the man who neither knows about professional politics nor understands the problems of government, but has arrived at a position of eminence through achievement in some quite different field: Grant, Hoover, Eisenhower.

EDMUND WILSON, *A Piece of My Mind*

Now suppose that a paragraph of this sort becomes too long; its subordinate sections are swollen with evidence, and the paragraph occupies one and a half or two pages. Such a paragraph could easily be converted into an essay. We could lift out the topic sentence and place it in a paragraph at the start of our essay-in-the-making. The topic sentence would become our *essay-idea,* the central idea of the essay. Next we could divide the rest of the original paragraph into its subordinate parts and turn each part into a separate paragraph. Each subtopic sentence would become a topic sentence. And now what was originally a paragraph would be a rudimentary essay. It would look something like this:

Essay-idea

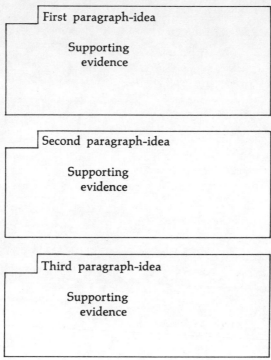

First paragraph-idea

Supporting
evidence

Second paragraph-idea

Supporting
evidence

Third paragraph-idea

Supporting
evidence

The following chapters deal with special problems of writing the essay. But you already know the basic framework: first the essay-idea, then the supporting paragraph-ideas and their paragraphs.

7

The Essay-Idea

Before starting an essay, the writer must have a tentative notion of what he will say. If he spews his thoughts out as they first occur to him, his essay will be filled with false starts, digressions, needless repetitions, unreasonable lines of reasoning—all sorts of troubles. It is particularly important that he think out his essay-idea, for the essay can be no stronger than its central proposition.

First he must put the essay-idea on paper, to be sure it is more than a nebulous feeling, a vague itch in the brain. Searching for the right words to express his idea will help him clarify it; and once he has committed his essay-idea to paper he will be better able to criticize it objectively. He must watch in particular for three possible defects.

One is *incoherence*, disunity. The several parts of the following essay-idea are not clearly connected:

> Since the revolution of 1917, Russia has increased its economic output considerably, and the Russian society has kept a class structure.

The reader will not understand what relationship the writer sees between Russia's economic output and her class structure unless the essay-idea is revised:

> Since the revolution of 1917, Russia has increased its wealth considerably; but it has not redistributed its wealth to achieve the revolution's ostensible goal: a classless society.

The split in the following essay-idea is too deep to be repaired with mere rewording:

> In Dostoevsky's *Crime and Punishment*, Raskolnikov is punished by being estranged from all people, especially from the people he loves most; furthermore, *Crime and Punishment* shows Dostoevsky's opposition to the socialist doctrines of his day.

This sentence consists of two separate ideas. One of the ideas must be abandoned, or the resulting essay will be split in two.

Another possible defect is *triteness*; the essay-idea may be superficial, obvious, commonplace. If a writer is satisfied with quick glances, if his thinking fails to penetrate beneath surfaces, he can produce banal ideas on any topic whatever:

> During his stay in New England, Mark Twain certainly produced some interesting writing.

> In the soliloquy beginning "To be or not to be," Hamlet shows that he is contemplating suicide.

> God's speech to Job convinces Job to stop his complaints.

Coming upon an essay-idea of this sort, the reader thinks "of course" and tosses the essay aside as a waste of time.

A writer need not be divinely inspired or extraordinarily intelligent to produce stimulating ideas. But he must cultivate certain habits of mind. First of all, he must be willing to study his subject thoroughly. If it is a book to be reviewed, he should read it several times (noting its chief ideas, weighing evidence, pondering crucial passages), and possibly he should consider other writers' comments on the book or the topic it deals with. By the time he knows his subject well, perhaps he will already have formulated several valuable ideas from which he can choose his essay-idea. But if no usable ideas have occurred to him, he can try the technique called "brainstorming." He can review the notes he has taken, then write down any strange, wild conclusions that come to mind, no matter how far-fetched or silly they seem. Once his thoughts are flowing, he will eventually hit on ideas that are not so silly and others that come close to fitting the details he has gathered. Then he can think in a more rigorous, analytical fashion and devise an essay-idea that not only fits the details but gives them a fresh and provocative interpretation.

The essay-idea he devises, instead of resembling the bland, superficial ones mentioned earlier, will probably be more like these:

> Under the influence of genteel New England society, Mark Twain's writings lost the humorous gusto that had characterized his earlier work.

> In the soliloquy beginning "To be or not to be," Hamlet indulges in self-pity and self-dramatization.

> In His speech at the end of the Book of Job, God admits having created Evil and declares that Evil is necessary in the universe.

Far from being restatements of the obvious, these ideas sound a note of challenge and controversy.

The writer who works too hard at being controversial may find that he has overstated his case. The writer of the above essay-idea about Mark Twain might have to admit that during the New England years Twain did not decline in skill but rejected his earlier style to be capable of new and better accomplishments. The essay-idea would need thorough revision:

> Under the influence of sophisticated New England society, Mark Twain replaced the raw, extravagant humor of his earlier work with a new capacity for subtle irony and shrewd social satire.

This idea is just as interesting as the other, but closer to the truth.

The third possible weakness is that the essay-idea may be *too general:*

> Capitalism is superior to socialism in some respects but not in others.

> Shakespeare's ideas about human nature and the human condition are similar to those of the Greek tragedians.

> The stories and novels of F. Scott Fitzgerald satirized the manners and morals of the Roaring Twenties.

Even the simplest of these, the statement about Fitzgerald, would require a book: an explanation of the term "Roaring Twenties"; a depiction of the "manners and morals" of the period; then a discussion of "the stories and novels of F. Scott Fitzgerald"—all of them, it seems. The following essay-ideas are more limited and therefore more likely to be capably defended in short essays:

> Fitzgerald's *The Great Gatsby* portrays various kinds of love— all of them shallow, most of them basically self-serving.

> Several of Fitzgerald's works of fiction satirize the sort of woman for whom money and comfort are more important than people.

The essay-idea about Mark Twain in New England also needs trimming. Consider the idea again:

> Under the influence of sophisticated New England society, Mark Twain replaced the raw, extravagant humor of his earlier work with a new capacity for subtle irony and shrewd social satire.

The essay would have to cover all of Twain's early works, establish that Twain was influenced by New England society, and show that all his later works contain "subtle irony" and "shrewd social satire"—an enormous task! The writer would be doing well to handle just one feature of one of Twain's later works:

> In *The Adventures of Huckleberry Finn,* Mark Twain employed subtle irony in satirizing conventional religion.

This essay-idea would meet the three criteria we have discussed: it would have unity; it would say something important; and it would be specific enough to be supported in a short essay.

Practice

I. Rearrange the five statements in each group below so that they form a sequence moving from specific to general.

1. a. *Mrs. Warren's Profession,* George Bernard Shaw's second play, was banned from public performance in England for thirty years by the state censor.
    b. The early career of British playwright George Bernard Shaw was damaged by the state censor.
    c. Despite the Theatre Act of 1843, the subsequent development of English drama has been impeded by state censorship.
    d. The history of English drama has been repeatedly blighted by state censorship and banning.
    e. *Mrs. Warren's Profession,* George Bernard Shaw's second play, received abominable treatment from the state censor.

2. a. President Ulysses S. Grant was tricked into letting financiers Jay Gould and Jim Fisk gain control of the nation's gold market.
    b. At least three times during the administration of President Ulysses S. Grant, schemers made use of the federal government to swindle the public.
    c. Ulysses S. Grant was extraordinarily capable as a soldier but shockingly inept as a politician and statesman.
    d. Although President Ulysses S. Grant helped scoundrels swindle the public, Grant himself was not corrupt, merely ignorant of the workings of government.
    e. Ulysses S. Grant was extraordinarily competent in some fields but shockingly inept in others.

3. a. Throughout his novels Samuel Butler satirized the religious

beliefs of his society, the very beliefs he had been trained in as a youngster.

b. In his novel *Erewhon* Samuel Butler satirized those people of his time who believed that by mere church-going they could save their souls.

c. In both his novels about the imaginary land of Erewhon, Samuel Butler satirized the religious beliefs of his society.

d. In his novel *Erewhon* Samuel Butler satirized several of his society's religious beliefs.

e. Samuel Butler satirized the hypocrisy and narrow-mindedness he found in Victorian society.

II. Most of the fifteen statements in the previous exercise would be unsuitable as essay-ideas for short essays; the majority are either so specific as to warrant no more than a paragraph or two, or so general as to require fifteen or twenty paragraphs or more. But the remaining statements might serve as central ideas in essays of five to ten paragraphs. From each group of statements, choose one that might serve as the essay-idea for an essay of that length.

III. Below are seven would-be essay-ideas. Examine each one for flaws. Does the idea lack unity? If so, could the disunity be repaired with a few changes in wording, or is the split too deep for easy repair? Is the idea too general to be dealt with in a short essay? Is the idea trite—so obvious and superficial as not to be worth developing into an essay?

1. Even now the legend of John Barrymore retains its strength with the general public and with many people of the theater, but the truth is that although Barrymore was interesting as a person, he was not the great actor he is commonly thought to be.

2. During his childhood Theodore Dreiser experienced dire poverty, and several of his later novels deal with a "financier" and "titan" of industry—Frank Cowperwood.

3. The influence of philosopher John Dewey has damaged the academic standards of our public schools.

4. Ring Lardner served for many years as a newspaper sportswriter, then began to write fiction about athletes, mostly about baseball players and prizefighters.

5. In Chaplin's early short film *Shoulder Arms*, he introduced

several themes that were also prominent in his later, more important film about war—*The Great Dictator*.

6. Lytton Strachey's biographies punctured the inflated reputations of famous people, and his example has had a lasting influence on the art of biography.

7. The novels of Sinclair Lewis dissected and ridiculed typical American figures, and his writings became enormously popular.

IV. Compose three essay-ideas about subjects you know well.

8

Planning the Paragraph-Ideas

If the paragraph-ideas are not planned carefully, an essay will be cluttered with irrelevant material and will probably not succeed in defending its essay-idea.

The writer can formulate a dependable set of paragraph-ideas if he remembers that their primary purpose is the defense of the essay-idea. He must use all paragraph-ideas necessary for the defense and reject all others.

The writer will have no trouble devising paragraph-ideas when his essay-idea is like these:

> Of the three forms of execution used in the United States, the gas chamber is the least inhumane; both the electric chair and the gallows are barbaric in their cruelty.

> The history of English prose contains several noted proponents of "the plain style."

The first of these virtually announces that its supporting paragraph-ideas must deal with the three forms of execution; perhaps each form can be handled in one paragraph. The second essay-idea obviously calls for paragraph-ideas about the "noted proponents of 'the plain style' "—perhaps one paragraph for Ben Jonson, one for Swift, and so on.

Other essay-ideas are not so obvious in indicating the direction their development must take. The following idea would require a more careful analysis:

> In many Western films the career of the professional gunslinger follows a conventional pattern.

But the writer would soon recognize that his paragraph-ideas must focus on the gunslinger's stereotyped career; he could let each paragraph deal with one stage of the career, as in this *paragraph outline:*

> *Essay-idea:* In many Western films the career of the professional gunslinger follows a conventional pattern.
> I. At first the gunslinger is unfeeling and reckless.
> II. Then, remorseful for his killings, he attempts to reform.
> III. He discovers that he cannot escape the role of gunfighter: "It's too late to change."
> IV. He "dies as he lived"—through a gunfight.

Another essay-idea requiring careful analysis is this one concerning the central figure of Joseph Conrad's novel *Victory:*

> Despite his initial cynicism toward human nature, Axel Heyst eventually became capable of love and trust.

The writer could begin by displaying Heyst's "initial cynicism," then show Heyst gradually becoming capable of love and trust. The transformation could be divided into phases, with each phase treated in a paragraph.

> *Essay-idea:* Despite his initial cynicism toward human nature, Axel Heyst eventually became capable of love and trust.

    I. Even in childhood Heyst learned to distrust human na-
       ture, and his cynicism stayed wih him.
   II. He fell in love with a woman who had come to him for
       help.
  III. Still warped by his cynicism, he doubted the woman's
       loyalty.
  IV. He finally discovered her to be worthy of his love.

But what seems to be a paragraph-idea may be too general or too specific for development in a paragraph. This idea is
too general:

> Even in childhood Heyst learned to distrust human nature,
> and his cynicism stayed with him.

A discussion of Heyst's cynicism requires more supporting evidence than could be crammed into a single paragraph. The paragraph-idea must be divided into several more limited ones:

> During Heyst's childhood his father trained him to distrust
> human nature.
>
> As Heyst grew older, his cynicism stayed with him.

On the other hand, a paragraph-idea may be too specific. Such
an idea will result in a skimpy paragraph. Consider these paragraph-ideas concerning Arthur Dimmesdale, the hypocritical
Puritan minister of Hawthorne's *The Scarlet Letter:*

> Arthur Dimmesdale committed a sin but concealed it from
> his parishioners.
>
> Ironically, his secret guilt made him all the more effective as
> a minister.

The second is a true paragraph-idea. It calls for an explanation
of the complex psychological process by which Dimmesdale's
guilt enabled him to instill in his parishioners a fear of sin. But
the first idea does not require a paragraph. The minister's secret
sin can be revealed in a few sentences. The writer could combine
the two ideas to form one satisfactory paragraph-idea:

> When Dimmesdale concealed his own sin from his parish-
> ioners, he became, ironically, a more effective minister.

The writer must remember two principles, then, as he devises his paragraph-ideas. First, the ideas must form a solid defense for the essay-idea. Second, each must be a true paragraph-idea.

Let us watch these principles work together as they help to formulate a set of paragraph-ideas.

Suppose that a writer is planning an essay comparing the prose styles of George Bernard Shaw and H. L. Mencken. He has read extensively, pondered his notes, and stated his essay-idea:

> In criticizing their societies' values and institutions, Shaw and Mencken employed similar techniques of satire.

The writer tries the following paragraph-ideas:

I. Shaw used forceful techniques of satire to criticize his society.

II. Mencken used some of the same techniques in his own social criticism.

These form an adequate defense for the essay-idea, but they are not true paragraph-ideas. Each one is too general to be developed in a paragraph.

The writer divides his argument into smaller parts:

> *Essay-idea:* In criticizing their societies' values and institutions, Shaw and Mencken employed similar techniques of satire.
>
> I. Shaw criticized many of his society's values and institutions.
>
> II. In his social criticism Shaw used several forceful techniques of satire.
>
> III. Mencken criticized many of his own society's values and institutions.
>
> IV. Mencken's critical writings employed some of the same techniques that were used by Shaw.

This is still unsatisfactory. The essay-idea focuses on Shaw's and Mencken's *techniques* of satire, not the *objects* of their satire. But only two of the above paragraph-ideas concentrate on the techniques (II and IV); the others deal with the objects.

The writer tries again:

Essay-idea: In criticizing their societies' values and institutions, Shaw and Mencken employed similar techniques of
satire.

  I. Both Shaw and Mencken often used a blunt, plain-speaking style that could attack their societies' values with
vigorous directness.

 II. Both authors sometimes employed hyperbole: they exaggerated certain features of society in order to ridicule
them.

III. Both authors filled their prose with comical metaphors,
comparisons between things their societies held to be
good and things obviously vile or ridiculous.

Now the writer has emphasized satirical techniques. But his paragraph-ideas are still too general—the paragraphs would be
enormous.

By dividing the ideas into smaller ones, the writer
finally produces a satisfactory outline:

Essay-idea: In criticizing their societies' values and institutions, Shaw and Mencken employed similar techniques of
satire.

  I. Shaw often used a blunt, plain-speaking style that could
attack his society's beliefs with vigorous directness.

 II. Mencken, in attacking the beliefs of his own society,
used the same kind of bluntness.

III. Another of Shaw's techniques was hyperbole: he exaggerated certain features of his society in order to ridicule
them.

IV. Mencken used hyperbole in the same way.

 V. Shaw made frequent use of comical metaphors, comparisons between things his society held to be good and
things obviously vile or ridiculous.

VI. Mencken, too, filled his prose with satirical comparisons.

The paragraph-ideas are neither too general nor too specific; and
they work together effectively to defend the essay-idea.

Writers who prefer a more detailed outline can use a
sentence outline, which includes not only paragraph-ideas but

subtopic sentences and subordinate details. Here is a sentence outline for the final paragraph of the essay on Shaw and Mencken:

> VI. Mencken, too, filled his prose with satirical comparisons.
>   A. He used comparisons to satirize schools.
>   1. He often called schools penitentiaries.
>   2. Teachers he called guards and wardens.
>   B. He used comparisons to ridicule politics.
>   1. He compared politicians to confidence men.
>   2. He once compared a political convention to a swarm of jungle animals gathering at a waterhole.
>   C. Mencken used comparisons to show his scorn for organized religion.
>   1. He likened church services to seances and tent meetings.
>   2. He likened ministers to swamis, witch doctors, and pitchmen.

The writer who would rather not do this much outlining can use a paragraph outline, even for essays more difficult to plan than the one on Shaw and Mencken. And if his essay is particularly easy to plan, he can use merely a *scratch outline*, which, instead of stating paragraph-ideas in full, substitutes phrases:

> *Essay-idea:* In many Western films the career of the professional gunslinger follows a conventional pattern.
>   I. Unfeeling bravado
>   II. Remorse and attempted reform
>   III. Inability to escape his role
>   IV. Death by gunfight

No matter how carefully the writer plans, he must regard his outline as tentative. As he turns the outline into an essay, he may discover new ideas that strengthen his argument, or he may encounter unexpected difficulties—paragraph-ideas too general or specific, holes in the argument, problems with arrangement, and so forth.

But although an outline is tentative, it is far from being unnecessary. Sometimes a beginning writer insists that all outlining is useless drudgery; he wants to plunge right into his essay, and is confident that he can produce one cogent paragraph after another in perfectly logical sequence. He will almost certainly run into trouble. He may race through an entire draft without sensing problems, but if he can review the draft objectively, he will probably have to admit that the ideas are fuzzy and the argument weak. Then he must rewrite big sections of the essay or throw the whole thing out and start again.

Practice

I. Tell how you would develop each of the following essay-ideas into an essay. Do not try to write out the paragraph-ideas that would be needed—to do so would require much research. Merely tell what sorts of topics the paragraphs would have to deal with. For instance, suppose you were planning the development of an essay-idea examined earlier: "In many Western films the career of the professional gunslinger follows a conventional pattern." Though it might be difficult to tell exactly what the paragraph-ideas would be, you could probably tell, at least roughly, what topics the paragraph-ideas would have to cover: they would cover the *stages* of the gunslinger's career.

1. At least three times during the administration of President Ulysses S. Grant, schemers made use of the federal government to swindle the public.

2. In his novel *Erewhon* Samuel Butler satirized several of his society's religious beliefs.

3. In Chaplin's early short film *Shoulder Arms*, he introduced several themes that were also prominent in his later, more important film about war—*The Great Dictator*.

4. In the fiction of Tobias Smollett, several leading characters are deluded by imagination, a faculty Smollett distrusted.

5. Despite the efforts of government inspectors, the public is still sold many worthless drugs and some drugs that are dangerous.

6. Several of today's leading jazz musicians, well trained in mod-

ern musical theory, often use practices derived from such composers as Bartok and Stravinsky.

7. At the outset of Nabokov's *Lolita,* Humbert Humbert is a grotesque person, scarcely pitiable; but towards the end of the novel he briefly rises above the perverse obsessions that have dominated him.

II. In exercise IV on p. 79 you were asked to write three essay-ideas. Choose one idea to work with further. Write out the paragraph-ideas that could defend it.

9

The Introduction: Presenting the Essay-Idea and Its Clarification

The beginning of an essay can convince the reader that he is in capable hands. It can present the essay-idea, the gist of the argument, and thus prepare him to understand the supporting ideas and evidence.

In the briefest of essays the writer can state the essay-idea in a single sentence (and then begin the first supporting paragraph):

Several writers for the *New Yorker* magazine have entertained their readers by describing people from New York's lower classes.

John McNulty, for instance, used to search New York's

streets and taverns for worthwhile stories, and he found so many that he was a *New Yorker* staff writer for almost twenty years. . . .

If the one-sentence introduction seems too abrupt, the essay-idea can be expanded into several sentences:

> Although the *New Yorker* contains stories about all sorts of people from all sorts of places, it has always focused mainly on New Yorkers. And several of the magazine's writers have concentrated on just one segment of the city. They have entertained their readers by describing people from New York's lower classes.
>
> John McNulty, for instance, used to search New York's streets and taverns. . . .

In most essays, however, the essay-idea is not a sufficient introduction by itself. Usually it needs clarification.

If only a few words are unclear, the writer can provide *explanation of vague or unfamiliar words*. Suppose this were the essay-idea: "The Cravenfield Police Department has long been guilty of Comstockery." Seventy years ago readers would have recognized "Comstockery" as a reference to Anthony Comstock, leader of the New York Society for Suppression of Vice—that is, for suppression of controversial literature. Today, since the name is no longer familiar, the writer should offer an explanation: "The Cravenfield Police Department has long been guilty of Comstockery, *the suppression of controversial literature.*" Abstractions such as *democracy, freedom, selfishness, faith,* and *leftist* are also likely to need clarification. Such terms can signify one thing to the writer, another to the reader. George Bernard Shaw, immediately after asserting that Joan of Arc was a "genius," explains what he means: "A genius is a person who, seeing farther and probing deeper than other people, has a different set of ethical valuations from theirs, and has energy enough to give effect to this extra vision and its valuation. . . ."

A second technique of clarification is *restatement in more specific terms*. (This was recommended on pp. 13–17 for clarifying a paragraph-idea.) Consider the following.

The trouble is everything is too big. There are too many people, for example, in the city I live in. In walking along the street, one passes scores of other people every minute; any response to them as human beings is impossible; they must be passed by as indifferently as ants pass each other in the corridors of the anthill. A style of behavior which refuses to recognize the human existence of the others has grown up of necessity. Just the scale on which people congregate in such a city breaks down human solidarity, alienates people from each other. There are so many people that there aren't any people; 7,000,000 becomes 0; too big.

DWIGHT MACDONALD, "Too Big," *Memoirs of a Revolutionist*

"The trouble is everything is too big." This opening statement is so abstract that Mr. Macdonald immediately restates the essay-idea in more specific terms: "There are too many people, for example, in the city I live in." But this is still too general to be clear. Is Mr. Macdonald thinking of crowded housing, congested streets, or what? His third sentence becomes more specific and tells exactly what he is worried about—overcrowding causes indifference: "In walking along the street, one passes scores of other people every minute; they must be passed by as indifferently as ants pass each other in the corridors of the anthill."

A third technique of clarification is *helpful rewording*. Several examples appear in the introduction by Dwight Macdonald. In his first three sentences, as we have seen, Mr. Macdonald restates his essay-idea in progressively more specific terms until he reaches this statement: "In walking along the street, one passes scores of other people every minute; they must be passed by as indifferently as ants pass each other in the corridors of the anthill." Notice what happens after that third sentence:

> ... A style of behavior which refuses to recognize the human existence of others has grown up of necessity. Just the scale on which people congregate in such a city breaks down human solidarity, alienates people from each other. There are so many people that there aren't any people; 7,000,000 becomes 0; too big.

These sentences repeat the essay-idea several times, but not for the purpose of being more specific. (They are more general than the third sentence, not more specific.) Instead, they are merely *helpful rewordings* of the essay-idea. They express it in a variety of ways, each of which offers the reader another slant on the idea, another way of looking at it, so that perhaps he can see aspects of it that he had not seen before.

Another technique may be called *rejection of wrong meanings*. This tells what the writer does *not* mean and thus rules out wrong interpretations. Though Mr. Macdonald's introduction is clear as it stands, the following rendition shows how the introduction might have used *rejection of wrong meanings*. Note the italicized additions.

> The trouble is everything is too big. There are too many people, for example, in the city I live in. *I am not speaking of the over-crowding in the streets, or the inadequacy of housing and public services, or the inefficiency of the government bureaucracy.* In walking along the street, one passes scores of other people every minute; any response to them as human beings is impossible; they must be passed by as indifferently as ants pass each other in the corridors of the anthill. A style of behavior which refuses to recognize the human existence of the others has grown up of necessity. *A few people resist the influences that lead to indifference, but those few are a tiny remnant among the impersonal hordes.* Just the scale on which people congregate in such a city breaks down human solidarity, alienates people from each other. There are so many people that there aren't any people; 7,000,000 becomes 0; too big.

At the start of the paragraph, it might seem as if the writer were proposing to deal with all the problems of big-city bigness, but the first italicized passage cites problems he will not discuss. In the middle of the paragraph the reader might think that all city people, without exception, were being accused of indifference; but the second italicized passage notes exceptions. Both passages guard against misinterpretation. By telling what the writer does not mean, they help pin down what he does mean.

Another technique is *illustration,* the use of a concrete example. Mr. Macdonald pictures a busy street where people hurry past one another without a word or a glance, like ants in an anthill. In addition to speaking of alienation and the breakdown of human solidarity, he turns his abstractions into an illustration and *shows* what he means. Suppose a writer were trying to explain the following idea: "According to our American conception of justice, all men should be equal before the law." He might begin with *rejection of wrong meanings:* "This does not mean that all men are to be regarded as equal in height or strength or intellect." He might offer a *restatement in more specific terms:* "But our courts should regard all men as equal in their right to impartial treatment and a fair trial." Now an *illustration* would be helpful. The writer might picture a night court where two men are brought in for drunken driving. One was driving a Cadillac, is dressed in formal evening wear, and is vice-president of the city's largest bank; the other was driving a dilapidated, third-hand Ford, is dressed in third-hand clothes, and is out of work. Yet the judge must give the men equal treatment. Both must be granted legal counsel; both must be allowed to post bail; and the punishment for both must fit the crime, not the social background. "All men should be equal before the law." The illustration makes the idea clear.

We have now discussed five techniques of clarification:
1. Explanation of any vague or unfamiliar words
2. Restatement in more specific terms
3. Helpful rewording
4. Rejection of wrong meanings
5. Illustration

Some essay-ideas can be clarified with one or two of these techniques, but even if the writer must use all five, the effort will be worthwhile. An introduction that succeeds in clarifying the essay-idea will prepare the reader to understand the rest of the essay. If an introduction leaves him confused, he is likely to find the whole essay confusing.

Practice

I. Find the essay-idea in each introduction below. Then determine which techniques are used to clarify the idea.

1. (1)Money is the cause of athleticism in the American colleges. (2)Athleticism is not athletics. (3)Athletics is physical education, a proper function of the college if carried on for the welfare of the students. (4)Athleticism is not physical education but sports promotion, and it is carried on for the monetary profit of the colleges through the entertainment of the public.

ROBERT MAYNARD HUTCHINS, "Gate Receipts and Glory,"
Saturday Evening Post, Dec. 3, 1938

2. (1)The birds, who ought to know all about flying, cannot fly blind; but men can. (2)The proudest skill of airmanship, painfully learned only yesterday, blind flying does not mean, of course, flying with eyes closed or bandaged. (3)It means flying in clouds or fog when you can see nothing but vapor— no horizon, no ground, no stars. (4)Rather than to attempt flight where he can't see, a bird will invariably ground himself—for a reason which he must feel quite clearly within himself: his sense perceptions are not good enough for such a task. (5)Neither are a man's. (6)But the modern professional pilot has learned to fly by the artificial sense organs on the instrument panel before him.

WOLFGANG LANGEWIESCHE, "Flying Blind," *Harper's*, April, 1947

3. (1)In this century the basic character of astronomy has been undergoing a drastic change: traditionally the most precise of sciences, it has become perhaps the most boldly speculative. (2)For three centuries after Galileo made his first telescope astronomers were preoccupied with detail. (3)The first great observatories were founded three hundred years ago at Greenwich and Paris to refine navigational techniques and the keeping of time. (4)Through the early years of this century the main business of astronomy continued to be determination of the orbits of the moon and planets and cataloguing nearby stars with their positions, motions, and brightness calculated meticulously to a fraction of a percent.

(5)Today, however, most astronomers have lost interest in the details of nearby space.... (6)The new astronomy takes for its province nothing less than the whole of the universe, including its origin and destiny. (7)In much of their work astronomers no longer aspire to absolute accuracy; estimates that may be wrong by a factor of ten are considered quite acceptable. (8)From this freewheeling approach have come fascinating, if somewhat uncertain, theories of how stars and planets are born and evolve.

GEORGE A. W. BOEHM, "Great American Scientists: The Astronomers," *Fortune*, May, 1960

4. (1)Every part of movie production is circumscribed by a very specific code of taboos. (2)We know [that] all societies, from primitive ones to modern Hollywood, have their "thou-shalt-nots." (3)In the South Seas they are a way of dealing with the supernatural to avoid certain dangers and to insure success, particularly in those situations in which luck or chance plays a part. (4)In Hollywood they are also a technique to escape dangers which, although of this world, are so fearful as to appear almost supernatural; and here too they are part of a formula for trying to make success more certain.

(5)Among Stone Age Melanesians in the Southwest Pacific there is a taboo on sex relations before a fishing expedition, to insure a good catch. (6)In Hollywood there is a taboo on portraying in a movie any indication that a marriage has been consummated, and for the same reason: to prevent hostile forces from interfering with the catch—at the box office. (7)The most important and universal taboo in all primitive culture is the prohibition of incest far beyond the limits of the immediate family; in some places half the females are forbidden to the males, and vice versa. (8)If individuals are caught in an incestuous act, they either commit suicide or are killed by their relatives. (9)The breaking of this taboo is thought to endanger the very life of the society in some terrible but indefinable way, and the death of the violators serves as a kind of appeasement. (10)In the Hollywood production of movies, there is an equally important taboo prohibiting any reference to the biological nature of man or other animals. (11)There can be no dialogue, serious or farcical, about the mating of men, elephants, horses, moths, or butterflies; even a wet baby in need of being diapered is absolutely forbidden. (12) Violators of these taboos do not commit suicide nor are they killed by members of their clan. (13) But they are refused its seal of approval, which is considered a form of business suicide.

HORTENSE POWDERMAKER, *Hollywood: The Dream Factory* (1950)

II. The statements below (taken from H. L. Mencken's *New Dictionary of Quotations*) are provocative but rather vague. If any were used as an essay-idea, it would need clarification. Choose the two statements you can best explain (not necessarily ones you agree with) and write a paragraph of clarification for each, using the techniques discussed in this chapter. Because the statements are concerned with education, you need not do any special research to explain them but can rely on first-hand experience.

1. We need education in the obvious more than investigation of the obscure.

—O. W. HOLMES II

2. You can send your child to the schoolmaster, but 'tis the schoolboys who educate him.

—R. W. EMERSON

3. There is no royal road to learning.

—EUCLID

4. Knowledge is a process of piling up facts; wisdom lies in their simplification.

—MARTIN FISCHER

5. The effects of infantile instruction are, like those of syphilis, never completely cured.

—ROBERT BRIFFAULT

6. Man can be set free from the yoke of his own nature only by education.

—M. A. BAKUNIN

7. A little learning is a dangerous thing.

—ALEXANDER POPE

8. The important thing is not so much that every child should be taught, as that every child should be given the wish to learn.

—JOHN LUBBOCK

9. In large states the public education will always be mediocre, for the same reason that in large kitchens the cooking is usually bad.

—F. W. NIETZSCHE

10. The things taught in schools and colleges are not an education, but the means of education.

—R. W. EMERSON

11. Learn to unlearn.

—BENJAMIN DISRAELI

10

The Introduction: Catching the Reader's Attention

Offered nothing but essay-idea and clarification, a reader may find the introduction dull and assume that the rest of the essay will be the same. The introduction must somehow catch the reader's interest and convince him that the essay is worth reading.

The following pages present eight techniques by which this may be accomplished.

1 PROVOCATIVE ESSAY-IDEA
The essay-idea may do the job by itself. If the idea startles the reader or angers him, he will probably read further to see what defense can be offered for such a controversial view.

It is a pity that true history is not taught in schools.

HILAIRE BELLOC, "The Barbarians," *One Thing and Another*

It would be difficult to find a more shattering refutation of the lessons of cheap morality than the life of James Boswell. One of the most extraordinary successes in the history of civilization was achieved by an idler, a lecher, a drunkard, and a snob.

LYTTON STRACHEY, "James Boswell," *Portraits in Miniature*

The writer who works too hard at being controversial will produce exaggerations:

Barring sociology (which is yet, of course, scarcely a science at all but rather a monkeyshine which happens to pay, like theology) psychology is the youngest of the sciences, and hence chiefly guesswork, empiricism, hocus-pocus, poppycock.

H. L. MENCKEN, "The Genealogy of Etiquette," *Prejudices: First Series*

This is more bombast than reason: half-truths in extravagant language. Although such shenanigans may entertain the reader or stir up his thinking, they will hardly win his trust.

2 REJECTION OF WIDELY ACCEPTED OPINIONS

This technique, too, involves the assertion of a provocative essay-idea; but to begin with, the writer rejects a more conventional view.

Most American parents want to send their children to college. And their children, for the most part, are anxious to go. It is an American tradition that there is something about a college that transforms an ordinary infant into a superior adult. Men and women who have been to college sometimes suspect that this is not the case, but they seldom say so. They are alumni, and, as such, it is their life work to maintain the tradition that college—their college anyway—is the greatest place in the world.

College is the greatest place in the world for those who ought to go to college and who go for the right reasons. For those who ought not to go to college or who go for the wrong reasons, college is a waste of time and money.

ROBERT M. HUTCHINS, "Why Go to College?" *Saturday Evening Post*, Jan. 22, 1938

In his first paragraph Mr. Hutchins sets forth a popular belief: any student who *can* go to college *should* go. But Mr. Hutchins ridicules this notion even as he presents it. Then his second paragraph denounces it altogether and counters with his own controversial views.

3 POSING A PROBLEM OR QUESTION

The introduction may present a puzzle:

> Suppose there were no critics to tell us how to react to a picture, a play, or a new composition of music. Suppose we wandered innocent as the dawn into an art exhibit of unsigned paintings. By what standards, by what values would we decide whether they were good or bad, talented or untalented, successes or failures? How can we ever know that what we think is right?
>
> MARYA MANNES, "How Do You Know It's Good?" *But Will It Sell?*

Perhaps the reader will be snagged—curious about the answers to Miss Mannes's questions and eager to read on.

4 THE OCCASION FOR WRITING

The writer can begin by telling what caused him to write. Here is the opening of John Lardner's satirical essay on a certain television show:

> Sunday, June 22, was the tenth anniversary of "The Ed Sullivan Show" (originally "Toast of the Town"), by proclamation of the Columbia Broadcasting System. It was also Ed Sullivan Day in twelve states, by proclamation of twelve governors.
>
> "A Happy Sullivan Day," *The World of John Lardner*

Almost any kind of event can be the occasion for writing: a hot skirmish in the Cold War, the writer's encounter with a zany character, the appearance of a new motion picture or book. The occasion mentioned in this next introduction is the popularity of a mediocre novel:

> The most alarming literary news in years is the enormous success of James Gould Cozzens' *By Love Possessed*. It sold 170,000 copies in the first six weeks of publication—more than all eleven of the author's previous novels put together.

At this writing (December, 1957) it has been at the top of the best-seller list for two months. Hollywood and the *Reader's Digest* have paid $100,000 apiece for the privilege of wreaking their wills upon it.

DWIGHT MACDONALD, "By Cozzens Possessed,"
Against the American Grain

5 NARRATIVE DETAILS

The following introduction offers a dramatic anecdote, complete with punch line. Its author was a "muckraker" who, at the turn of the century, spoke out against social injustices such as child labor.

Once, so the story goes, an old Indian chieftain was shown the ways and wonders of New York. He saw the cathedrals, the skyscrapers, the bleak tenements, the blaring mansions, the crowded circus, the airy span of the Brooklyn Bridge. "What is the most surprising thing you have seen?" asked several comfortable Christian gentlemen of the benighted pagan whose worship was a "bowing down to sticks and stones." The savage shifted his red blanket and answered in three slow words, "Little children working."

EDWIN MARKHAM, "The Hoe-man in the Making," *Cosmopolitan*, 1906

An anecdote can help support the essay-idea even before the idea is made explicit. Certainly the next opening has that effect.

Not long ago a professor in a Midwestern university, concerned about evidence of cheating, set up an experiment to discover the extent of it. He gave a difficult assignment and announced there would be a quiz. On the morning of the test he mentioned that the correct answers were on his desk. Then by prearrangement he was called from the room.

Unknown to the others, two graduate students had been enrolled in the class to observe and report on what then might happen. It exceeded the teacher's worst imaginings. No sooner was he out the door than there was a stampede to the desk. With the exception of two dean's-list geniuses, every student present copied the answers and handed them in as his own.

JEROME ELLISON, "American Disgrace: College Cheating,"
Saturday Evening Post, Jan. 9, 1960

This incident not only catches the reader's interest but prepares him to accept the essay-idea: college cheating is alarmingly widespread.

6 HISTORICAL EVENTS

Incidents may also serve as historical background. They may be historical *causes* of a phenomenon discussed in the essay; they may serve as *parallels;* or they may offer a *contrast,* as in the following introduction from an essay about our new abundance of leisure time.

> Recently I discovered among some papers that my mother had stowed away in a deserted file a clipping from a magazine of the 1920's. It was headed "Schedule for a One-Maid House." The house, it said, "had seven rooms: a living-room, dining-room, porch, kitchen, maid's room and bath, three bedrooms, and two baths." The schedule starts with:
>   6:45 A.M.   Wash and Dress
> and ends with:
>   8:00 P.M.   Plans for the evening will be adapted to household convenience.
> Bridget, if that was her name, was busy in the intervening hours with cleaning, cooking, bed-making, baking, and polishing silver and brass. Her respite came sometime between 1:30 and 3:00 P.M. when, according to the schedule, she was to "clear table, wash dishes, go to own room to rest, bathe, and change dress." At 3:00 she was back in the kitchen, "ready to answer door, etc."
>   RUSSELL LYNES, "Time on Our Hands," *Harper's*, July, 1958

Today, the author goes on to assert, people have so much new leisure time that they have not yet learned to enjoy it.

7 DESCRIPTIVE DETAILS

The introduction may offer a graphic portrayal of an interesting subject. Here are two macabre examples from the essays of George Orwell.

> As the corpse went past, the flies left the restaurant table in a cloud and rushed after it, but they came back a few minutes later.
>   "Marrakech," *Collected Essays, Journalism and Letters,* I

It was in Burma, a sodden morning of the rains. A sickly light, like a yellow tinfoil, was slanting over the high walls into the jail yard. We were waiting outside the condemned cells, a row of sheds fronted with double bars, like small animal cages. Each cell measured about ten feet by ten and was quite bare within except for a plank bed and a pot for drinking water. In some of them brown silent men were squatting at the inner bars, with their blankets draped round them. These were the condemned men, due to be hanged within the next week or two.

"A Hanging," *Collected Essays, Journalism and Letters,* I

8 QUOTATION

If the essay is about a person, it can open with one of his characteristic statements. If the topic is a book, the essay can begin by quoting an important passage. And with any topic the introduction can quote someone who supports the essay-idea—a respected authority, an eyewitness, anyone whose words carry weight. Mr. Derek Colville, in his essay on British and American schools, argues that American students are poorly trained in fundamental skills; and Mr. Colville's introduction quotes someone whose words are right to the point—a British teacher who has visited American schools.

"The class was keen and intelligent," said the visiting professor from England. "They were excited by the poems we read, and they had insight. They talked more readily than classes do at home. It was a delightful teaching experience. But when I asked them to write on those same poems they were lost. Their papers were appalling. They couldn't plan, construct, find words for their meaning, or even punctuate and spell. It was a shattering anticlimax."

"British and American Schools," *Harper's,* Oct., 1957

Note that Mr. Colville combines three attention-getters in a single paragraph. He uses a *quotation;* he announces a *provocative essay-idea* (that American students are poorly trained); and he presents *narrative details* (the professor's anecdote about students unable to write). If an introduction seems dull with only one attention-getter, the writer can use two or three and make sure his essay gets off to a lively start.

Having discussed the three elements of an introduction (essay-idea, clarification, and attention-getter), we must consider the problems of combining them.

First comes the problem of finding a clear arrangement. There are many possibilities worth trying, but one arrangement is particularly dependable: (1) attention-getter, (2) essay-idea, (3) clarification. The writer captures the reader's attention, then presents the essay-idea, then clears up any obscurities.

When these three elements are combined in an introduction, each element tends to help the others. Descriptive details intended mainly as an attention-getter can help with clarification; an illustration used primarily for clarification can also serve as an attention-getter; and so on.

The following introduction shows that material brought in to serve one purpose can help serve another. The introduction also exemplifies the sequence recommended above (attention-getter → essay-idea → clarification).

(1)Before the present era of great material abundance in America began, it was assumed that prosperity would eliminate, or greatly reduce, class differences. (2)If everybody enjoyed the good things of life, as defined by mass merchandisers, it was thought the meanness of class distinctions would disappear. (3)Unfortunately, the theory didn't work. (4)Today, instead of being indifferent to outward evidence of rank and affluence, millions of prosperous Americans are becoming anxious status seekers.

Sentences 1–3:
The author opens with an attention-getter: rejection of widely accepted opinions. He states the popular notions, then denounces them.
The passage also helps with clarification. The essay-idea has not appeared yet, but this passage prepares the reader to understand it. By expressing what the writer does not believe, the passage prepares the reader to understand what the writer does believe. In other words, the passage employs the technique referred to in the last chapter as rejection of wrong meanings.

Sentence 4:
After building his reader's interest the author here states his essay-idea. And the statement is also an attention-getter: a provocative essay-idea. It insults "millions of Americans," accuses them of becoming "anxious status seekers."

(5)Many of us seek possessions as status symbols. (6)We draw social lines to try to prove our own superior status. (7)We rate acquaintances on whether it is smart or not to be seen with them, and we are rated in turn.

This paragraph is primarily clarification. Sentences 5–7:
First comes the technique we have called restatement in more specific terms. The author tells the particular ways in which Americans reveal their "status-seeking": we "seek possessions," "draw social lines," and "rate acquaintances."
This passage also acts as attention-getter. It continues the insult begun in the first paragraph, and makes the insult more personal by applying it to "many of us" and telling the contemptible activities of which "we" may be guilty.

(8)In so doing, we are intensifying social stratification in the United States.

VANCE PACKARD,
"The Pursuit of Status,"
Look, April 28, 1959

Sentence 8:
To finish the job of clarifying the essay-idea, the author now offers a helpful rewording.

The three components of this introduction work together harmoniously. The reader can move easily from attention-getter to essay-idea to clarification; and each element helps the others to do their jobs well.

Practice

I. What techniques do these introductions employ to catch the reader's interest? Each introduction uses several techniques in combination.

1. (1)Englishmen boast that theirs is the freest nation on earth. (2)All political parties are allowed to advocate their views in full and public liberty; no one need take refuge in a Fifth Amendment to conceal his beliefs; and on the soapboxes in Hyde Park speakers with turbans or kilts, bowler hats or flaming beards, can freely expound doctrines ranging from anarchism to theosophy. (3)But there is one great medium of ideas, one great arena in which free minds have clashed and debated, to which the Englishman's access is barred by ancient inhibitions and rigorous censorship. (4)It is the theatre.

(5)The English theatre of today is less free than that of any other Western nation and is, in certain aspects, more severely controlled than the theatre behind the Iron Curtain.

GEORGE STEINER, "Close-Up of Britain's Censor," *New York Times Magazine,* Sept. 2, 1956

2. (1)Hollywood was his invention. (2)Charlie Chaplin said, "The whole industry owes its existence to him." (3)Yet of late years he could not find a job in the town he had invented. (4)He clung to the shadows, a bald, eagle-beaked man, sardonic and alone. (5)At parties, he sat drinking quietly, his sharp eyes panning the room for a glimpse of familiar faces most of them long gone. (6)David Wark Griffith had been The Master, and there was nobody quite like him afterwards.

JAMES AGEE, *Agee on Film: Reviews and Comments*

3. (1)The people who work at Ward, West Virginia, live in little flat yellow houses on stilts that look like chicken-houses. (2)They seem mean and flimsy on the sides of the hills and at the bottom of the hollow, in contrast to the magnificent mountains, wooded now with the forests of mid-June. (3) Between those round and rich-foliaged hills, through the middle of the mining settlement, runs a road which has, on one side of it, a long row of obsolete coal-cars, turned upside down and, on the other, a trickle of a creek, with bare yellow banks, half-dry yellow stones, yellowing rusty tin cans and the axles and wheels of old coal-cars. (4)There are eight hundred or so families at Ward, two or three in most of the houses, and eight or ten children in most of the families. (5) And these families are just as much prisoners, just as much at the mercy of the owners of their dwellings as if they did live in a chicken-yard with a high wire fence around it.

EDMUND WILSON, "Frank Keeney's Coal Diggers," *The American Earthquake*

4. (1)The ordeal and spectacular death of King Kong, the giant ape, undoubtedly have been witnessed by more Americans than have ever seen a performance of *Hamlet, Iphigenia at Aulis,* or even *Tobacco Road.* (2)Since RKO-Radio Pictures first released *King Kong,* a quarter-century has gone by; yet year after year, from prints that grow more rain-beaten, from sound tracks that grow more tinny, ticket-buyers by thousands still pursue Kong's luckless fight against the forces of

technology, tabloid journalism, and the DAR. (3)They see him chloroformed to sleep, see him whisked from his jungle isle to New York and placed on show, see him burst his chains to roam the city (lugging a frightened blonde), at last to plunge from the spire of the Empire State Building, machine-gunned by model airplanes. . . .

(4)Why does the American public refuse to let King Kong rest in peace? (5)It is true, I'll admit, that *Kong* outdid every monster movie before or since in sheer carnage. (6)Producers Cooper and Schoedsack crammed into it dinosaurs, headhunters, riots, aerial battles, bullets, bombs, bloodletting. (7)Heroine Fay Wray, whose function is mainly to scream, shuts her mouth for hardly one uninterrupted minute from first reel to last. (8)It is also true that *Kong* is larded with good healthy sadism, for those whose joy it is to see the frantic girl dangled from cliffs and harried by pterodactyls. (9)But it seems to me that the abiding appeal of the giant ape rests on other foundations.

X. J. KENNEDY, "Who Killed King Kong?"
Dissent, Spring, 1960

II. Leaf through an issue of *Atlantic* or *Harper's* or some other magazine that contains a number of essays.

1. Find two introductions that use techniques of attention-getting mentioned in this chapter.

2. Find two introductions that use techniques not mentioned here.

3. Find one introduction that is not as interesting as it could have been. Tell in a few sentences how it could have been improved.

III. Each of the following introductions does the three jobs mentioned in the last two chapters: catches the reader's attention, presents the essay-idea, and provides necessary clarification—though not necessarily in that order. Analyze each introduction and answer these questions about it:

a. What is the earliest statement of the essay-idea?

b. What techniques are used to clarify the statement?

c. What techniques are used to catch the reader's attention?

Don't be surprised if some passages in the introductions serve several of these functions at once.

Here is a list of the techniques for clarification and attention-getting.
For clarification:
1. Explanation of any vague or unfamiliar words
2. Restatement in more specific terms
3. Helpful rewording
4. Rejection of wrong meanings
5. Illustration
For attention-getting:
1. Provocative essay-idea
2. Rejection of widely accepted opinions
3. Posing of a problem or question
4. The occasion for writing
5. Narrative details
6. Historical events
7. Descriptive details
8. Quotation

1.   (1)To most Americans the Slavery Convention now being
debated in the United Nations' Social and Economic Council
seems more a part of the 19th century than the 20th. (2)Yet
the Convention actually dates only from 1956, and has been
made necessary by the startling fact that slavery, far from
being a vanishing anachronism, seems to be increasing.

(3)Across great sections of Arabia and Africa, both in
fully independent nations and in the protectorates of Western
powers, the buying and selling of slaves is a flourishing
business. . . .

RUPERT WILKINSON, "The Slave Trade,"
New Republic, Sept. 17, 1962

2.   (1)Everyone knows the popular conception of Florence
Nightingale. (2)The saintly, self-sacrificing woman, the delicate maiden of high degree who threw aside the pleasures of
a life of ease to succour the afflicted, the Lady with the Lamp,
gliding through the horrors of the hospital at Scutari, and
consecrating with the radiance of her goodness the dying
soldier's couch—the vision is familiar to all. (3)But the truth
was different. (4)The Miss Nightingale of fact was not as
facile fancy painted her. (5)She worked in another fashion
and towards another end: she moved under the stress of an

impetus which finds no place in the popular imagination. (6) A Demon possessed her. (7)Now demons, whatever else they may be, are full of interest. (8)And so it happens that in the real Miss Nightingale there was more that was interesting than in the legendary; there was also less that was agreeable.

LYTTON STRACHEY, "Florence Nightingale," *Eminent Victorians*

3. (1)On a winter day some years ago, coming out of Pittsburgh on one of the expresses of the Pennsylvania Railroad, I rolled eastward for an hour through the coal and steel towns of Westmoreland County. (2)It was familiar ground; boy and man, I had been through it often before. (3)But somehow I had never quite sensed its appalling desolation. (4)Here was the very heart of industrial America, the center of its most lucrative and characteristic activity, the boast and pride of the richest and grandest nation ever seen on the earth—and here was a scene so dreadfully hideous, so intolerably bleak and forlorn that it reduced the whole aspiration of man to a macabre and depressing joke. (5)Here was wealth beyond computation, almost beyond imagination—and here were human habitations so abominable that they would have disgraced a race of alley cats.

(6)I am not speaking of mere filth. (7)One expects steel towns to be dirty. (8)What I allude to is the unbroken and agonizing ugliness, the sheer revolting monstrousness, of every house in sight. (9)From East Liberty to Greenburg, a distance of twenty-five miles, there was not one in sight from the train that did not insult and lacerate the eye.

H. L. MENCKEN, "The Libido for the Ugly," *A Mencken Chrestomathy*

4. (1)"The average Yaleman, Class of '24," *Time* magazine reported last year after reading something in the New York *Sun*, a newspaper published in those days, "makes $25,111 a year."

(2)Well, good for him!

(3)But, come to think of it, what does this improbably precise and salubrious figure mean? (4)Is it, as it appears to be, evidence that if you send your boy to Yale you won't have to work in your old age and neither will he? (5)Is this average a mean or is it a median? (6)What kind of sample is it based on? (7)You could lump one Texas oilman with two hundred hungry free-lance writers and report *their* average income as $25,000-odd a year. (8)The arithmetic is impeccable, the figure is convincingly precise, and the amount of meaning there is in it you could put in your eye.

(9)In just such ways is the secret language of statistics, so appealing in a fact-minded culture, being used to sensationalize, inflate, confuse, and over-simplify. (10)Statistical terms are necessary in reporting the mass data of social and economic trends, business conditions, "opinion" polls, this year's census. (11)But without writers who use the words with honesty and understanding and readers who know what they mean, the result can only be semantic nonsense.

DARRELL HUFF, "How to Lie with Statistics," *Harper's*, Aug., 1950

IV. Write an introduction that contains attention-getter, essay-idea, and clarification. Perhaps you can base the introduction on one of the essay-ideas you wrote for exercise IV on p. 79 or on one of those listed in exercise II on pp. 95–96.

11

Continuity

In order to secure continuity between paragraphs, the writer must place the paragraphs in a clear order and then link them with transitions.

The arrangement should be planned before the writer turns his paragraph-ideas into paragraphs. At that point he can easily juggle the ideas about and consider one arrangement after another until he finds the clearest.

Two principles of clear arrangement discussed earlier (in Chapter 5) will prove useful in planning most essays. One is the principle of chronological order; the second is that separate topics should be kept separate. At this point a third principle may be added: The writer should save his most difficult ideas for the end of the essay, so that early in the essay he can prepare the reader for the complexities coming later. If the essay were concerned with *Lucky Jim*, the novel by Kingsley Amis, the writer could discuss its characters first, then its social situations, then its themes. The characters are easily understood; the social situations are ludicrously complicated; and the themes can be fully comprehended only after one knows the characters and their social entanglements.

When these principles fail to solve the problems of arrangement, the writer can seek help from the more general principle mentioned in Chapter 5: Always be considerate of the reader. Regard the arrangement from the reader's point of view, decide where he might bog down, and rearrange accordingly.

Once the arrangement is satisfactory and the writer has begun composing his paragraphs, he can connect the paragraphs with transitions.

One way of doing this is to link the last sentences of one paragraph to the first sentence of the next. The transitional devices discussed in Chapter 6 will serve the purpose: explicit *markers* (see pp. 56–57) and *repetition of words or ideas* (pp. 57–58). Consider three illustrations (from Arthur Schlesinger's *The Age of Jackson*), each of which contains the end of one paragraph and the beginning of a second. In each case the opening sentence of the second paragraph achieves continuity by means of transitions. (Explicit markers are italicized; words echoing previous words are underlined.)

> 1. . . . A pious Jeffersonian, [Van Buren] . . . more than once counseled new kinds of governmental action, but he justified them always in terms of sacred texts.
>
> *Yet,* for all his reluctance to abandon dogma, Van Buren was fertile in introducing new methods. Endowed with practical political intuitions of the highest order, he was the first national leader really to take advantage of the growing demand of the people for more active participation in the decisions of government. . . .
>
> 2. . . . Though the Round Hill School flourished in the twen-

ties, Bancroft was no great teacher, and Northampton [was] too restricted a stage. More and more his writings won him attention as a rising young literary man.

Politics, *too,* vaguely attracted <u>him.</u> In 1826, in a Fourth of July speech at Northampton, he declared bravely in favor of "a democracy, a determined, uncompromising democracy," at a time when the word still sounded in some Massachusetts ears with the horrors of the French Revolution. . . .

3.   . . . The planters of the South, the workingmen of the North, . . . small farmers of the North and West . . . could not but have grave misgivings over the workings of the American System. It seemed to them . . . a betrayal of the Jeffersonian promise of equal rights in favor of special benefits for a single class.

<u>This widespread conviction,</u> which would by itself have caused trouble, was aggravated by local grievances. The new Western states felt their development hampered and thwarted by economic and political institutions too much under Eastern control. . . .

Besides linking one paragraph to the next, transitions can link all the paragraphs to the central argument of the essay. They do this by linking the paragraph-ideas to the essay-idea. An illustration from *The Reader over Your Shoulder,* by Robert Graves and Alan Hodge, can show the technique at work. One section of the book proposes this central idea: *The present confusion of English prose has several causes.* Below are some paragraph-ideas from this section. Note the italicized transitions.

In spoken *English* haste has been the chief *cause* of the increasing *confusion.*

Probably the habit of dictation to a typist has been *responsible* for a good deal of *confusion.*

To haste as a *cause* of *confusion* must be added distraction.

A *third* general *cause* of *confusion* has been timidity.

A *fourth cause* of *confusion* has been dividedness of mind.

The transitions link the paragraph-ideas to the central thesis so clearly that the reader could hardly go astray. If he became engrossed in the details of one paragraph and temporarily lost his sense of the argument as a whole, he could pick up the line of reasoning again when he reached the next paragraph-idea.

Yet for all their usefulness, transitions alone cannot guarantee continuity. The paragraphs must first be placed in a clear order, or the transitions will be ineffectual.

Practice

I. Here are three scrambled paragraph outlines. Rearrange the paragraph-ideas so that each outline will be the basis for a clear essay.

1. *Essay-idea:* Robert Owen, as an enterprising young businessman, set up a successful model factory town, but his later experiments in social change were failures.

   a. In his mid-twenties he bought a group of mills in the squalid Scottish village of New Lanark and set about transforming the village into a model factory community.

   b. Not only was New Lanark successful as a social experiment, but it was financially successful and made Owen a wealthy man.

   c. Owen's early life is a poor-boy-makes-good story that might have been taken straight from Horatio Alger.

   d. Encouraged by the success of New Lanark, in 1826 Owen set up a would-be utopia in Indiana, calling it New Harmony; but the experiment failed within two years.

   e. Working conditions in the New Lanark factories were far superior to those in most factories of that era.

   f. In 1791, at the age of twenty, Owen was the boy wonder of the English textile industry.

   g. Owen's final venture was his campaign to establish a nationwide union of English workingmen.

   h. Within a few years New Lanark was world-famous.

   i. Too many forces were opposed to the setting-up of a Grand National Union, and Owen's campaign was a fiasco.

   j. Instead of working in the factories, the children of New Lanark attended a first-rate school, free of charge.

k. The factory workers in New Lanark lived in clean, comfortable surroundings.

Information from Robert L. Heilbroner's
The Worldly Philosophers

2. *Essay-idea:* Hollywood motion pictures are usually not written by a single person but by a team of people—with the result that the scripts are usually not good.

a. It is usually at this point that the director has his say about the script, and if he decides it needs changes, additional writers might have to be brought in.

b. Under these circumstances a single script might be the product of as many as fifteen writers—as was the case with one "A" film.

c. The original conception for a film is not always a writer's but often that of a producer or the executive head of a studio.

d. Even after the movie is being filmed, someone might insist on changing the script further—sometimes a star who wants the script to make him shine more brightly.

e. Basing his work on this initial plan, the writer begins the script, but always under the close supervision of the producer.

f. The script turned out by this assembly line of writers was just what might be expected—a hodge-podge of fragments and inconsistencies.

g. If the producer is not pleased with the progress of his first writer, he is likely to hire a second or third or however many more he thinks he needs.

h. If the present writers refuse to satisfy the star's every whim, the producer may have to find other, more pliable scriptwriters.

i. It would seem that any script written in this way would be mediocre at best.

j. When the chief writers have finished their task, the producer is likely to call in a team of rewrite specialists to work the script over.

Information from Hortense Powdermaker,
Hollywood: The Dream Factory

3. *Essay-idea:* I have always hoped that by reading the

books of philosophers I could absorb wisdom and strength of character, but I find that when I finish reading, I am still much the same man that I was before.

   a. Unlike Epictetus, I am impatient with all discomforts, even small ones.

   b. As soon as I was able, I procured a copy of Epictetus, and I found that I agreed with nearly everything he said.

   c. In spite of my repeated failures to follow the teachings of philosophers like Epictetus, I continue to believe that he and Socrates and Emerson and Marcus Aurelius must be men of wisdom.

   d. The other day I overheard a conversation in which someone praised the teachings of Epictetus.

   e. Unlike Epictetus, I am far from being indifferent to material possessions, and if anything of mine is stolen I become angry and upset about it.

   f. I am convinced that to practice the teachings of these sages, one would have to become a saint and ignore the things most people regard as valuable.

   g. Though I agree in theory with the teachings of Epictetus, I know I can't follow them in practice.

Thoughts from Robert Lynd's "On Not Being a Philosopher"

II. For exercise II on p. 87 you wrote a paragraph outline. Go back to it now and arrange the paragraph-ideas in the clearest order.

III. 1. Below is the paragraph outline for one section of Marchette Chute's *Shakespeare of London*. Each paragraph-idea contains transitional words that link it to the central idea. Find those transitional words.

Central idea: A young man up from the country would find that London . . . people [were] . . . intent on enjoying themselves.

    I. Many London shows cost the happy population nothing at all.

    II. Another source of public entertainment was executions, and the criminals knew what was expected of them by the public.

    III. If a Londoner liked to look at strange animals there was the zoo in the Tower.

    IV. Betting members of the population spent much of

their time watching cock fights in an arena near Smith-
field.

   V.   Best of all, however, there were plays, and whatever a
Londoner's interests might be, there was sure to be a
play in town that would suit him.

2.   Here is another paragraph outline, this time for a section of
Norman Holland's article on Horatio Alger: "Hobbling with
Horatio, or The Uses of Literature." Alger was an enormously popular American author of the late 1800's who
specialized in rags-to-riches novels—novels, that is, about
boys whose honesty and diligence carried them from
poverty to wealth.

     Again, find the transitional words by which the para-
graph-ideas are linked to the central idea.

Central idea: The Horatio Alger story is a simple wish-
fulfilling fantasy.

   I.   Certainly one wish Alger gratifies is the boy's desire to
become a man.

   II.   Alger . . . does more than simply gratify a boy's wish
to become a man. He provides a foil, the Other
Boy. . . . The Other Boy represents the infantile wish
to get the symbols of adulthood without sacrificing the
privileges of childhood.

   III.   The Alger mother . . . plays her part in the wish-ful-
filling constellation.

   IV.   By far the most satisfying figure . . . is the Alger
father. . . .

IV.   This exercise is concerned with the use of transitions to connect
the final sentences of one paragraph with the opening sentence
of the next.

     In the essay "Winged Bullets," an account of the history
and habits of the dragonfly, Edwin Way Teale makes skillful use
of this technique. Below are portions of "Winged Bullets"—the
endings of several paragraphs and the beginnings of the ones
that follow. Seven opening sentences have been italicized and
numbered. Find the transitional words in each of those sentences.

     A dragonfly, slanting over the pool [of tar] on glittering
wings, had swooped too low. Writhing and twisting, it lay
gripped by the black glue of the tar pit. . . . Finally . . . it sank

deeper and deeper into the tar just as, long ago, so many of its ancestors had done at this identical spot on the changing, eroding face of the earth.

1. *For the dragonflies . . . were insect pioneers, one of the earliest forms to appear.* In the prehistoric jungles . . . dragonflies as big as hawks soared through the steaming air. . . . Possessed of wings that measured nearly thirty inches from tip to tip they were the largest insects that ever lived.

2. *The towering trees of that day have been dwarfed to the club moss and the ground pines of the present, and the dragonfly has shrunk with them.* . . . Yet, in many of its habits and characteristics, the dragonfly is still a creature from the distant past.

3. *Often it rushes through the air, scooping up its victims in a basket formed of spine-fringed legs, sucking their bodies dry and letting the carcasses fall to the ground, all without slackening its headlong pace.* . . . Its veined and transparent wings, moving on the average twenty-eight times a second, can carry it through the air at speeds approaching sixty miles an hour.

4. *So completely is the dragonfly a creature of the air that the female often remains upon the wing when laying her eggs.* . . . She usually bumps along the surface of a pond, dipping the tip of her abdomen in the water at intervals, leaving behind clumps of tiny eggs. . . . Sometimes the female dives completely under the surface to attach her eggs to the leaves or stems of plants. . . .

5. *The shape of the dragonfly's egg varies.* . . . Nobody knows how many eggs a dragonfly is capable of laying. Dr. Leland O. Howard tells of finding 110,000 separate eggs in a single clump.

6. *What would happen if all these eggs hatched out and reached maturity is indicated by the "dragonfly year" of 1839.* Over a large part of . . . Europe . . . immense swarms of the insects followed the rivers and darkened the sky. . . . Hunger drove millions of dragonflies to seek new feeding grounds.

7. *Occasionally dragonflies migrate in great numbers.* . . . Off the coast of Europe, vessels have sometimes sighted small swarms far out at sea.

12

The Conclusion

Rather than stopping short or fading away, an essay should leave the reader with a strong final impression.

In a brief essay, one of perhaps six or seven paragraphs, the writer need not add a separate conclusion but can let the last of his supporting paragraphs serve as a conclusion.

That final paragraph should be an important one. If the essay maintains that the Roman emperor Caligula committed vile atrocities, some of the most atrocious should be saved for the last paragraph. If the essay argues that America's "Gilded Age" had some surprisingly big spenders, the last paragraph should cite one of the biggest. In many essays the argument will naturally end with a climactic paragraph. Suppose the essay-idea were this: "Only toward the end of Sinclair Lewis's novel *Babbitt* does George Babbitt achieve self-knowledge." The early paragraphs would be concerned with the Babbitt who evades self-knowledge by various dodges and delusions; the final paragraphs would deal with Babbitt's discovery that he has been a prisoner of his society. The essay would naturally lead toward its most important paragraph.

If the final supporting paragraph is to serve as a conclusion, it must not only be important as a whole but must end with important sentences. These last sentences of the essay should be a *forceful reminder of the essay-idea*. The essay on Babbitt might end:

> . . . Thus Babbitt recognizes that he has been living in odious traps. The Athletic Club, his business, his church, even his family—they have all been traps. In the last speech of the book, Babbitt puts his new self-knowledge into words: ". . . I've never done a single thing I've wanted to in my whole life! I don't know's I've accomplished anything except just get along. I figure out I've made about a quarter of an inch out of a possible hundred rods. . . ." He has seen his prison for what it is. After years of self-evasion, Babbitt has finally gained self-knowledge.

In a longer essay, however, this sort of ending might seem abrupt and ineffectual. An essay of ten paragraphs or so is likely to need a separate conclusion.

If the essay on Babbitt were that long, the writer might add a separate paragraph of *summary*.

> . . . He has finally seen his prison for what it is.
> During most of his life George Babbitt has refused to know himself. Only toward the end of the novel, when Babbitt is well into his middle-age years, does he achieve self-recognition.

In addition to providing a summary, the writer may sometimes hazard a *prediction*.

> . . . He has seen his prison for what it is.
> After years of self-evasion, Babbitt has finally gained

self-knowledge. Perhaps with his new insight he can make his life more satisfying. If he cannot escape his dungeon he can at least appreciate more keenly the pleasures his imprisonment allows him, the beams of light that occasionally come through the bars. His last act in the novel shows that his self-knowledge makes a difference. He condones his son's marriage and tells him:

> "Don't be scared of the family. No, nor all of Zenith. Nor of yourself, the way I've been. Go ahead, old man! The world is yours!"

Notice that the writer is cautious in his conjectures, and wisely so. A reckless prediction might convince the reader that the writer's ideas are not to be trusted—hardly the final impression an essayist wishes to make.

Another way of ending the essay is to mention *further implications of the essay-idea*—implications for subjects other than the one the essay has been discussing. In the essay on Babbitt the writer might conclude by telling whether the essay-idea applies to characters in other novels by Sinclair Lewis or characters created by other American authors. Or the writer could apply the essay-idea to present-day American society.

> . . . He has finally seen his prison for what it is.
>
> After years of self-evasion, Babbitt has finally gained self-knowledge. He has been living the sort of unexamined life that most people fall into much of the time, especially in these days of the "other-directed," "organization" man. He has engaged in only those kinds of work and play that his society told him were acceptable. He has valued other people's assessment of him more than his own; he has hardly ever looked at himself except through their eyes. Only towards the end of the novel does he discover the old truism that James Thurber said we must all reconsider: "All men should strive to learn before they die what they are running from, and to, and why."

Try an ending of this sort if you can do it convincingly. Or try a prediction if it is plausible. But if neither kind of ending comes easily, don't force it, or the result may strike the reader as being farfetched and false. You would do better to offer merely a brief summary of the essay's central thesis.

Practice

I. Read the essay on pp. 127–129. It has no separate concluding paragraph but lets the end of the final supporting paragraph serve as conclusion. Is that conclusion adequate or not? Explain your answer in a few sentences.

II. Each of the following paragraphs serves as a separate conclusion in an essay too long to do without one. What does each conclusion offer the reader? Summary? Prediction? Further implications of the essay-idea? A combination of several of these?

1. (See the introduction on p. 105.)

In Hollywood last week, many people were offering epitaphs for Griffith. But perhaps the most succinct was the one presented years ago by another man who could claim to know about such things, the Frenchman René Clair. "Nothing essential," he said, "has been added to the art of the motion picture since Griffith."

JAMES AGEE, *Agee on Film: Reviews and Comments*

2. (See the introduction on pp. 104–105.)

Despite the social revolution of the last decade, loyalty to the crown is stronger than ever and dramatic censorship is safely barricaded behind palace walls. Perhaps feelings will change if some major playwright is discovered in the next generation and if a play, which enough people consider outstanding and more wish to see, is barred from regular production. But as far as one can see at present, and unless the Earl of Scarborough bans "My Fair Lady" on the ground that it contains dangerous social doctrines, the censor's job is safe. And the delightful day may come when the Lord Chamberlain will caution a troupe of visiting Russian actors against putting on a play with too much controversy or freedom of ideas!

GEORGE STEINER, "Close-Up of Britain's Censor,"
New York Times Magazine, Sept. 2, 1956

3. (See the introduction on pp. 105–106.)

Every day in the week on a screen somewhere in the world, King Kong relives his agony. Again and again he expires on the Empire State Building, as audiences of the devout assist his sacrifice. We watch him die, and by extension kill the ape within our bones, but these little deaths of ours occur in prosaic surroundings. We do not die on a tower, New York before our feet, nor do we give our lives to smash a few flying machines. It is not for us to bring to a momentary standstill the civilization in which we move. King Kong does this for us. And so we kill him again and again, in much-spliced celluloid, while the ape in us expires from day to day, obscure, in desperation.

x. j. kennedy, "Who Killed King Kong?"
Dissent, Spring, 1960

4. (See the introduction on p. 102.)

The conclusion can hardly be avoided: American schools (mostly grade and high, but even some private schools) *must* achieve the means of satisfactory basic training. They must spend more time on more central subjects. They must do thoroughly the grinding work of inculcating basic facts and logical principles. I am almost ashamed at having reached so simple and pedestrian a conclusion. But it cannot be over-stressed: it must be done at any cost, even that of accepting some central control. If we look after the schools, the colleges will look after themselves.

derek colville, "British and American Schools,"
Harper's, Oct., 1957

5. (See the introduction on p. 107.)

Let me finish—rashly—with a prediction. The slave trade will drag on. The U.S. and Britain will continue to subsidize it, as the unfortunate requirement for obtaining Middle Eastern oil and Middle Eastern alliances. And then, suddenly, bewilderingly, the political picture will change, as it is always changing. The revolutions that occured in Egypt and Iraq will occur again, elsewhere. Already, Egypt has used the slavery issue in its attacks on Saudi Arabia. The Western powers will again be discredited, as the "friends of dictators" and, what is worse, the friends of dictators who lost out. In the United States and Britain thinking people will go into agonies of hindsight; they may start asking whether in fact their governments could have put more pressure on Middle East rulers to ameliorate their regimes, and whether this pressure could have been applied without "playing into the hands of the Russians" or bankrupting oil companies. But by then such questions will be academic.

rupert wilkinson, "The Slave Trade,"
New Republic, Sept. 17, 1962

13

The Title

Accuracy is the chief requisite of a title. Sometimes it is the only requisite; the title of a scientific report or scholarly article can be merely a clear indication of the content ("The Characterization of Edmund in Shakespeare's *King Lear*"; "A Survey of the Techniques for Draining Swamps"). But ordinarily the title should meet a second requirement: it should be interesting enough to catch the reader's attention.

A simple, straightforward title may be able to satisfy both requirements—may be interesting as well as accurate. Montaigne was content with such unadorned titles as "Of Liars," "Of Cannibals," and "How We Cry and Laugh for the Same Thing";

and the tradition of the straightforward title is still observed in modern writing:

> "On Pleasure-Seeking" (G. K. Chesterton)
>
> "In Defense of James Baldwin" (Norman Podhoretz)
>
> "You Americans Are Murdering the Language" (Lord Conesford)
>
> "In Favor of Capital Punishment" (Jacques Barzun)
>
> "What Use Is Poetry?" (Gilbert Highet)
>
> "Is Our Common Man Too Common?" (Joseph Wood Krutch)

A straightforward title can catch the reader's attention by referring to a particularly interesting topic (as does "On Pleasure-Seeking") or by raising a provocative issue (as do "In Favor of Capital Punishment" and "Is Our Common Man Too Common?").

Another kind of title is the clever, catchy phrase that snares the reader's attention but leaves him guessing about the topic. An essay by Paul Jacobs, for instance, is concerned with Los Angeles's Forest Lawn Memorial Park, whose management tries to comfort both the living and the dead with sentimental inscriptions, soft music, and lush landscape. Mr. Jacobs might have used the title "The Policies of Forest Lawn Memorial Park" —entirely clear but quite dull. He preferred something less clear but more likely to catch the reader's interest: "The Most Cheerful Graveyard in the World."

Here are other catchy titles that only hint at subject or thesis:

> "They Made the Cigar Respectable" (Keith Monroe). The essay explains how advertising has changed the public "image" of the cigar.
>
> "Science Has Spoiled My Supper" (Philip Wylie). Mr. Wylie argues that the new scientific processing of food has made it tasteless.
>
> "A Way of Death" (Dwight Macdonald). The essay is concerned with the "way of life" of our Southern sharecroppers.
>
> "The Know-Nothing Bohemians" (Norman Podhoretz).

This essay censures Jack Kerouac and his cult, who scorn reason and worship spontaneity.

"Who Cares Who Killed Roger Ackroyd?" (Edmund Wilson). Mr. Wilson ridicules murder mysteries, including Agatha Christie's *Who Killed Roger Ackroyd?*

"The Vigilantes" (Fred B. Millett). Mr. Millett denounces the suppressors of literature.

An essay may have a second title—a *sub-title*.

"They Made the Cigar Respectable: How Advertisers Changed Public Opinion"

"A Way of Death: The Plight of Our Sharecroppers"

"The Vigilantes: The Censors Are Still Among Us"

The first title can be a teaser; the second, an explicit label.

The writer who wishes to use a catchy phrase in a title must use one consistent with his essay. The title "The Vigilantes" suits an essay deriding suppressors of literature, but if the essay had praised such people it would have needed a title with different implications, one such as "Defenders of Good Taste." And a title may have to reflect attitudes more subtle than praise or derision. Because Mr. Macdonald's essay is concerned with the hopelessness of sharecroppers' lives, his title, "A Way of Death," reflects their despair. Because Mr. Monroe's essay notes something comical in the fact that "They Made the Cigar Respectable," his title has a touch of the comical. The titles are accurate as well as interesting, and thus possess both requisites of a good title.

Practice

I. Choose five essay-ideas about which you might wish to write essays. Then devise two titles for each of your five hypothetical essays. One title should be a straightforward label, interesting but explicit. The other should be a puzzling attention-getter.

Below are some essay-ideas you can choose from. Others may be found in exercise II on pp. 95–96. Or use essay-ideas of your own, such as you devised for exercise IV on p. 79.

1. Several of Fitzgerald's works of fiction satirize the sort of woman for whom money and comfort are more important than people.
2. Of the three forms of execution used in the United States, the gas chamber is the least inhumane; both the electric chair and the gallows are barbaric in their cruelty.
3. In many Western films the career of the professional gunslinger follows a conventional pattern. (See the paragraph outline on p. 81.)
4. Since the revolution of 1917, Russia has increased its wealth considerably; but it has not redistributed its wealth to achieve the revolution's ostensible goal: a classless society.
5. In the soliloquy beginning "To be or not to be," Hamlet indulges in self-pity and self-dramatization.
6. In His speech at the end of the Book of Job, God admits having created Evil and declares that Evil is necessary in the universe.
7. In criticizing their societies' values and institutions, Shaw and Mencken employed similar techniques of satire. (See the paragraph outline on p. 84.)
8. At least three times during the administration of President Ulysses S. Grant, schemers made use of the federal government to swindle the public.
9. In his novel *Erewhon* Samuel Butler satirized those people of his time who believed that by mere church-going they could save their souls.
10. Several of today's leading jazz musicians, well trained in modern musical theory, often use practices derived from such composers as Bartok and Stravinsky.
11. Robert Owen, as an enterprising young businessman, set up a successful model factory town, but his later experiments in social change were failures. (See the paragraph outline on pp. 113–114.)

Further Practice on the Short Essay

I. Evaluate the following essays, two samples of student writing. The first essay is concerned with works of literature. The second essay portrays a college student who, by the standards of the 1950's or early 1960's, was a most daring journalist. In evaluating the essay, remember that its author was writing about the campus life of another era.

1. Trying to Cancel the Past

More than two thousand years ago, the Psalmist expressed remorse for his sins:

... My iniquities have gone over my head;
they weigh like a burden too heavy for me.
5 *My wounds grow foul and fester*
because of my foolishness ...
I am utterly spent and crushed;
I groan because of the tumult of my heart.

Psalm 38, *Revised Standard Version*

10 Yet the Psalmist went on to utter the hope that he might still achieve salvation.

In modern literature, too, we come upon figures whose "iniquities" have become "like a burden too heavy" and who reach out for some kind of salvation. In several modern
15 American novels a central character engages in sordid duplicity for much of his life but then seeks to realize a dream that will absolve him of his past. He gropes for something that will give his life meaning. He fears that he has been a mere "drunken beggar on horseback," dissolute and directionless,
20 but he hopes to change all that and reach some goal of high value, so that the ugliness in his past will be canceled.

In *All the King's Men* by Robert Penn Warren, Willie Stark reaches toward a goal whose goodness might be able to justify his past, but he fails to achieve absolution. Stark
25 has made himself a powerful governor, almost a dictator, by ruthlessly manipulating the people around him and by channeling the will of the voters without regard for law or traditional ethics. In the process of acquiring power he has employed bribery and blackmail without hesitation. He has
30 played upon popular sentiments with little concern for truth or justice. But Stark keeps insisting that power itself is not his real goal. He insists that goodness and evil are unavoidably interrelated and that to achieve good, one must use evil or tarnished materials. Everything is made of dirt; what
35 matters is how one shapes dirt into instruments that can help

the common people. Stark believes that through evil means he can create something good. The symbol in his mind of the good he can achieve is the construction of a new public hospital. His dream of building a great hospital for the people of
40 his state becomes an obsession with him. He desperately needs to create something undeniably good, something undeniably beneficial to the common people for whom he claims he has fought. Otherwise the sordidness of his past will be without justification. But Stark is never able to build his hos-
45 pital. The evil he has set in motion not only destroys his dream of building a hospital but destroys Stark himself.

In much of this, Willie Stark is similar to Jay Gatsby, of F. Scott Fitzgerald's novel *The Great Gatsby*. Though Gatsby is not concerned with creating goodness, he too is reaching
50 toward a goal that he hopes will justify his sordid past. He wishes to realize his dream of love between himself and Daisy Buchanan. Like Stark, Gatsby is utterly obsessed with his dream, and he believes that only the realization of that dream can make his past seem worthwhile. Hints scattered
55 throughout the novel suggest that Gatsby has engaged in criminal activities. And the money he has made by these questionable activities he spends on lavish parties that are really tawdry, meaningless affairs. But Gatsby has done all this to win Daisy. After each night's party is over he stares
60 across the bay in back of his mansion, stares at the green light on the dock behind Daisy's house. Gatsby believes that if he wins Daisy his life would be made worthwhile. But, like Stark, Gatsby is destroyed without having realized his dream.

In Bernard Malamud's *The Assistant*, Frank Alpine
65 reaches for a goal that will absolve him of his past and help him become a better person. Like Gatsby, Frank dreams of a love that might be able to cancel the rottenness of his past. Frank has been a vagrant without a purpose. And he has been a thief. He took part in the holdup of Morris Bober's
70 grocery store, and later, after becoming the grocer's assistant, he stole from the cash register. But Frank clutches the belief that he can atone for his past mistakes—by confessing his sins, by helping the Bobers survive, and by winning Helen Bober's love. By the end of the novel he has confessed, has
75 carried the Bobers through difficult times, and still has hope

of winning Helen. Perhaps he will succeed in absolving himself of his past and in reaching a new way of life with Helen. This is his dream—like Willie's shining hospital, like Gatsby's green light, beckoning him across the bay of past failures.

2. A Majority of One

Last Monday *Minority Report* came out for the first time this year. Some friends and I were hurrying over to the Student Union for a quick lunch. But right outside the main doors we were held up by a crowd gathered around a card table.
5   Sale of football tickets? Free passes to a local movie-house? No. It was *Minority Report,* on sale for thirty cents a copy and selling as fast as the boy behind the table could hand copies out and make change. Short of time though we were, we waited ten minutes to buy copies. Then we read most of
10 the magazine while eating lunch, and argued about it on our way back to the library and for twenty minutes after we got there.

      Minority Report, a weekly mimeographed magazine on our campus, is probably our most exciting publication. Certainly it's the most popular. The quarterly literary magazine
15 sells about 1500 copies. The *Daily Sentinal,* the traditional school paper, sells about 1900. But *Minority Report* sells more than 2300 every time it comes out. And yet *Minority Report* is a one-man show. It was originated and set in motion
20 by one person, and the same person does all the writing for it. So it may seem a miracle that the magazine survives. How could one person handle all the details of production? And how could one person have enough to say each week to outsell the other campus magazines? The answer lies in the
25 nature of that one person: Clyde Hooker. Only someone of his remarkable abilities could keep *Minority Report* going. Clyde has a tremendous capacity for hard work, a managerial skill that would seem more appropriate in a chief executive for IBM, and an unwearying talent for lively, incisive writing.
30   Yet he doesn't look like someone with those abilities. He's tall—about six-foot, four—and loose, sometimes limp. As he walks around the campus every afternoon, hunting down news and chatting with people, he never hurries. He

droops his head much of the time, lets his belly hang out, and
lets his long feet slap the sidewalk like so much loose leather.
His hair is cut in what would be called crew-style except that
it's rarely short. He does get a crew-cut to begin with, but
then he lets it grow out for ten or twelve weeks until it becomes downright uncomfortable around the ears and neck;
then he gets another crew-cut. He wears round, colorless
glasses and has a round, colorless face. The face has only
three expressions: one, a big, happy grin; two, a lost-in-
thought expression, with mouth and eyes hanging open;
three, a serious, worried look, with mouth pursed and eyes
narrowed. Except on the Sundays when he attends chapel, he
wears only one outfit: long-sleeved white shirt, not ironed,
buttoned in some places, mostly hanging loose; khaki pants,
loose and baggy; and brown loafers, loose and flappy. Yet,
despite appearances, Clyde is a remarkably hard-driving person. Because his family has little extra money, even the
scholarship money Clyde receives does not pay all the bills,
and he has been working his way through college. For his
freshman and sophomore years he worked at any jobs he
could find. For six months he worked twenty to thirty hours a
week in a downtown art theater. "At least I got to see a few
good movies," he says, with the big-grin expression. Then,
because he needed more money, he switched to being bus-boy
and cashier in the Student Union cafeteria. But when he came
back to school at the beginning of his junior year, last year,
he decided to become self-employed. "If I had to work so
much of the time," he explains with the serious expression,
"I could at least do work that I liked." He was asked the obvious question: "If you decided to earn your money by writing, why didn't you go to work for the *Daily Sentinal?*" Big-
grin response: "That wouldn't be doing the kind of work I
like. The *Sentinal* is near-sighted, and doesn't much care
what's going on around it anyway." With the serious expression: "I wanted to start a paper that would come out less
often maybe, but would say things worth saying."

But of course Clyde had to do much more than merely
want a paper of his own. He had to be good at getting things
done—at a profit. At the start, last September, besides writing
all the copy himself, he had to organize and oversee the entire

production and sales of his new magazine. He had to hire
reliable people—a typist, a student salesman, and someone to
do the mimeographing; he had to help these people out when
something went wrong; and he had to handle all the banking
and paying-out of money. At first he was mostly paying out.
During that chancy period he was taking a tremendous
gamble with his money, his time, and his health. By the end
of November, however, he had made the magazine a success.
The operation was running smoothly, and there was money in
the bank. He had proved his managerial ability. But he had lost
so much sleep in the process that he began to suffer dizzy
spells at least once a day. "The only remedy was black coffee
run through the strainer twice." So he boosted the price per
copy from twenty-five cents to thirty and hired sophomore
Gerry Morrison as business manager, at the rate of $80 a
week.

Clyde himself has been earning at least $130 a week.
And he deserves it—partly because he worked so hard at the
start of *Minority Report* but also because he has continued to
work hard. He follows a strict regimen for himself. Each
weekday morning he starts in on his course work at six, two
hours before breakfast. And after breakfast he makes use of
every spare minute. If he has ten minutes between classes or
just five minutes during a slow-moving lecture, out comes a
book. By working this steadily he usually finishes his course
work by two in the afternoon. After that he concentrates on
gathering material for *Minority Report*. He goes "on the
prowl," as he says, stalking all the places where people might
know some news. He visits the deans' offices, the athletic
training fields, and the rooms of club presidents and campus
politicians. He chats with secretaries and campus police, people who are usually closemouthed but occasionally have a
juicy piece of news that they can't resist telling. He banters
with janitors and groundskeepers, who know a surprising
amount about life on the campus. And at least once a week
he visits a few off-campus sources of news—particularly the
local newspaper office and the police station. Then, in the
evening, Clyde retires to his room and writes out what he has
seen and heard and thought during the day. When Saturday
morning comes he revises and polishes all that he has written

during the week. Then he takes in the week's major athletic
event and the most important new movie in town, writes up
his comments on both, decides whether any "letters to the
editor" are worth printing, gets the copy into final shape, and
has it ready for George Morrison by two o'clock sharp every
Sunday afternoon.

The amount that Clyde writes each week is not so surprising as the fact that it is consistently entertaining. How is
it that week after week he can keep us eager to buy the next
issue? One answer is that he refuses to print dull, trivial news
items. "I let the *Sentinel* print the stuff that people already
know about or don't care about," he explains. "People *know*
when the Big Prom is coming, and they don't *care* whether
the theme' is Orange Blossom Time or Jet Set Time or whatever nonsense it is. At least, the ones that *do* care had better
read the *Sentinel* and skip *Minority Report*." Clyde aims for
the kind of story that newspapermen used to call a "scoop."
Last year, when the Society for Open Debate invited members of a fascist party to speak on campus, Clyde found out
from the president of the Society, then pledged him to secrecy
until after *Minority Report* appeared. Clyde was also the first
to tell us that the president of the college was thinking about
barring the fascists from the campus. Clyde does write other
news articles besides "scoops," but only if he can make them
interesting by means of the slant he takes or the style of his
writing. His sportswriting is excellent. Though not much of
an athlete himself, he sees far more from the sidelines than
most spectators do, and reports his observations with honesty
and vigor. The *Sentinel* sportswriting, by comparison, is
ineffectual. Here is part of the *Sentinel's* description of a play
that scored against us last year:

As their halfback (Marino, number 37) came around the
end, our left end (Collins, number 52) made a game try
to stop him, but was not quite able to.

Clyde wrote:

Halfback Marino headed wide around our left side.
Sammy Collins, our end there, saw what was coming. A
fast, solid 230 pounds, he speared his way right between
the two men trying to block him, took three, four, five
long strides to his left, and dove for Marino's legs. If he

155 had caught one of those high-stepping feet, it would have been the tackle of the season. But he missed.

While the "news" occupies about one third of each *Minority Report,* the rest is devoted to editorials and reviews or to what newspapers call "feature articles" and "stories in depth." These are invariably worth reading. Through them 160 all Clyde keeps his intellect working at high speed. He never settles for the hackneyed or the obvious. His interviews with the chief of the campus police showed most of us for the first time just how far into petty crime some of our fellow students have been driven—some of them having been caught at 165 cashing bad checks or systematically stealing from the gymnasium locker rooms. And we all knew about the right-wing political group on campus, but it was only after Clyde had written his series of articles on the group that we knew how much encouragement and money it was receiving from alumni 170 of the college. In his movie reviews, too, Clyde is never satisfied with the obvious. When *Loneliness of the Long-Distance Runner* came to town for a rerun last year, the *Sentinel* gave it perfunctory praise: ". . . widely acclaimed . . . based on the excellent story by Alan Sillitoe, who also wrote the screen- 175 play . . . well worth seeing . . ." and more of the same. But Clyde wrote an analytical review that caused most of his readers to see the movie, read the book, and argue many hours about both. His editorials have the same ability to provoke argument, the same disdain for platitude. When about a 180 quarter of the students boycotted their classes last year, the *Sentinel* merely tried to console both students and teachers:

> The dissatisfied should remember that no education can be perfect, but that in our school education is carried out as well as anywhere in the country. And our teachers are 185 always trying to make it even better than it is.

But Clyde went into the matter more deeply. About the students, he said:

> I am not convinced that the boycotting students truly want a better education. Though it's hard to tell 190 from their muddled list of "Basic Principles of Education," they seem to want not so much a better education as an easier one, one that requires less time and strain. The "basic principles" really demand no basic changes

195
in the system of education, but merely seem to want *less* of the same old thing. And what else are we to make of the boycotters' picketing techniques last week? Beer cans were more in evidence than books.

200
Perhaps the boycotters are right to want an easier time of it. But let them say straight out that that's what they want, instead of taking a few days' vacation in the name of "basic principles."

To the teachers, on the other hand, Clyde said:

205

210
Even if last week's boycotts were based on "principles" that didn't have much thinking behind them, still the boycotts should not be ignored. They are a symptom that something is wrong with the school. Perhaps the admissions system is at fault for admitting too many students who would rather not be studying, who go to college only because parents tell them that they'd better go. Or perhaps the education itself, the system of departments and lectures and classes and exams, is somehow at fault. As Dean Arnold has admitted, the last time the faculty engaged in a thorough evaluation of the system was twenty years ago.

215
No easy answers here. *Minority Report* avoids easy answers. This is to be expected. Clyde doesn't do things the easy way. If he did he would still be a cashier at the Student Union, and *Minority Report* would be nothing but a daydream occasionally fluttering through his mind.

II. Now write an essay of your own. It might be concerned with literature, like "Trying To Cancel the Past." It might be a portrayal of an interesting person, like "A Majority of One." It might be about education, in which case the essay-ideas listed on pp. 95–96 can offer suggestions. Or it might be based on one of the essay-ideas you wrote for exercise IV on p. 79.

The Complex Essay

III

The short essay on pp. 127–129 has a crucial weakness, as may be seen from this paragraph outline.

Trying to Cancel the Past

Essay-idea: In several American novels a central character engages in sordid duplicity for much of his life, then seeks to realize a dream that will absolve him of his past.

  I. In *All the King's Men* by Robert Penn Warren, Willie Stark reaches toward a goal whose goodness might be able to justify his past, but he fails to achieve absolution.

II. In *The Great Gatsby* by F. Scott Fitzgerald, Jay Gatsby reaches for a goal that he hopes will justify his sordid past.

III. In Bernard Malamud's *The Assistant*, Frank Alpine reaches for a goal that will absolve him of his past and help him to enter a new life.

Perhaps the first problem one spots is that the paragraph-ideas are not really paragraph-ideas. Even someone who has not read the novels mentioned may be able to see that each of the so-called paragraph-ideas is too general to be defended in a paragraph. And if we search for the cause of this difficulty, we find the essay's fundamental weakness. Its essay-idea is too general to be defended in a short essay. If the writer wishes to handle this large a topic, a study of three characters from three novels, then his short essay must be converted into a *complex essay.*

He must make two basic changes. First, each paragraph-idea must become a *section-idea:* each must be developed not in a single paragraph but in an entire section of the essay. Second, each section-idea must be supported by several paragraph-ideas. Thus the outline for a complex essay on the three American novels could take the following form:

Trying to Cancel the Past

Essay-idea: In several modern American novels a central character engages in sordid duplicity for much of his life, then seeks to realize a dream that will absolve him of his past.

First section-idea: In *All the King's Men* by Robert Penn Warren, Willie Stark reaches toward a goal whose goodness might be able to justify his past, but he fails to achieve absolution.

Paragraph-idea: For many years Willie Stark has used the political tactics of a tyrant.

Paragraph-idea: In his personal dealings Stark has been a bully and a cheat.

Paragraph-idea: But Stark wishes to benefit the people of his state and prove to himself that he is capable of goodness.

Paragraph-idea: The hospital he hopes to build is meant to be evidence of his goodness.

Paragraph-idea: But Stark learns that no single act, not even the building of a hospital, can compensate for years of cruelty and opportunism.

Second section-idea: In *The Great Gatsby* by F. Scott Fitzgerald, Jay Gatsby reaches for a goal that he hopes will justify his sordid past.

Paragraph-idea: Throughout the novel there are hints that Gatsby has been engaged in criminal activities.

Paragraph-idea: Gatsby's extravagant parties are actually sordid.

Paragraph-idea: The aim of all these activities has been to win Daisy's love; if Gatsby can win her over, he will feel that his wrongdoings have been justified.

Paragraph-idea: But Gatsby learns that he has been mistaken to value Daisy so highly.

Third section-idea: In Bernard Malamud's *The Assistant*, Frank Alpine reaches for a goal that will absolve him of his past and help him to enter a new life.

Paragraph-idea: Frank has been a thief and a liar.

Paragraph-idea: But he suffers remorse, and hopes to become a better person.

Paragraph-idea: His love for Helen Bober is largely the result of his remorse and his hopefulness.

Paragraph-idea: At the end of the novel Frank is still struggling to change himself and still has a chance of winning Helen's love.

Note that each section of a complex essay is like a short essay, with a section-idea in place of the essay-idea. In evaluating each section, the writer can ask the questions he would ask about a short essay. (Is the central idea, the section-idea, clear and coherent? Are the paragraph-ideas relevant to the section-idea? Do they defend it persuasively?) Then he can ask whether the section-ideas work together to support the essay-idea. When the answers are satisfactory, the outline may be turned into an essay.

14

The Outline

To prevent the many section-ideas, paragraph-ideas, and supporting details from getting out of control, the writer can outline his complex essay with the following procedure.

1. Initial acquaintance with the subject. If the writer is planning an essay on *All the King's Men, The Great Gatsby,* and *The Assistant,* then obviously he begins by reading the novels.

2. Limiting the topic. After reading the novels and recognizing that he cannot discuss all their characters and themes, the writer concentrates on one central figure from each work, then on a few salient features the three characters have in common.

3. *Stating the essay-idea.*   A tentative formulation like the following serves the purpose: "Each of these characters did wrong, then felt remorse, then looked for some kind of absolution." This is an adequate guide; later it can be revised for style and precision.

4. *The preliminary outline.*   This is a tentative listing of subtopics. For example:

> *Essay-idea:*   Each of these characters did wrong, then felt remorse, then looked for some kind of absolution.
> I. Willie Stark
>   A. Wrongdoing
>   B. Remorse
>   C. Search for absolution
> II. Gatsby
>   A. Wrongdoing
>   B. Remorse
>   C. Search for absolution
> III. Frank Alpine
>   A. Wrongdoing
>   B. Remorse
>   C. Search for absolution

5. *Taking notes.*   The writer returns now to his sources, the three American novels, reads them closely, and quotes or paraphrases important passages on 3 x 5 or 4 x 6 index cards, until he has ample evidence to support his ideas.

But if he indiscriminately jots down something from every page he reads, the notes will become so inclusive as to be useless. He should record only passages relevant to the preliminary outline. In *The Great Gatsby* he finds a passage suggesting Gatsby's involvement in criminal activities. Because the subject is relevant to entry *IIA* in the rough outline (Gatsby's "wrongdoing"), the writer makes a note of the passage. Further reading discloses that members of the respectable elite were also involved in criminal ventures; no better than Gatsby really, they engaged in crime if the profit was big and their reputations could stay clean—an interesting irony. But since it is irrelevant to the preliminary outline, the writer passes it by without making a note.

(This is not to imply that the preliminary outline should tyrannize over the planning of the essay. The outline is tentative. A rereading of the sources may lead the writer to revise both his essay-idea and the outline.)

On each card the writer must indicate the subtopic the note pertains to (for reasons that will become clear at step 6). A quick way of doing this is to use a shorthand based on the rough outline. If the note card mentions an instance of Stark's "wrongdoing," entry *IA* in the outline, the writer can mark the card *IA*. A *IIC* would refer to Gatsby's "search for absolution," a *IIIB* to Alpine's "remorse." Or the writer may prefer using explicit labels, such as *Stark's wrongdoing* and *Alpine's remorse*.

The card can hold other useful notations. A note card on Frank Alpine, from Malamud's *The Assistant*, might take this form:

III B   Malamud

                                          24-25

Even during hold-up, Frank shows remorse.
Offers Morris water. And he "waved
frantically" trying to stop the other thief
from striking Morris.

The *IIIB* in the upper left-hand corner indicates the topic: Alpine's "remorse." The notation in the upper right-hand corner tells the exact source of the note: *Malamud* indicates the book; *24–25*, the pages. This information, apart from other uses, becomes especially valuable when the essay is finished and the writer must insert footnotes.

6. *Arranging the note cards.* Now the writer groups his note cards by topic. He locates all cards pertaining to the first topic in his preliminary outline—the cards marked *IA* or *Stark's*

wrongdoing—then finds the *IB*'s, the *IC*'s, and so on until the rearrangement is complete.

    7. *The final outline.* After refining his essay-idea, the writer composes, one by one, the subsidiary sections of his final outline. Let us see how he works out the section on Willie Stark.

    The writer reviews the material relevant to that section: the note cards and the first part of the preliminary outline.

    I. Willie Stark
        A. Wrongdoing
        B. Remorse
        C. Search for absolution

Now he writes the section-idea.

> *Section-idea:* In *All the King's Men* by Robert Penn Warren, Willie Stark reaches toward a goal whose goodness might be able to justify his past, but he fails to achieve absolution.

Next the writer formulates his paragraph-ideas. Rereading the notes for entry *IA*, he finds that it requires two paragraph-ideas—one on Stark's political wrongdoing and one on his arrogance and duplicity in personal matters.

> *Paragraph-idea:* For many years Willie Stark has used the political tactics of a tyrant.

> *Paragraph-idea:* In his personal dealings Stark has been a bully and a cheat.

The writer proceeds to entry *IB* in the preliminary outline: Stark's "remorse." The note cards show that the topic warrants only one paragraph.

> *Paragraph-idea:* But Stark wishes to benefit the people of his state and prove to himself that he is capable of goodness.

Entry *IC* (Stark's "search for absolution") requires two paragraphs.

> *Paragraph-idea:* The hospital he hopes to build is meant to be evidence of his goodness.

> *Paragraph-idea:* But Stark learns that no single act, not even the building of a hospital, can compensate for years of cruelty and opportunism.

The first section of the outline is complete. The others will be composed in similar fashion.

This seven-step procedure is no magical planner of essays. The writer who hurries his planning and tries every apparent shortcut may reach a dead end and have to start over. But the writer who does a thoughtful job at each stage, and varies the procedure only with good reason, will produce a competent outline. He must still regard it as tentative, since no amount of planning can anticipate all the difficulties he may encounter in composing his essay or all the new ideas that may occur to him as he writes, but his outline almost certainly will not require major revision.

Practice

I. Make an outline with the following sentences, which are in scrambled order. The outline will contain one essay-idea, four section-ideas, and sixteen paragraph-ideas.

The outline is based on information from the delightful essay "Who Is This King of Glory?" by A. J. Liebling and St. Clair McKelway, from *True Tales from the Annals of Crime and Rascality* by St. Clair McKelway.

1. A turning point in George's life was his acquaintance with Samuel Morris, an evangelist who came to Baltimore in 1900.
2. For most of his residence in Baltimore, George Barker was a member of the Eden Street Baptist Church, where he served as Sunday school teacher.
3. Another indication of the size of Father Divine's following in 1933 is that in the New York mayoralty campaign of that year, both leading candidates courted the favor of Father Divine.
4. In 1919 Father Divine set up living quarters for himself and his followers in Sayville, Long Island.
5. After establishing himself and his followers in the Harlem area of New York City, Father Divine expanded his holdings even further and achieved his greatest prominence.
6. In their gratitude to Father Divine, the Sayville disciples gave him all their earnings, and some gave him bank savings, real estate, and the cash value from their insurance policies.

7. At about the turn of the century, a man named George Barker lived in Baltimore and worked there as a groundskeeper and handyman.

8. Eventually George became a follower, a "disciple," of Morris, and renamed himself "The Messenger."

9. Though Father Divine was once a mere groundskeeper, he discovered that quasi-religious evangelism could be profitable business, and he eventually became a wealthy man.

10. By 1933 Father Divine's followers had become so numerous that he decided to move himself and them to Harlem.

11. George became fascinated with Morris's belief that he, Morris, was actually God Himself.

12. During his residence in Long Island, George Barker became "Father Divine" and perfected his techniques for gathering money.

13. At the Wednesday night meetings at the Baptist Church, George occasionally spoke out in a manner that might have suggested his later demagoguery.

14. Father Divine must have profited considerably from his growing Sayville "Heaven," as he called it, for in 1930 and 1931 he expanded his Sayville holdings.

15. During the time in Sayville, Father Divine took care of his followers' needs—food, lodging, and job placement.

16. While still living in Baltimore, George Barker became interested in evangelism, though he was only an apprentice evangelist at the time.

17. Before leaving New York City in 1942, Father Divine had become Harlem's most prominent proprietor of rooming houses and the guiding spirit of countless other enterprises.

18. Father Divine's lowly origin scarcely suggested his future career.

19. By 1936 Father Divine had such extensive holdings in New York that he needed the services of a secretarial staff and a full-time lawyer.

20. Shortly after his arrival in Long Island, George Barker dropped the title of "Messenger," began calling himself "Father Divine," and let it be made public that he was actually God the Father.

21. George (now "The Messenger") studied evangelism also under St. John Divine Bishop, during the years from 1908 to 1915.

15

The Introduction and the Conclusion

The longer an essay becomes, the longer its beginning and ending may be. If the middle of a complex essay occupies about fifteen paragraphs, even a three-paragraph introduction or conclusion would not be out of proportion.

THE INTRODUCTION

The explanation of the essay-idea may have to be long enough to include all the techniques of clarification at the writer's command. In an essay by Aldous Huxley which argues that "the great writers of the past" have rarely given us "the whole truth," the clarification of this idea occupies two pages.

The introduction may also have to announce, or suggest, what will be dealt with in the middle of the essay. In a short essay this would not be necessary, but as a reader prepares to take in fifteen paragraphs or so, he welcomes an indication of their content. Nathan Glazer's essay "The Wasted Classroom" asserts that "a very large part of what students and teachers do in the best colleges and universities is sheer waste"; his introduction announces the kinds of waste the essay will discuss:

> There are . . . three main sources of waste in college teaching: the classroom system, the examination system, the departmental system.
>
> "The Wasted Classroom," *Harper's*, Oct., 1961

Donald Hall's essay about Washington Woodward, an old man Mr. Hall knew in New Hampshire, is concerned with another kind of waste, for Woodward "lived a half-life, a life of casual waste." While clarifying this thesis, Mr. Hall suggests the content of his essay:

> . . . Washington hated corruption and spied it everywhere like a prophet. Yet unlike a prophet he retired from corruption to the hills, meditated it, and never returned to denounce it. He bought a few acres high up New Canada Road, on Ragged Mountain, in 1895. He lived there alone, with few forays into the world, for the more than fifty years until he died.
>
> "A Hundred Thousand Straightened Nails,"
> *String Too Short to Be Saved*

Now the reader knows that the essay will discuss the life and thoughts of a backwoods hermit. Though Mr. Hall's advance notice is not so explicit as Mr. Glazer's, it accomplishes the purpose. Bergen Evans accomplishes the same purpose in another way in his essay defending the much-attacked *Webster's Third New International Dictionary*. Mr. Evans asks certain questions early in his essay:

> Just what's a dictionary for? What does it propose to do? What does the common reader go to a dictionary to find? What has the purchaser of a dictionary a right to expect for his money?
>
> "But What's a Dictionary For?" *Atlantic*, May, 1962

And the reader knows that the essay will answer these questions.

THE CONCLUSION

Although a short essay may require no separate conclusion (see pp. 118–119), a complex essay needs at least one paragraph of conclusion, and perhaps two or three paragraphs. Chief among the possible components of the conclusion are *summary, prediction,* and *further implications of the essay-idea* (see pp. 119–120).

The most important is *summary.* As the reader finishes a complex essay, he is perhaps fifteen paragraphs away from the introductory statement of the essay-idea. Having been entangled in section-ideas, paragraph-ideas, and subordinate details, he will welcome a reiteration of the essay's central proposition. Bergen Evans, after arguing the superiority of the 1962 *Webster's* over the 1934 edition, finishes with this summary:

> . . . One thing is certain: anyone who solemnly announces in the year 1962 that he will be guided in matters of English usage by a dictionary published in 1934 is talking ignorant and pretentious nonsense.

Nathan Glazer's "The Wasted Classroom" ends in this way:

> . . . The fact that higher education . . . is largely a huge waste for our young people who spend some of their best years there, and for the thousands of teachers who spend most of their lives there, does not seem to bother many people. It should.

A longer summary appears in Donald Hall's study of the wasted life of Washington Woodward:

> . . . The waste that he hated . . . was through him like blood in his veins. He had saved nails and wasted life. He had lived alone, but if he was a hermit he was neither religious nor philosophical. His fanaticisms, which might have been crea-

tive, were as petulant as his break from the church. I felt that he was intelligent, or it would not have mattered, but I had no evidence to support my conviction . . . He worked hard all his life at being himself, but there were no principles to examine when his life was over. It was as if there had been a moral skeleton which had lacked the flesh of the intellect and the blood of experience. The life that he could recall totally was not worth recalling; it was a box of string too short to be saved.

Outright summary is not the only way to remind the reader of the essay-idea. Mentioning *further implications of the essay-idea* may serve the same purpose. Mr. Glazer, having accused higher education of being wasteful, reapplies this thesis by praising experimental colleges that have maximized education and minimized waste. Thus he fixes the thesis more firmly in the reader's mind. A concluding *prediction* may achieve the same result. Donald Hall's essay about Washington Woodward ends with a prediction made at the hermit's deathbed:

> Standing beside him in the nursing home, I saw ahead for one moment into the residue, five years from then, of Washington Woodward's life: the shack has caved in and his straightened nails have rusted into the dirt of Ragged Mountain; though the rocks stay where he moved them, no one knows how they got there; his animals are dead and their descendants have made bad connections; his apple trees produce small and sour fruits; the best built hayracks rot under rotting sheds; in New Hampshire the frost tumbles the cleverest wall; those who knew him best are dead or dying, and his gestures have assumed the final waste of irrelevance.

In predicting the decay of Washington Woodward's retreat, Mr. Hall offers a final harsh reminder of the essay-idea: the hermit's life has been wasted.

Mr. Hall's conclusion, which includes both summary and prediction, is two paragraphs long; and sometimes the conclusion, or the introduction, of a complex essay can be even longer and yet not seem out of proportion.

Practice

Chapters 9, 10, and 12 offered much practice with introductions and conclusions. But study the introduction and conclusion from one complex essay—or rather from a full-length book, Michael Harrington's *The Other America*.

I.　Here are four questions about Mr. Harrington's introduction.

1. Where is the earliest statement of his essay-idea?
2. What techniques does he use to clarify the idea?
3. What techniques does he use to capture the reader's interest? (A list of techniques for clarification and attention-getting appears on p. 107.)
4. Where does Mr. Harrington indicate the particular topics likely to be discussed in his essay? What are the topics?

(1)There is a familiar America. (2)It is celebrated in speeches and advertised on television and in the magazines. (3)It has the highest mass standard of living the world has ever known.

(4)In the 1950's this America worried about itself, yet even its anxieties were products of abundance. (5)The title of a brilliant book was widely misinterpreted, and the familiar America began to call itself "the affluent society." (6)There was introspection about Madison Avenue and tail fins; there was discussion of the emotional suffering taking place in the suburbs. (7)In all this, there was an implicit assumption that the basic grinding economic problems had been solved in the United States. (8)In this theory the nation's problems were no longer a matter of basic human needs, of food, shelter, and clothing. (9)Now they were seen as qualitative, a question of learning to live decently amid luxury.

(10)While this discussion was carried on, there existed another America. (11)In it dwelt somewhere between 40,000,000 and 50,000,000 citizens of this land. (12)They were poor. (13)They still are.

(14)To be sure, the other America is not impoverished in the same sense as those poor nations where millions cling to hunger as a defense against starvation. (15)This country has escaped such extremes. (16)That does not change the fact that tens of millions of Americans are, at this very moment, maimed in body and spirit, existing at levels beneath those necessary for human decency. (17)If these people are not starving, they are hungry, and sometimes fat with hunger, for that is what cheap foods do. (18)They are without adequate housing and education and medical care.

(19)The Government has documented what this means to the bodies of the poor.... (20)But even more basic, this poverty twists and deforms the spirit. (21)The American poor are pessimistic and defeated, and they are victimized by mental suffering to a degree unknown in Suburbia.

(22)This book is a description of the world in which these people live; it is about the other America. (23)Here are the unskilled workers, the migrant farm workers, the aged, the underworld of American life.

II.   Now here is Mr. Harrington's conclusion. Does the conclusion offer *summary? Prediction? Further implications of the essay-idea?* Or does it offer some combination of these?

(1)These, then, are the strangest poor in the history of mankind.

(2)They exist within the most powerful and rich society the world has ever known. (3)Their misery has continued while the majority of the nation talked of itself as being "affluent" and worried about neuroses in the suburbs. (4)In this way tens of millions of human beings became invisible. (5)They dropped out of sight and out of mind; they were without their own political voice.

(6)Yet this need not be. (7)The means are at hand to fulfill the age-old dream: poverty can now be abolished. (8)How long shall we ignore this underdeveloped nation in our midst? (9)How long shall we look the other way while our fellow human beings suffer? (10)How long?

16

Continuity

The complex essay is so large a collection of ideas and evidence that if its parts are illogically arranged and poorly connected, it can be an impenetrable maze.

Most of the techniques needed for securing continuity have already been discussed. The techniques that ensure continuity in a short essay (see pp. 110–113) can serve the same purpose in each large section of a complex essay. And the problems of arranging the several sections of the complex essay can be solved with the principles of clear arrangement discussed on pp. 110–111.

But the linking of one section to the next is not accomplished by any means discussed earlier. The *transitional para-*

graph solves the problem. It bridges two sections by first referring back to the section just finished and then introducing the
next section-idea.

An illustration may be taken from our essay-in-the-
making concerning three characters from American fiction (see
the outline on pp. 138–139). Suppose the writer were finishing
the introduction and entering the section on Willie Stark.

... This kind of person fears that his life has been meaningless and clutches for something to give it meaning. Like the Psalmist he has committed "iniquities" that weigh like a "heavy burden," his "wounds stink and are corrupt," and he yearns for salvation.	*(End of introduction)*
One such figure is Willie Stark, from *All the King's Men* by Robert Penn Warren. For much of his life Stark has bullied people and cheated them, but he hopes to justify himself through one great act of generosity. His hope is futile.	*(Transitional paragraph)*
During his years as governor of his state, Stark has used the political tactics of a tyrant. ...	*(Opening of first supporting paragraph on Stark)*

Note the dual function of the transitional paragraph. On the one
hand, it links itself to the introduction with the phrases *one such
figure* (referring back to *This kind of person*), *bullied people and
cheated them* (referring to *"iniquities"*), and *hopes to justify
himself* (echoing *yearns for salvation*). On the other hand, the
paragraph serves as a brief introduction to the section on Stark,
complete with a statement of the section-idea: "... Stark has
bullied people and cheated them, but he hopes to justify himself
through one great act of generosity. His hope is futile."

The writer needs another transitional paragraph when he
has finished the last paragraph on Stark and is about to begin
the section on Gatsby.

... A few days later Willie is assassinated. He will never build his hospital. Ironically, the assassin is Adam Stanton, the doctor Willie wanted as director of the hospital because Adam was the best. Having	*(End of last supporting paragraph on Stark)*

learned of Willie's affair with Anne, Adam is no longer the skilled preserver of life; he has become a killer. Willie's double-dealing has corrupted even Adam. The corruption has spread beyond the Tiny Duffys of state politics, beyond Tom Stark and Sadie Burke and Jack Burden, all the way to the Stantons—to Anne and then to Adam. And through Adam the corruption comes back to ruin the chances for Stark's hospital and destroy Stark himself.

Stark's one hope of redemption is blasted. And even if he had been able to live and build his hospital, it would not have compensated for the wrongs he has done and the anguish he has caused. In much of this, Willie Stark is similar to Jay Gatsby, of Fitzgerald's *The Great Gatsby.* Gatsby, too, defiles himself with sordid activities, reaches for a goal he believes will justify his wrongs, yet fails to achieve justification or redemption.   *(Transitional paragraph)*

Throughout the novel we find hints that Gatsby has engaged in criminal activities. . . .   *(Beginning of first supporting paragraph on Gatsby)*

The first and second sentences of the transitional paragraph summarize the section concerning Willie Stark. The third sentence leads the reader away from Stark and toward Gatsby. The final sentence presents the section-idea concerning Gatsby. When a transitional paragraph does its work this well, the reader will have no trouble moving from one section of a complex essay to the next.

Practice

I.   In unscrambling the outline on pp. 145–146, perhaps you placed the ideas in a clear order. If not, do so now.

II.   The following transitional paragraphs come from *The Inside Story: Psychiatry and Everyday Life,* by Fritz Redlich and June Bingham. Analyze each paragraph to determine (1) the section-idea of the section coming before the transitional paragraph and (2) the section-idea of the section coming after.

1. Although these basic urges of man do not vary from era to era, the way they are expressed does vary greatly from culture to culture and within the same culture from time to time and from class to class.

2. Whereas small children learn what society expects of them through their parents, after starting school they also learn from other children. And this later learning, despite its sometimes conflicting with what is taught in the home, may well be remembered long after the content of the school's courses has been forgotten.

3. The case of Mary was like Jim's, in that her trouble also was the kind that people do not ordinarily recognize as being emotionally based. While Jim, until his attack of amnesia, had expressed his repressed conflicts mainly through the physical symptoms of headaches, Mary expressed hers through obnoxious behavior as well as through physical symptoms.

4. There are not enough psychiatrists to go around, but there is great work being done by the allied professions of clinical psychology and psychiatric social-work. . . .

5. . . . Although psychiatrists are often able to alleviate inner problems, they are relatively helpless in respect to outer ones. Doctors must always work within the frame of what *is*, not of what might have been. And one of their aims is to help the patient recognize what the realities of his life are and, when these cannot be altered, adjust to them as best he can.

III. 1. You should have no difficulty writing a transitional paragraph for the hypothetical complex essay on Stark, Gatsby, and Alpine. Write the third transitional paragraph the essay would need, the one that would join the sections on Gatsby and Alpine. The outline on pp. 138–139 will be helpful.

2. Or turn to the scrambled outline concerning Father Divine, on pp. 145–146. You have probably already unscrambled the outline so that it could serve as the basis for a complex essay. Write the transitional paragraphs the essay would require.

Prose Style

IV

If the writer worries about style as he begins his essay, he is likely to do more worrying than writing—he may never finish a first draft. Therefore most writers favor a procedure like the following.

(1) When all note-taking and outlining is finished, write a rough draft quickly ("Compose in fury," said William James) —not brooding about diction or sentence structure but intent merely on getting the ideas and information down on paper. (2) Evaluate the content and organization of each paragraph and of the essay as a whole. (3) Make a *working draft:* recopy the essay, writing neatly or typing, with two or three spaces between

lines. While recopying, correct any obvious stylistic crudities. (4) Polish the style, slowly and carefully.

Between these stages the writer should relax for a few hours (or longer if the essay is long)—not only because he can then come back to the essay refreshed and alert but because he can be more objective about its strengths and weaknesses.

In polishing the style, what qualities should the writer aim to achieve? One is *forcefulness:* incisiveness and vigor. A second is *fluency:* quick, easy movement from one idea to the next. And the chief requisite is *clarity.* As Eric Partridge has said, "The ideal at which a writer should aim . . . is that he write so clearly, so precisely, so unambiguously, that his words can bear only one meaning to all averagely intelligent readers that possess an average knowledge of the language."[1] Or, as Orwell put it, "Good prose is like a window-pane."[2]

The following chapters discuss the means for achieving these three cardinal virtues of prose style.

[1]*Usage and Abusage.*
[2]"Why I Write," *Collected Essays, Journalism and Letters,* I.

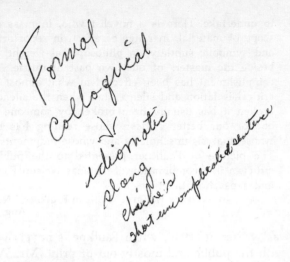

Formal v. Colloquial
idiomatic
slang
cliché's
short uncomplicated sentence

17

Extreme Formality and Extreme Colloquialism

FORMALITY AND ORNATENESS

The *formal style* is appropriate for occasions of special importance and subjects of great seriousness. It maintains an impersonal, dignified tone; its sentences tend to be long and elaborate; its wording is that of highly educated people. The *Declaration of Independence* and Lincoln's *Gettysburg Address* are examples of formal style. And here is an example from contemporary prose:

> The study of [William] Faulkner is the most challenging single task in contemporary American literature for criticism

to undertake. Here is a novelist who, in mass of work, in scope of material, in range of effect, in reportorial accuracy and symbolic subtlety, in philosophical weight, can be put beside the masters of our own past literature. Yet this accomplishment has been effected in what almost amounts to critical isolation and silence, and when the silence has been broken it has usually been broken by someone (sometimes one of our better critics) whose reading has been hasty, whose analysis unscholarly and whose judgments superficial. The picture of Faulkner presented to the public by such criticism is a combination of Thomas Nelson Page, a fascist and a psychopath. . . .

ROBERT PENN WARREN, "William Faulkner," *New Republic*, Aug. 12, 26, 1946

This was written in 1946, when Faulkner's novels were out of favor with the public and mostly out of print. Mr. Warren was so desirous of directing attention to Faulkner that in this central passage of the essay he raised his style to the formal level.

At important points in an essay, then, particularly at the conclusion, a writer may well employ the stately rhythms and resounding phrases of high formality. But some writers become so caught up in formality that they cannot escape. They grow so fond of fancy words and complicated sentences that they become addicted to *the ornate style*. The prose of John Ruskin, for instance, is often like a string of gaudy trinkets. Here is his description of Venice as he imagines it must have been in 1600:

. . . Deep-hearted, majestic, terrible as the sea—the men of Venice moved in sway of power and war; pure as her pillars of alabaster, stood her mothers and maidens; from foot to brow, all noble, walked her knights; the low bronzed gleaming of sea-rusted armour shot angrily under their blood-red mantle-folds. Fearless, faithful, patient, impenetrable, implacable—every word a fate—sate her senate. In hope and honour, lulled by flowing of wave around their isles of sacred sand, each with his name written and the cross graved at his side, lay her dead. A wonderful piece of world. Rather, itself a world. It lay along the face of the waters, no longer, as its captains saw it from their masts at evening, than a bar of sunset that could not pass away; but for its power, it must have seemed to them as if they were sailing in the expanse of heaven, and this a great planet, whose orient edge widened through ether. A world from which all ignoble care and petty thoughts were banished, with all the common and poor elements of life. No foulness, nor tumult, in those tremulous streets, that filled, or fell, beneath the moon, but rippled music of majestic change, or thrilling silence. No weak walls could rise above them; no low-roofed cottage nor straw-built shed. Only the strength as of rock, and the finished setting of stones most precious. And around them, far as the eye could reach, still the soft moving of stainless waters, proudly pure; as not the flower, so neither the thorn nor the thistle, could grow in the glancing fields. . . .

Modern Painters

The ornate style always tends to be obscure, even in the hands of a Ruskin. The writer who refuses to use it is in good company. William Hazlitt denounced it for being "pompous and unwieldy," and said, "I hate to see a parcel of big words without anything in them." Matthew Arnold scorned the notion that style should be a display of fancy rhetoric: "What stuff it all is! Have something to say and say it as clearly as you can. That is the only secret of style." And Samuel Butler declared that the writer's chief goal should be "just common simple straightforwardness."

COLLOQUIAL STYLE

At the opposite extreme from ornateness is a style that sounds like casual conversation:

(1)I've been reading some stuff by this fellow Hemingway. And in each thing there's something pretty unhappy just waiting for you. (2)Just about all the characters are about to get beaten up or think they might wind up dead. (3)But I've got to admit, things weren't all bad. Somehow or other the guy in the story hangs on to something. (4)And, you know, maybe that's why Hemingway likes all those dangerous situations. (5)Because he can show how the people in the story hold up. How they make it through. He can show how they last it out or at least stick with it. And most of them do stick with it. (6)At least they don't turn yellow. Or just turn squealer or welcher. Or just give in or run away. Guts! They can take it. The old stiff upper lip. So they don't lose everything. (7)Do you know what I mean? Even if they get beaten up or killed off or something, they don't give up without a fight. Never say die. A lot of them even go in with the odds against them. But they stuck it out. That's the thing. So they've still got their self-respect. (8)And they've still got their pride. It's like someone said, "Are you a man or a mouse?" And the guy in the story says, "I'm a man!" It's like they are base-ball players that lose but know they played the game right. "Messy" is what Hemingway calls people that don't play right.

This extreme form of the colloquial style would be inappropriate even in the most popularized of popular magazines or the chattiest of newspaper gossip columns. Nevertheless the writer might unwittingly let too many characteristics of the style creep into his prose, with the result that the prose would sound too much like idle talk.

These are the characteristics to watch out for.

1. A tone of personal intimacy. The speaker assumes the role of an old pal, freely using *I* and *you* and *you know*.

2. Simple, inexact wording. The speaker uses only easy words and does not care about precision. He tends to express an idea sloppily, then repeat it several times to explain his meaning. For example: "He can show how the people in the story *hold up*. How they *make it through*. He can show how they *last it out*, or at least *stick with it*." And the speaker frequently uses those handy but vague words *thing* and *something*.

3. Colloquialisms. This term refers to words more suited to conversation than to written prose. Colloquialisms in the illustrative passage are: *stuff* by *this fellow* Hemingway, *pretty* unhappy, *guy, a lot of,* and *get* or *got* as they are used in the passage.

4. Slang. This is extreme colloquialism, the sort of colloquialism that might seem vulgar in polite conversation. Slang words in the illustrative passage are: *beaten up, turn yellow, squealer, welcher,* and *guts.*

5. Idioms. This kind of expression is readily used in conversation, usually as a verb. The typical idiom is a phrase of short words used in place of a single more formal word. In the illustrative passage the idiom *wind up* is used in place of *finish.* One mark of an idiom is that it defies logical analysis and has meaning only for someone intimately familiar with the language; *wind up* would be nonsense to anyone not familiar with conversational English. Other idioms in the passage are: *hold up* and *take it,* both meaning *endure;* and *give in* and *give up,* both meaning *surrender.*

6. Contractions. These are frequent in conversation and in the kind of prose that resembles it. The illustrative passage uses fifteen.

7. Hackneyed language. This kind of wording has been "worn out by overuse so as to become dull and meaningless" (*Webster's Seventh New Collegiate Dictionary*). Yet people frequently use a hackneyed phrase (a *cliché*) in conversation rather than pausing to think of a fresh wording. Hackneyed phrases from the illustrative passage are: *the old stiff upper lip / don't give up without a fight / never say die / go in with the odds against them / are you a man or a mouse? / players that lose but know they played the game right.*

8. Short, uncomplicated sentences. The speaker in our illustration divides his ideas into easy units of thought.

9. Latitude in matters of grammar and usage. The speaker refuses to worry about the niceties of good English. He freely uses sentence fragments, blithely switches the tense of verbs, uses *like* as a conjunction, and so on.

Occasional marks of colloquial style can keep prose from sounding solemn or pompous, can help keep it lively. But if the marks become too frequent, the prose will sound loose and unconsidered, like casual talk that should not be taken seriously.

Practice

I. This order was issued by a government agency during World War II:

> Such preparations shall be made as will completely obscure all Federal Buildings and non-Federal buildings occupied by the Federal Government during an air raid for any period of time from visibility by reason of internal or external illumination. Such obscuration may be obtained either by blackout construction or by termination of the illumination.

Asked for an explanation, President Roosevelt laughed at this puffed-up prose and offered a translation: "Tell them in buildings where they have to keep the work going, to put something across the window; and in buildings where they can afford to let the work stop for a while, to turn out the lights."

Here are other samples of ornate prose. Can you translate them into plain English?

1. From Samuel Johnson:

> The proverbial oracles of our parsimonious ancestors have informed us that the fatal waste of our fortune is by small expenses, by the profusion of sums too little singly to alarm our caution, and which we never suffer ourselves to consider together. Of the same kind is the prodigality of life; he that hopes to look back hereafter with satisfaction upon past years, must learn to know the present value of single minutes, and endeavour to let no particle of time fall useless to the ground.

2. From a present-day literary critic:

> Reference back to philosophic principles to expose erroneous assumptions and to establish common grounds for judgments of fact or value could not be justified easily by the record of its success in producing agreement. Philosophers have frequently expressed the expectation that philosophic disagreements would be resolved by applying scientific principles to a subject matter for the first time or that doctrinal disagreements in particular fields of inquiry or action would be removed by discovering and expounding philosophic principles. Yet doctrinal differences seem to have persisted, after each such effort at resolution, translated into more inclusive and

more obstinate philosophic oppositions, and the differences of philosophers have disappeared because they have been forgotten more frequently than because they have been resolved.

RICHARD MCKEON, "The Philosophic Bases of Art and Criticism,"
Critics and Criticism, ed. R. S. Crane

3. From a sociologist—the first paragraph in Chapter 13 of Thorstein Veblen's *The Theory of the Leisure Class:*

In an increasing proportion as time goes on, the anthropomorphic cult, with its code of devout observances, suffers a progressive disintegration through the stress of economic exigencies and the decay of the system of status. As this disintegration proceeeds, there come to be associated and blended with the devout attitude certain other motives and impulses that are not always of an anthropomorphic origin, nor traceable to the habit of personal subservience. Not all of these subsidiary impulses that blend with the bait of devoutness in the later devotional life are altogether congruous with the devout attitude or with the anthropomorphic apprehension of sequence of phenomena. Their origin being not the same, their action upon the scheme of devout life is also not in the same direction. In many ways they traverse the underlying norm of subservience or vicarious life to which the code of devout observances and the ecclesiastical and sacerdotal institutions are to be traced as their substantial basis. Through the presence of these alien motives the social and industrial regime of status gradually disintegrates, and the canon of personal subservience loses the support derived from an unbroken tradition. Extraneous habits and proclivities encroach upon the field of action occupied by this canon, and it presently comes about that the ecclesiastical and sacerdotal structures are partially converted to other uses, in some measure alien to the purpose of the scheme of the devout life as it stood in the days of the most vigorous and characteristic development of the priesthood.

II. A good college dictionary supplies definitions for the most widely used idioms and tells the writer which idioms may be too informal for his essays. (Not all dictionaries labeled "college" provide this information. See p. 252, where three are recommended that do.) When you need information about an idiom, consult the dictionary entry for one of the main words in the idiom. (Consult *mind* for *bear in mind,* and *put* for *put up with.*)

To familiarize yourself with your own dictionary's handling of idioms, list those entered under *call, mind,* and *put,* and indicate which ones are labeled "slang," "colloquial," or "informal."

III. For the italicized idioms below, substitute expressions of greater formality. For example:

The housewife was *put out* when the dishwasher would not
(a)

get going.
(b)

For (a) you could substitute *irritated* or *angered;* for (b), *start* or *operate.*

1. The producer *had half a mind* to *call off* the opening night
(a)   (b)

performance.

2. The chief executive *kept on putting off* the meeting.
(a)   (b)

3. Harry *called to mind* that the agreement was *for keeps.*
(a)   (b)

4. If the truck corps fails to *come through with* some rations,
(a)

the regiment will have to *call it quits* and *give up.*
(b)   (c)

5. After *coming out with* those heretical thoughts, he would
(a)

certainly *be in line* to *get it* from the Inquisition.
(b)   (c)

IV. Read the sentences below and check the italicized expressions in your dictionary. If you find that an expression is labeled "slang," "colloquial," or "informal," replace it with a more formal wording.

1. Mr. Peters had the *notion* that if this latest business ven-
(a)

ture *drove* him into *going broke,* he would be too old to make
(b)   (c)

a *comeback.*
(d)

2. Smith's candidacy for the governorship seemed to be a
put-up job by the *bigwig politicos.*
   (a)   (b)   (c)

3. The *chief* executives of the Think-Young Automobile
     (a)
Company are *downright chuckleheads.*
          (b)   (c)

4. The latest advertising campaign for Think-Young *cars*
                                     (a)
is a *bunch* of *bombast* and *drivel.*
   (b)   (c)   (d)

5. But the *loony* executives think the public will be *suckers*
     (a)   (b)
enough to *fall for* those *nonsensical ads.*
     (c)   (d)   (e)

V. The following sentences are derived from Allen Tate's *Stonewall Jackson* (specifically from Mr. Tate's account of the Con-
federate surprise attack on the Federal Eleventh Corps at Chan-
cellorsville); but the sentences have deliberately been mangled
by the substitution of slang, colloquialisms, and sloppy idioms
for some of Mr. Tate's wording. If you find the italicized expressions unsatisfactory (as most of them are), replace them
with more formal wordings.

1. Before the men of the Eleventh Corps could *hop up to*
                                           (a)
their feet, *a whole slew of yelling* demons, *rising out of* the
         (b)   (c)   (d)
earth, were upon them.

2. Far to the north and south the long and ~~pretty~~ *ragged*
                                          (a)
gray lines *made their way on ahead* forward *sort of like a*
                            (b)   (c)
machine.

3. The *good-for-nothing* pickets of the Federals *let loose*
       (a)
with a few scattered shots, and *lit out.*
                                (b)

4. The Confederates *came* steadily on like *some kind of a*
                               (a)   (b)
giant harvester, *laying out* the men *who were making a stab*
                  (c)   (d)
at putting up a fight.
     (e)

5. At Talley's farm [Federal] regiments ~~from all over the~~ *from all over everything* ~~place lined up~~ *grouped* behind breastworks to ~~meet up with~~ *chop up* the onset.
(a) (b)

6. In the ~~mess~~ *cloud* of smoke the defenders ~~looked~~ *peered* out and got a
(a) (b)
~~peek~~ *glimpse* at the ~~vast bunch~~ *mass-horde* of Confederates: they ~~got a glimmer~~ *saw*
(c) (d) (e)

~~of~~ the flash of the rifles, the *oncoming* battle flags, the tanned
(f)
faces, the *blazing* eyes of their mysterious, ~~scary~~ *terrible* foe.
(g) (h)

7. The ~~whole lot~~ *mass out* of their mounted officers ~~keeled~~ *dropped* over like
(a) (b)
bags of *meal* to the ground.
(c)

8. The *defending soldier-boys took off in panic.* *Troops fled in panic*
(a) (b) (c)

VI. The following is a travesty of a passage by James Thurber about an unhappy phase of his life at college. The passage has been cluttered with hackneyed phrases and thus made slow-moving and simpleminded. Rewrite it and remove all worn-out expressions. Some can be replaced with new wordings; others can simply be deleted.

I passed every single one of the other courses that I was fortunate enough to take at my alma mater, but I couldn't for the life of me pass botany. This was because each and every one of the botany students had to spend countless ages in a laboratory with his eyes glued to a microscope, looking at plant cells—and I could never in a million years see one iota through a microscope. In the last analysis I was doomed to disappointment. This used to make my instructor mad as a hornet. He would wander hither and yon around the laboratory, pleased as punch with the great strides forward all the students were making in putting pen to paper and drawing the involved and, as has been said so often, fascinating structure of flower cells. But sooner or later he would have to put in an appearance where I was standing. "I can't see one single solitary thing," I would say. He would begin with the patience of Job, with implicit confidence that anybody can see through a microscope, but each and every time he would end up mad as a hatter, claiming that it was as certain as death and taxes that I could see through a microscope but that I was plain and simple pulling his leg and just pretending to draw a blank.

VII. Write a parody of the hackneyed style. Choose a subject that lends itself to clichés and platitudes: love at first sight, the first day of spring, a New Year's Eve party, a mighty clash between rival football teams, a candidate's qualifications for office, your first days at a new school—anything of that sort. And try to make every sentence a display case of worn-out phrases.

Frank Sullivan does this sort of thing with his "cliché expert," who professes to know *all* clichés and, in various mock interviews, gives us his worn-out words on love, war, politics, motion pictures, etc. See the interviews in Mr. Sullivan's books *A Pearl in Every Oyster* and *A Rock in Every Snowball*.

VIII. Reread the paragraph about William Faulkner, by Robert Penn Warren, on pp. 161–162. Then rewrite it in an extremely colloquial style, the same style used in the passage on Hemingway on pp. 163–164. Make your revision display all the traits of colloquialism discussed in this chapter.

I passed ~~every~~ all the courses that I took at my alma mater, ~~but I paid~~ except botany. I felt the reason for my ~~ailing~~ this course ~~was~~ stemmed from the fact that all the students were required to spend several hours in the laboratory looking at plant cells through a microscope, ~~moreover, and~~ I could never see one iota through a microscope. ~~This~~ used to make my instructor angry when he would appear where I was standing. I would say, " I can't see one single botany thing." He would begin with the patience of Job, with emphatic confidence that anybody can see through a microscope, but ~~each~~ every time he would ~~leave~~ angry, claiming that it was as certain as death and taxes that I could see through a microscope, but that I was simply pretending to draw a blank.

18

The Informal Style

The highly formal style is too ornate. The colloquial style is too casual. Therefore the modern essayist steers between the extremes. As William Hazlitt advised, the essayist avoids "the solemnity of the pulpit" but does not just "gabble on" or "resort to vulgar dialect"; he steers a "middle course" between high formality and low vulgarity, the middle course known as *informal style*.

Between the colloquial and formal extremes there is room for many levels of informality. To simplify, we can divide them into three main levels. The first, which might be termed *low informal*, is the near-colloquial style found in some newspapers and in the magazines for movie-star worshipers and people who read "confidential confessions." Second is the *middle informal* style, which appears in the majority of articles in popular magazines— *Sports Illustrated, Newsweek, Time,* and the like. Moving further toward formality we come to the *high informal* style, which is found in the most serious articles of *Harper's* and *Atlantic.* Most of the best contemporary essay-writing, then, is done at the middle and high informal levels.

Here is a passage written at roughly the high informal level. The passage may seem familiar, since we examined a colloquial version of it in the last chapter.

> (1) The shadow of ruin is behind the typical Hemingway situation. (2) The typical character faces defeat or death. (3) But out of defeat or death the character usually manages to salvage something. (4) And here we discover Hemingway's special interest in such situations and such characters. (5) His heroes are not defeated except upon their own terms. (6) They are not squealers, welchers, compromisers, or cowards, and when they confront defeat they realize that the stance they take, the stoic endurance, the stiff upper lip mean a kind of victory. (7) If they are to be defeated they are defeated upon their own terms; some of them have even courted their defeat; and certainly they have maintained, even in the practical defeat, an ideal of themselves, some definition of how a man should behave, formulated or unformulated, by which they have lived. (8) They represent some notion of a code, some notion of honor, that makes a man a man, and that distinguishes him from people who merely follow their random impulses and who are, by consequence, "messy."
>
> ROBERT PENN WARREN, Introduction to Hemingway's
> *A Farewell to Arms*

This prose displays the virtues of "the middle course." While avoiding extreme formality and extreme informality, it keeps the best features of both extremes.

1. Tone. The informal style is neither so chummy as the colloquial nor so cool and remote as the formal. Low informal makes frequent use of *I, we,* and *you;* middle informal uses them sometimes; high informal, occasionally. In the sample passage Mr. Warren twice uses *we*.

2. *Range and exactness of diction.*   The informal style, unlike the formal, avoids bookish, unfamiliar words; yet its wording is much more precise than that of colloquial prose. Mr. Warren's words, though familiar enough for most readers, express his meaning precisely. Hazlitt's advice is again valuable: the writer should choose "the best word in common use."

3. *Colloquialisms.*   Informal style is lightly sprinkled with colloquialisms—not enough to distract the reader or make the prose sound like aimless talk, but enough to keep it relaxed and natural. Mr. Warren's paragraph, though high informal in style, contains touches of colloquialism. His third sentence begins with *but*, the next one with *and*. There is also colloquial flavor in *manages to salvage something* (in the third sentence), *makes a man a man* (in the final sentence), and Hemingway's word *messy* (the last word of the paragraph).

4. *Slang.*   Middle and high informal styles use occasional slang, though usually none that would startle the reader. Mr. Warren uses two slang words: *squealers* and *welchers*.

5. *Idioms.*   Informal styles differ widely in their use of idioms. The writer of low informal uses idiomatic phrases liberally, not caring whether they make his prose wordy. He readily says *go in for* instead of *enjoy*, or *put up with* instead of *tolerate*. The writer of middle informal is more cautious with idioms. He likes the fluency they impart to his prose but not the wordiness. High informal uses few idioms; Mr. Warren uses none.

6. *Contractions.*   Informal styles vary in the use of contractions just as in the use of idioms. Contractions are frequent in low informal, rare in high informal. Mr. Warren uses none.

7. *Hackneyed language.*   Though the low informal syle may contain some hackneyed phrases, the writer using middle or high informal generally avoids them. Mr. Warren uses only one hackneyed expression—*stiff upper lip* in sentence six. And possibly he should have eliminated even the one. After millions of reiterations it has lost whatever force it originally had.

8. *Length and complexity of sentences.*   Again infor-

mal style follows a middle course. On one hand, it avoids the skimpy sentences of the colloquial style. Even Mr. Warren's first five sentences, though fairly short, are more substantial than the abrupt sentences often found in colloquial style. And Mr. Warren is soon using longer sentences—sentences six, seven, and eight. On the other hand, informal style avoids the intricate sentences of highly formal prose. Sentences six, seven, and eight, though fairly long, are not difficult to follow.

9. *Attitude toward grammar and usage.* Informal style observes fine distinctions more carefully than colloquial style, generally following the standard conventions of written English; but informal style sometimes disobeys tired old laws that would be followed only by a strictly formal style—the laws concerning *shall* and *will,* for instance.

Thus informal style remains "the middle style." It avoids the extremes of gossip and oration but keeps the best features the extremes can offer. While avoiding colloquial sloppiness, informal style keeps a conversational naturalness and lucidity. While avoiding the pomposity of ornateness, informal style remains generally serious and exercises care in the choosing of words and shaping of sentences. Midway between the extremes, informal is the style best able to achieve clarity, fluency, and force.

Practice

I.   Although these five passages have roughly the same meaning, they vary in degrees of formality. One passage, the original by Robert Penn Warren, is formal. Of the others, one is colloquial, one is low informal, another is middle informal, and another high informal.

Determine the level of formality (or informality) of each passage.

1.   If a book is going to deal with the problems that really bother us way down deep, it will have to be a critical book. It'll make us uneasy about the times we cheat a little bit because we think we have to. And we'll wonder why we're

bored stiff so much of the day, and why we hanker every minute of the day after luxuries. We might start suspecting we're just fooling ourselves when we appear cool and comfortable on the outside, but are scared on the inside by the fears and frustrations that heckle us each day more times than we can count. But a book that does all that can still be a good thing. It can give us the will-to-win and gumption to face up to our most basic problems and maybe do something about them. As the Bible puts it, if the rock is hit hard enough, it will give us helpful waters.

2. If a literature struggles to engage the deep, inner issues of life, the literature will be critical. It will produce impatience with the compromises, the boredom, the desire for luxuries, the self-deception, the complacency, and the secret, unnamable fears and frustrations that come to us even during an ordinary day. But a critical literature is still affirmative. It affirms the will and courage to confront life at the deepest levels. If the rock is struck hard enough, it will give us the living waters.

3. If a book tries to deal with the deep, inner problems of life, it will be a critical book. It will make us impatient with our compromises, our boredom, our constant chasing after luxuries, and our attempts to fool ourselves, to look comfortable and composed, even while fears and frustrations are gnawing continually at our insides. But even though a critical book may give us these worries, it can still be valuable. It can give us the will and courage to face our most basic problems and try to solve them. As the Bible says, if the rock is struck hard enough, it will give us the living waters.

4. If a book is going to really tackle some important problems, well then it's got to do some criticizing. Yes, and it's going to make you think twice about some things. It'll make you wonder about all the times you cheat a little bit because you think you've just got to. And you'll wonder why you're bored stiff so much of the day. And why you hanker after things you don't really need every minute of the day. And you might start to think you're just kidding yourself—a lot of the time. You know what I mean? Like when you're trying to put on the cool front, but are really scared silly by those

deep, dark thoughts that come to you like the jimjams more times than you can count. That's what happens. A good bit of reading can put a notion or two like that in your noggin. But I say a book like that is an OK thing. Because it can really make you face up to the harsh realities of the real world. You know—the big problems. And then maybe you'll have the will-to-win and guts to do something about them. So a book like that—even if it's tough to take—can help you lead a better life.

5. Insofar as a literature struggles to engage the deep, inner issues of life, the more will that literature be critical—the more, that is, will it engender impatience with the compromises, the ennui, the materialism, the self-deception, the complacency, and the secret, unnamable despairs that mark so much of ordinary life. Such a critical literature is at the same time affirmative because it affirms the will and courage to engage life at fundamental levels: the rock, if struck hard enough, will give forth the living waters.

II. Most of your essays will be written in the upper ranges of the informal style—as are the passages listed below. Reread each passage and decide whether it is written at the middle informal level or the high informal. (There are six at middle informal and five at high.) Though not all prose is easily placed at one level or another, the following passages are fairly easy to categorize.

1. George Orwell on "the secrecy attaching to poverty" (pp. 16–17).
2. Mark Twain on "Cooper's word-sense" (pp. 17–18).
3. W. Macneile Dixon on the illogic of nature (p. 19).
4. Vance Packard on the effects of polluted waters (p. 27).
5. Vance Packard on some problems of people who "sell to our subconscious" (pp. 27–28).
6. Frederick Lewis Allen on "the young J. Pierpont Morgan" (pp. 37–38).
7. Joseph Mitchell on the winter of 1933 (pp. 44–45).
8. Thomas B. Morgan on Marcucci and his "promising raw material" (p. 50).
9. Edmund Wilson on Houdini (p. 59).
10. "Trying to Cancel the Past" (pp. 127–129).
11. "A Majority of One" (pp. 129–134).

III. Reconsider the passages listed in exercise II. Having decided at which stylistic level each is written, can you tell why the passage is written at that level? In a few sentences, tell why the subject matter or probable audience would lead the author to write at the level he has chosen.

IV. Reread Frederic Morton's paragraph about "romance" as part of the "American dream" (p. 32). Is the prose too near the low informal level? Does it contain too many colloquialisms? In a few sentences, tell whether the style seems appropriate to the subject and audience.

19

Choosing the Right Synonym

denotation - meaning of a word.

Synonyms have roughly the same meaning because they
have the same *denotation*. They refer to or *denote* the same
thing, as do *maiden, young lady, hussy, minx,* and *slut.* But these
words are certainly not interchangeable. For though synonyms
share the same denotation, they differ in *connotations,* the suggested shades of meaning that can make a crucial difference.
Slim, slender, scrawny, svelte, lithe, and *skinny* are synonyms
because they could all refer to one girl's figure, but they imply
widely different assessments of the figure.

implied meaning

The writer who ignores shades of meaning (and refers
to all 95-pound females as *thin girls*) will render his prose vague

and lifeless. But the writer who uses exact words rather than rough approximations will express his thoughts with incisive clarity. As Mark Twain insisted, "the difference between the right word and the almost right word is the difference between lightning and the lightning bug."

As a rule, the writer does best to hunt for synonyms only after he has composed his working draft (see p. 159). Then, without being distracted by problems of organization or argumentation, he can sharpen his wording at leisure—with two reference books at hand to make the job easier. One is a book of synonyms. The kind generally preferred does not define words or illustrate their uses but merely lists synonyms to jog the writer's memory. By looking up a word that almost expresses his meaning, he can usually find one that expresses it exactly. And when he has doubts about a word he finds, then he can consult his second reference book—a dictionary. This may supply not only definitions of the word but also a synonymy: a list of synonyms with an explanation of fine distinctions. (Particular dictionaries and books of synonyms are recommended on pp. 251–252.)

With these books to help, the writer need not wander aimlessly in his search for precise words. Suppose his working draft uses the word *atheist* for a woman who was not exactly that. The writer consults his dictionary, which defines an atheist as "a person who believes that there is no God" (*Webster's New World Dictionary*). The word is too strong. The woman did not assert that God could not possibly exist; she merely doubted His existence, on the grounds that mortals cannot find concrete evidence of God. The synonymy at the entry for *atheist* may help the writer find a word for this idea.

> SYN.—an *atheist* rejects all religious belief and denies the existence of God; an *agnostic* questions the existence of God, heaven, etc. in the absence of material proof and in unwillingness to accept supernatural revelation; *deist*, a historical term, was applied to 18th-century rationalists who believed in God as a creative, moving force but who otherwise rejected formal religion and its doctrines of revelation, divine authority, etc.;

freethinker, the current parallel term, similarly implies rejection of the tenets and traditions of formal religion as incompatible with reason; *unbeliever* is a more negative term, simply designating, without further qualification, one who does not accept any religious belief; *infidel* is applied to a person not believing in a certain religion or the prevailing religion.

Webster's New World Dictionary

Agnostic seems the best word. The writer consults the entry for *agnostic* and ascertains that the word fits: "a person who thinks it is impossible to know whether there is a God or a future life, or anything beyond material phenomena" (*Webster's New World Dictionary*).

Or suppose the working draft uses *nasty* to characterize a crime that was worse than nasty. The word makes the crime sound like a child's foolishness, whereas this crime was truly *bad.* Then is *bad* the word needed? No—it is too often used and too vague. But by consulting the entry for *bad* in his book of synonyms, the writer finds an abundance of words to choose from:

1. bad, ill, untoward, arrant, as bad as can be, dreadful; horrid, horrible; dire; rank, peccant, foul, fulsome; rotten, rotten at the core, decayed, decomposed, putrid, tainted. *Slang,* chessy, punk, lousy.
2. hurtful, harmful, baneful, baleful; injurious, deleterious, unhealthy, detrimental, pernicious, mischievous, full of mischief, mischief-making, malefic, malignant, noxious, nocuous, noisome; prejudicial; disserviceable, disadvantageous; unlucky, sinister; obnoxious; disastrous; inauspicious; oppressive, burdensome, onerous; malign, malevolent; corrupt, virulent, venomous, envenomed, corrosive; poisonous, toxic, septic, deadly, killing, pestilent; destructive.
3. mean, paltry; injured, deteriorated, unsatisfactory, exceptionable, indifferent; below par, inferior, imperfect; ill-contrived, ill-conditioned; wretched, pathetic, sad, grievous, deplorable, lamentable; pitiable; woeful, painful, unfortunate.
4. evil, wrong; depraved, vile, base, villainous; shocking,

flagrant, scandalous, nefarious; reprehensible, wicked, sinful; hateful; abominable, repugnant, abhorrent, revolting, repulsive, repellant, disgusting, odious, detestable, execrable, cursed, accursed, confounded; damned, damnable; infernal, diabolic, malevolent, devilish; vicious. *Colloq.*, beastly, ungodly.

The New American Roget's College Thesaurus

The second and fourth divisions seem to offer the best candidates. Perhaps *vile* is the needed word. The writer consults his dictionary:

vile (vīl), *adj.* (ME & OFr. *vil*; L. *vilis*, cheap, base), 1. morally base or evil; wicked; depraved; sinful. 2. offensive to the senses or sensibilities; repulsive; disgusting. 3. cheap; worthless. 4. degrading; lowly; mean: said of conditions, situations, etc. . . .

Webster's New World Dictionary

Perfect. And the writer notices that both this entry and the one in his book of synonyms mention another word that may be apt: *repulsive*. The word *vile* can be used for its primary meaning: "morally base or evil; wicked; depraved, sinful." And *repulsive* can be used to emphasize another sense of *vile:* "offensive to the senses or sensibilities; repulsive; disgusting." Would it be repetitious to use both *vile* and *repulsive*? No, *repulsive* seems to point up an idea not fully conveyed by *vile* alone. Thus the writer changes the phrase *a nasty crime* to *a vile, repulsive crime,* and again his close attention to synonyms has produced clear, vigorous expression.

Practice

I. The term *malapropism,* meaning a ridiculous misuse of words, is derived from the figure of Mrs. Malaprop in Sheridan's play *The Rivals.* This lady is so eager to flaunt her erudition that she uses fancy words without knowing what they mean. She states that someone should not try to *extirpate* himself from a situation when she means *extricate,* and says that any young person should know something about *contagious* countries when she means *contiguous*.

Find and correct the malapropisms in these sentences.

1. This latest edition of Keats's letters is almost certainly definitive; in the future it will be an authoritarian source for all students of the poet.

2. The new Secretary of Commerce divested himself of all his holdings in large corporations so that his decisions in his new post could be as disinterested and judicial as possible.

3. Tom Paine's inflammable pamphlets made the British regard him as contemptuous.

4. The new laws, ingenuous though they are, have not had the desirous effect of lessening traffic fatalisms, but have succeeded only in arousing the anger and repulsion of all drivers, even the most cautious and law-abiding.

5. In his summation the attorney depreciated the state's crucial witness and inferred that her credulity was questionable.

6. This student organization is comprised of all the campus dissidents and malcontents who have the allusion that they can literally trample upon the school administration.

II. In their desire to create interest, many writers fill their prose with exaggerations; and as they strive for grandiose effects they frequently ignore the dictionary meanings of their superlatives. Every interesting book they review is *fascinating*; every wide-screen motion picture is *titanic*; every attractive woman is *breathtaking*.

Look up dictionary definitions for the italicized words below. Then substitute milder, more accurate words. If necessary, revise entire sentences.

1. This *sensational* novel tells the *fantastic* story of one man's *tremendous* inward search for the meaning of his life—a literally *dazzling* performance.

2. The battle ended with the *ferocious* Pabst eleven *slaughtering* the Winnetka Raiders by a score of 14–6.

3. *The Courage and the Agony* is a *colossal* film *epic*—a veritable *orgy* of front-line war experiences, complete with the *infinitely* ugly torment that men must undergo in wartime.

4. Rock-and-roll music has had a *stunning* impact on this country and has been *devastating* to the morals of the young.

beautiful *scene*

5. This Western movie is one of those *gorgeous spectacles* in which the *awe-inspiring* marshal and the *terrifically* brutal villain finally meet in a *superb* fast-draw reckoning.

marvelous

6. That young lady was not only *divine* in her appearance but also *terribly elegant* in her speech—a truly *fabulous* airline stewardess. *graceful* *Charming*

III. Decide which words should occupy the blank spaces in the following extracts. For each blank space you are given several words from which to choose. Pass over malapropisms, vague or exaggerated wordings, and synonyms that do not quite express the intended meaning; and single out, if you can, the word actually used by the author of the passage.

1. (Based on a passage by Edmund Wilson.)

[Houdini] now ___(a)___ any medium to show him ___(b)___ phenomena which he could not ___(c)___ and reproduce. To the demonstrations and lectures of this period, he brought a perhaps even ___(d)___ enthusiasm than he had to his earlier escapes: the deflation of this higher fakery had a certain intellectual and ___(e)___ interest, and Houdini's ___(f)___ against the mediums turned into a veritable ___(g)___ .

a. solicited, demanded, called on, asked, challenged, requested.

b. strange, supernatural, metaphysical, divine, marvelous, spirited.

c. descry, expose, detect, make bare, exhibit, show up, disclose.

d. fiercer, more violent, hotter, sharper, more ardent.

e. good, upright, moral, honorable, virtuous, ideal, laudatory.

f. war, crusade, campaign, drive, activities, battle.

g. major war, crusade, campaign, drive, activities, battle.

2. (Based on a passage by Vance Packard.)

Thousands of ___(a)___ fish have turned up in the Passaic River, from which several northern New Jersey communities had been ___(b)___ their drinking water. Fish can no longer ___(c)___ in parts of New Hampshire's Merrimack, once ___(d)___ for its fishing. ___(e)___ salmon runs of the North-

west are being ____(f)____ by the fact that the fish, in their
____(g)____ migrations up to the headwaters of streams,
____(h)____ in badly ____(i)____ stretches of these streams.

a. deceased, inanimate, dead, defunct, extinct, lifeless, moribund.
b. carrying, eliciting, drawing, extracting, withdrawing, pulling.
c. make do, subsist, last, persist, continue, survive, bear up.
d. notorious, reputable, famed, unique, egregious.
e. plentiful, abounding, innumerable, many of the, countless.
f. distracted, disturbed, disrupted, made miserable, worried, perturbed.
g. inflexible, unstoppable, unconquerable, decided, indomitable, relentless.
h. are exterminated, pass away, are obliterated, perish, are demolished, breathe their last.
i. corrupted, soiled, tainted, polluted, desecrated, dirtied, unkempt.

3. (Based on a passage by Herbert Muller.)

Let us spell out the worst about this ____(a)____ mass-man
and his mass-culture. He has ____(b)____ idea of the ____(c)____
life, ____(d)____ quantity with quality, size with greatness,
comfort with culture, gadgetry with genius. He has as little
appreciation of ____(e)____ science as of the fine arts, and as
little ____(f)____ the ____(g)____ that both ____(h)____ ; although
he may stand in ____(i)____ of them his real veneration goes to
the engineers and inventors, the ____(j)____ of True Romances
and Tin Pan Alley airs.

a. renowned, execrable, notorious, despicable, famous.
b. a poor, an insignificant, a meager, an infinitesimal, an emaciated.
c. abundant, overflowing, copious, abounding, lavish.
d. interspersing, mingling, mixing, blending, jumbling, confusing.
e. unsullied, unapplied, pure, unadulterated, real.
f. genius for, capacity for, power for, faculty of, efficiency at.

g. rigidity, drill, control, regulation, exercise, discipline.
h. require, solicit, request, want, requisition.
i. veneration, abashment, awe, terror, dread, reverence.
j. builders, manufacturers, creators, inventors, originators, designers.

4. (Based on a passage by Gilbert Highet.)

[Juvenal] received no appointment, however ___(a)___ . Possibly ___(b)___ censorious nature was apparent in his ___(c)___ even then. Lieutenants and assistant undersecretaries are expected to look bright and ___(d)___ , not coldly ___(e)___ ; to ___(f)___ and say "Certainly, sir," not to maintain ___(g)___ and dubious silence.

a. uneventful, immaterial, mediocre, poor, insignificant, bad, nonessential.
b. an unhappy, a bitter, an unpalatable, a sad.
c. carriage, guise, ways, appearance, manner.
d. neighborly, favorable, cooperative, obliging, supportive.
e. unpleasant, critical, abusive, detracting.
f. leer, smirk, sneer, smile, giggle, snicker, snigger, guffaw.
g. an unhappy, a moody, a sad, a glum, a morose, an unpleasant.

IV. Examine this prose by Stuart Chase—the first paragraph and last two paragraphs of his essay "The People, Yes." Leo Kirschbaum, in his book *Clear Writing*, accuses the prose of being slovenly and hackneyed in its wording. Do you agree? If so, what is your evidence?

(1)Carl Sandburg once wrote a stirring book ... [that] said the people were mostly right—but of course he was a poet. (2)William A. Lydgate ... has written another book proving that Sandburg was right. (3)Mr. Lydgate quotes chapter and verse to show where the people are often way ahead of Congress, ahead of the President, and several light years ahead of the editorials in most newspapers. (4) Again and again, the people leave the leaders of the people buried in a cloud of dust. ...

(5)The polls bring out one conclusion of great importance. (6)*Public opinion is changed by events, not rhetoric.*

(7)After the banks began to snap in 1932, people changed their political ideas rapidly. (8)They snowed Mr. Hoover under, and told Mr. Roosevelt to experiment as much as he pleased. (9)After the fall of France in 1940, they changed their ideas about international relations with great rapidity. (10)Following the event in Japan on August 6, 1945, their opinions may be taking another major shift. (11)Perhaps the bomb on Hiroshima has made a world state possible sooner than anyone expected!

(12)This is very cheerful news when all is said and done. (13)Also it makes sound biological sense. (14)If the mass of the people were swayed by every hurricane of political verbiage which came down the street, the human race would long since have become extinct. (15)The fact that *homo sapiens* keeps going—however waveringly—shows that somebody, somewhere, has stored up a little wisdom.

20

Familiar Words and Specific Words

The ornate style is still with us. Some writers, rather than expressing themselves as clearly as possible, seem more intent on dazzling their readers with high-sounding phrases. Here is a sample from a professor of sociology:

> In the long run, developments in transportation, housing, optimum size of plant, etc., might tend to induce an industrial and demographic pattern similar to the one that consciousness of vulnerability would dictate. Such a tendency might be advanced by public persuasion and governmental inducement, and advanced more effectively if the causes of urbanization had been carefully studied.
>
> Quoted by Samuel T. Williamson in
> "How to Write like a Social Scientist," *Saturday Review*, Oct. 4, 1947

The disease of ornateness can infect even literary critics. Irving Howe, who ordinarily writes in a plain style, loses control of his words in the following passage on "anti-utopian novels." (By this term he means such books as Huxley's *Brave New World*, which depicts a future society quite the opposite of a utopia.)

> ... [The novel] must be in the grip of an idea at once dramatically simple and historically complex: an idea that has become a commanding passion. This idea consists, finally, in a catastrophic transmutation of values, a stoppage of history at the expense of its actors. In reading the anti-utopian novel we respond less to the world it projects than to the urgency of the projection. And ... this involves the dangers of both monotony and monomania. ...
>
> "The Fiction of Anti-Utopia," *A World More Attractive*

A writer who wishes to avoid ornateness and express himself with clarity will follow this principle: *prefer the familiar word to the unfamiliar.* One trouble with "the sociological style" is its pretentious use of unfamiliar terms:

> ... Among sociologists in general there is a criminal fondness for using complicated terms when there are simple ones available. A child says "Do it again," a teacher says "Repeat the exercise," but the sociologist says "It was determined to replicate the experiment." Instead of saying two things are alike or similar, as a layman would do, the sociologist describes them as being either isomorphic or homologous. Instead of saying that they are different, he calls them allotropic. Every form of leadership or influence is called a hegemony.
>
> A sociologist never cuts anything in half or divides it in two like a layman. Instead he dichotomizes it, bifurcates it, subjects it to a process of binary fission, or restructures it in a dyadic conformation—around polar foci.
>
> MALCOLM COWLEY, "Sociological Habit Patterns in Linguistic Transmogrification," *Reporter*, Sept. 20, 1956

Not only academics strain to use fancy words. Many a beginning writer, fearful that his own words are too ordinary, rummages in a dictionary or thesaurus for farfetched substitutes. He uses *domicile* for *home, ubiquitous* for *widespread, gregarious* for *friendly* or *sociable, variegated* for *varied, metamorphosis* for *change,* and so on—not because the less familiar words express his meaning more precisely but because he hopes they sound more respectable.

A second principle of the plain style is this: *prefer specific wording to abstract or general wording.* As Brand Blanshard has said:

> Clearness and vividness often turn on mere specificity. To say that Major André was hanged is clear and definite; to say that he was killed is less definite, because you do not know in what way he was killed; to say that he died is still more indefinite because you do not even know whether his death was due to violence or to natural causes.
>
> *On Philosophical Style*

Not that a writer must use specific words only, with never a trace of the abstract or general—to do so would be impossible. But the writer should be as specific as he *can* be. The following sentence by James Baldwin, because it is concerned with death in the abstract and people in general, must use some abstract, general language; but Mr. Baldwin keeps the language as specific as he can:

> Life is tragic simply because the earth turns and the sun inexorably rises and sets, and one day, for each of us, the sun will go down for the last, last time.
>
> *The Fire Next Time*

A lesser writer might have produced something like this:

> Existence of the sort experienced by human beings is inevitably inclusive of some unpleasant phases, because all entities within the natural world move according to fixed and predetermined patterns, and at points somewhere in the future all mortal existences will reach their termination.

If the writer's first statement of an idea must be fairly abstract and general, he can add specifics afterward. Though the italicized statement in the passage below is fairly clear, the writer conveys his meaning more precisely when he adds specifics:

> ... *In Spain nothing, from a meal to a battle, ever happens at the appointed time.* As a general rule things happen too late, but just occasionally—just so that you shan't even be able to depend on their happening late—they happen too early. A train which is due to leave at eight will normally leave at any time between nine and ten, but perhaps once a week, thanks to some private whim of the engine-driver, it leaves at half-past seven. ...
>
> GEORGE ORWELL, *Homage to Catalonia*

Two principles, then, can help the writer avoid the obscurity and artificiality of the ornate style: (1) *prefer the familiar word to the unfamiliar;* (2) *prefer specific wording to abstract or general wording.* In order to watch the two principles working together to produce effective prose, we can examine another passage from the writings of George Orwell. His book *The Road to Wigan Pier* (1937) told the English public of a subject they had rarely considered: the hardships suffered by coal miners. Orwell spoke of the cheap, grimy housing, the dangers of working a thousand feet underground, and the brutal work of digging out the coal.

In describing the work of the shovelers (or "fillers") a mediocre writer might have said:

> The opportune moment for observing the mines is during the actual operation, so that one may witness the ordeal undergone by the laborers. At such a moment the setting is comparable to that of the *Inferno.* The surrounding atmosphere is filled with unpleasant particles of dust; the illumination is woefully inadequate; and the space is limited. There is a remarkable amount of noise and reverberation from the mechanical apparatus, and the temperature is extremely high. Moreover, the laborers must effect their operations in a kneeling position, with the result that they must expend considerably more effort than if they had been in an upright position. Despite these discomforts and disadvantageous conditions, the task is performed manfully. The laborers employ their earth-moving implements with a perfectly amazing dexterity. As a regular part of their daily routine, they must deal with

an enormous quantity of coal, which they must extract from the earth and place upon a machine that will transport it elsewhere. And yet the laborers are certainly capable of this task, quite as if they were deities rather than mundane creatures.

Now here is part of Orwell's account:

... The time to go there is when the machines are roaring and the air is black with coal dust, and when you can actually see what the miners have to do. At those times the place is like hell, or at any rate like my own mental picture of hell. Most of the things one imagines in hell are there—heat, noise, confusion, darkness, foul air, and above all, unbearably cramped space. ... In the hotter mines they [the "fillers"] wear only a pair of thin drawers, clogs and knee-pads; in the hottest mines of all, only the clogs and knee-pads. ... It is a dreadful job they do, an almost superhuman job by the standards of an ordinary person. For they are not only shifting monstrous quantities of coal, they are also doing it in a position that doubles or trebles the work. They have got to remain kneeling all the while—they could hardly rise from their knees without hitting the ceiling—and you can easily see by trying it what a tremendous effort this means. Shoveling is comparatively easy when you are standing up, because you can use your knee and thigh to drive the shovel along; kneeling down, the whole of the strain is thrown upon your arm and belly muscles. And the other conditions do not exactly make things easier. There is the heat—it varies, but in some mines it is suffocating—and the coal dust that stuffs up your throat and nostrils and collects along your eyelids, and the unending rattle of the conveyor belt, which in that confined space is rather like the rattle of a machine gun. ... You can never forget that spectacle once you have seen it—the line of bowed, kneeling figures, sooty black all over, driving their huge shovels under the coal with stupendous force and speed. ...

Orwell's language is plain and specific, especially in comparison with the feeble prose of the earlier version:

Earlier version	Orwell
the opportune moment for observing the mines is during the actual operation	the time to go there is when the machines are roaring
the setting is comparable to that of the *Inferno*	the place is like hell
the surrounding atmosphere is filled with unpleasant particles of dust	the air is black with coal dust

And so on.

But apparently Orwell felt that he had not yet conveyed the strength and endurance of the miners. He continued his account, first by calculating the amount of coal a miner shoveled out each hour, then by comparing the shoveling of coal (an activity not familiar to the reader) with the shoveling of dirt (an activity more familiar):

> Even when you watch the process of coal-extraction you probably watch it for a short time, and it is not until you begin making a few calculations that you realize what a stupendous task the "fillers" are performing. Normally each man has to clear a space four or five yards wide. The cutter has undermined the coal to the depth of five feet, so that if the seam of coal is three or four feet high, each man has to cut out, break up and load on to the [conveyor] belt something between seven and twelve cubic yards of coal. This is to say, taking a cubic yard as weighing twenty-seven hundredweight, that each man is shifting coal at a speed approaching two tons an hour. I have just enough experience of pick-and-shovel work to be able to grasp what this means. When I am digging trenches in my garden, if I shift two tons of earth during the afternoon, I feel that I have earned my tea. But earth is tractable stuff compared with coal, and I don't have to work kneeling down, a thousand feet underground, in suffocating heat and swallowing coal dust with every breath I take.... The miner's job would be as much beyond my power as it would be to perform on the flying trapeze or to win the Grand National. I am not a manual laborer and

please God I never shall be one, but there are some kinds of
manual work that I could do if I had to. At a pitch I could be
a tolerable road-sweeper or an inefficient gardener or even a
tenth-rate farm hand. But by no conceivable amount of effort
or training could I become a coal miner; the work would kill
me in a few weeks.

A writer's subject matter will often have a surprising
tendency to strike the reader as being new and difficult. Therefore George Orwell and other writers who can make hard thoughts
clear (such as philosopher Bertrand Russell, scientist George
Gamow, and economist Robert Heilbroner) observe the two principles set down as long ago as Aristotle—who urged that writers
should use common words rather than uncommon or "ornamental ones," and specific words rather than abstract or general.

Practice

I. The job of finding specific words is often a matter of choosing
    from among synonyms. If the word *small* is too vague, the
    writer can examine specific substitutes for it—*tiny, short, dwarf-
    ish, stunted, puny,* and so forth—and choose the one that best
    expresses his meaning.
        For each of the following words, give four or five
    specific substitutes.

    1. walk
    2. run
    3. weak
    4. strong
    5. seat (noun)
    6. intelligent
    7. big
    8. speak
    9. answer (noun)
    10. sad
    11. take
    12. weapon
    13. dog
    14. hold (verb)
    15. talk (noun)
    16. awkward
    17. see
    18. helpless
    19. dull
    20. absurd

II. Rewrite the following sentences to make them more specific.

    1. One person was addressing a group of people on a topic of
        doubtful importance.

2. As the young person approached the road, a large vehicle moved by at a high speed.

3. While one person walked across the room, a number of other people watched.

4. The mentor spoke to the group about a serious problem in their writing.

5. When the weather was at its best, the child showed signs of great happiness and played games outside with his friends.

6. Though the speaker gave only a brief talk, he surprised his listeners with what he said.

7. The dog uttered a strange sound, then ran across the road without paying attention to the amount of traffic.

8. The repairman spent a long time trying to fix the trouble in the kitchen.

9. The girl moved through the book slowly, giving it considerable attention.

10. John wanted to buy some gifts, but the store he went to already contained a great many people.

11. While working in a food store, Frank found out that women are often impolite and unpleasant.

12. He got to his feet, then made his way through the vegetation. (Rewrite sentence 12 twice—first supposing the "he" to be an escaped convict, then supposing him to be a drunkard.)

III.   This list contains words with which pretentious writers try to dazzle their readers. Though the words have legitimate uses, the bedazzlement of readers is not one of them. Replace each word with a synonym that is more familiar.

1. advent
2. behold
3. bereavement
4. beverage
5. converse (verb)
6. corpulent
7. demise
8. domicile
9. expectorate
10. imbibe
11. impecunious
12. indisposed
13. mentor
14. metropolis
15. missive
16. neophyte
17. prevaricate
18. transpire
19. underprivileged
20. visage

IV.   The following two pieces of prose employ a vague, pretentious wording. (The first was written in that style for the purposes of this exercise, but the second passage was taken word-for-word from a book about swindlers and confidence men.) Revise both passages to make the wording simpler and more specific.

1. A considerable proportion of the constituents of academe receive more motivation from the anticipation of their record of scholastic status than from any concern for the intellectual matter they might glean from their collegiate undertakings. They have more solicitude for the symbols registered on their record than for the learning manifested in those symbols. Representative students openly profess that they activate themselves more for the ultimate assessment incorporated in the record of academic achievement than for the absorption of academic material that might occur. They select a particular field of mental endeavor because they conceive that the field offers the least arduous courses of study, courses that afford maximum returns in terms of record of scholastic achievement, for minimum output of industry. These students often feel an aversion for the studies necessitated by their field of specialization, and they never deviate into areas of that field that are not made requisite by the syllabus of studies. They do occupy considerable time with endeavors necessitated by the area of investigation in which they are involved, but the essential impetus for this activity is not a motivation aroused by the investigation itself. When the results of such activity come back to them, they are oblivious to the mentor's evaluative glosses, but look with considerable animation for the simple signification of academic achievement, manifest gratification when they come to a symbol denoting relatively satisfactory accomplishment, then exhibit their indifference to the product of their cerebrations by disposing of it in a receptacle for refuse.

2. The fraudulent predatory parasites engage in a form of exploitation characterized by simulation or deceit. Their victims are induced to cooperate voluntarily with them under the mistaken impression that they are receiving a countervalue or counterservice for whatever they have been persuaded to give.

In sharp contrast to the methods of compulsive predators, which hinge upon force, stealth, or intimidation of some sort, the essential element in the parasitism of those who live by fraud is successful persuasion. The art of deception is their stock in trade, and they continually occupy themselves with schemes to gain access to the resources of others by false pretenses. Cunning decides the most effective bait, and the victims are inveigled into accepting semblance for reality.

JAMES WYATT MARRS, *The Man on Your Back*

V. Having converted the passages in exercise IV into simpler and more specific language, you may find it instructive to do the opposite: to ruin a clear piece of prose by making its wording vague and farfetched. Do this to a paragraph of your own or to one of those listed below.

1. George Orwell on "the secrecy attaching to poverty" (pp. 16–17).
2. Marya Mannes on the Lansings of Park Avenue (p. 39).
3. Joseph Mitchell on the painful winter of 1933 (pp. 44–45).
4. Gilbert Highet on Juvenal's search for employment (pp. 49–50).
5. Thomas B. Morgan on Marcucci, the promoter of teen-age idols (p. 50).
6. Joseph Mitchell on Joe Gould (p. 61).
7. George Orwell on the condemned Burmese prisoners (p. 102).

21

Tying Ideas Together: Coordination

    The child in elementary school writes short sentences that dole out one bit of information at a time: "John ran. Sam ran too. They ran to the edge of the woods. Then they walked. They walked into the woods." The mature writer, though he occasionally uses sentences as brief as these, generally uses longer sentences that combine single ideas into larger units of thought.

    One means of combining ideas is *coordination: the joining of elements that are equal in importance and similar in grammatical function.* For example: "John and Sam ran to the edge of the woods and then walked into them." *John and Sam* is one coordinate structure; *ran . . . and . . . walked* is another. The linked terms are equal in importance. And they are similar in grammatical function; a noun is linked to a noun, a verb to a verb.

Not only nouns and verbs can be coordinated. Nor is *and* the only word that can do the coordinating. *And* is merely one of the *coordinate conjunctions*. The following sentences show some of the most useful of these conjunctions, and show some of the various kinds of words, phrases, and clauses that can be coordinated. (The conjunctions are underlined; the coordinate terms are italicized.)

He earned some extra pocket-money *by working* as a lab assistant for the chemistry department <u>and</u> *by waiting* on tables in a local restaurant. [Coordinate gerund phrases]

He shot *quickly* <u>but</u> *accurately*, making four bull's-eyes in five shots. [Coordinate adverbs]

The book became a best seller, <u>for</u> *the publisher's advertising campaign convinced thousands of people that the book would put an end to their fears and frustrations.* [Coordinate independent clauses]

He wanted *to write* about *Sons and Lovers* <u>or</u> perhaps *to compare* several of D. H. Lawrence's novels. [Coordinate infinitive verbs]

The new governor refused to say whether he planned to raise the sales tax, <u>nor</u> *would he state his position on the issue of aid to schools* [Coordinate independent clauses]

He was unable to attend the charity dinner, <u>so</u> *he sent a telegram pledging his contribution.* [Coordinate independent clauses]

He *had studied* philosophy for all his adult years <u>yet</u> *could* not *solve* his own personal and domestic problems. [Coordinate verbs]

Sometimes the conjunction may be replaced by a mark of punctuation:

The raccoon paused for a moment at the edge of the clearing; then he darted across. [Semicolon joins independent clauses.]

The soft, easy flow of the river quickened until the water became a wild, white cascade. [Commas join coordinate adjectives.]

Coordinate elements, besides coming in twos, may occur in a *series* of three or more:

For breakfast he gorged himself with three *pieces* of toast, four scrambled *eggs*, a big *stack* of pancakes, and five or six corn *muffins*.

With only a hundred yards left in the race, he *gasped* for air, *pumped* his arms, and *strained* to lengthen his stride.

Another means of coordination is *correlative conjunctions*. These work in pairs:

James Agee was both a *scriptwriter* for the motion picture industry and an outspoken *critic* of the industry.
[The correlative conjunctions *both* ... *and* link coordinate nouns.]

The lawyer knew that the woman was not telling the truth. Either *she was making an honest mistake* or *she was deliberately lying to protect someone, perhaps herself*.
[Correlative conjunctions *either* ... *or* link coordinate independent clauses.]

Defoe's writings were popular not only *because the growing middle class wanted reading matter* but also *because he had good stories to tell and valuable information to convey*. [Correlative conjunctions *not only* ... *but also* link coordinate dependent clauses.]

That book was nothing but a labored reiteration of worn-out ideas; it was neither *informative* nor *entertaining*.
[Correlative conjunctions *neither* ... *nor* link coordinate adjectives.]

Coordination can improve some sentences greatly. Suppose a working draft contained mostly short, skimpy sentences.

The average man who uses a telephone could not explain how a telephone works. He takes it for granted. He also takes other things for granted. He doesn't think much about the linotype. He doesn't ponder the railway train. He even takes for granted the airplane, as our grandfathers took for granted the miracles of the gospels. He doesn't question these things. He doesn't understand them, either. It is as though each of us investigates only a tiny circle of facts. Only that small circle of facts do we make our own.

Although this prose is better than that found in most working drafts, a writer skilled in using coordination could make it even better:

The average man who uses a telephone could not explain how a telephone works. He takes for granted *the telephone, the railway train, the linotype, the airplane,* as our grandfathers took for granted the miracles of the gospels. He *neither questions nor understands* them. It is as though each of us *investigated and made* his own only a tiny circle of facts.

ROBERT LYND, *The Pleasures of Ignorance*

Note that the passage using coordination is not only more fluent but more forceful. Coordination has eliminated unnecessary words that made the earlier version lifeless. And at one point coordination has added the forcefulness that can result from repetition: "He takes for granted the telephone, the railway train, the linotype, the airplane. . . ." The point is emphasized by the insistent rhythm of the series. This technique is used more extensively in the following passage. The author employs two long series of parallel terms to convey the atmosphere of Henry Miller's *Tropic of Cancer:*

For the most part it is a story of bug-ridden rooms in workingmen's hotels, of fights, drinking bouts, cheap brothels, Russian refugees, cadging, swindling, and temporary jobs. And the whole atmosphere of the poor quarters of Paris as a foreigner sees them—the cobbled alleys, the sour reek of refuse, the bistros with their greasy zinc counters and worn brick floors, the green waters of the Seine, the blue cloaks of the Republican Guard, the crumbling iron urinals, the peculiar sweetish smell of the Metro stations, the cigarettes that come to pieces, the pigeons in the Luxembourg Gardens —it is all there, or at any rate the feeling of it is there.

GEORGE ORWELL, "Inside the Whale," *Collected Essays, Journalism and Letters*, I

The effect of this comes partly from the concreteness of the diction but also from the steady accumulation of parallel words and phrases.

A series may be forceful without being as long as those quoted above. For some reason a series of three terms (a *triplet* or *triad*) can be particularly effective:

I came, I saw, I conquered.

Life, liberty, and the pursuit of happiness.

Of the people, by the people, and for the people.

Consider these sentences from a discussion of Hemingway's *The Old Man and the Sea:*

The old man lives on plain water and raw fish, he goes almost without sleep, and his hands are cut open by his line.

Much later he succeeds in bringing the great thing [a giant marlin] alongside, in harpooning it, and in lashing it to the skiff. By this time his hands are cut badly, he is nearly blind from exhaustion, and he is too tired to think of anything.

. . . Santiago is a fighter whose best days are behind him, who is too old for what his profession demands of him and, worse, is wholly down on his luck. But he still dares, and sticks to the rules, and endures, and his loss therefore, in the manner of it, is itself a victory.

PHILIP YOUNG, *Ernest Hemingway: A Reconsideration*

These passages are taken from several pages of Mr. Young's book; this many triplets on one page would have seemed monotonous.

Even just two coordinate elements can be forceful if they are *balanced:* not only coordinate, but similar in form and word order.

Coordinate but not balanced	Balanced
Preacher Jim Casy states several themes of *The Grapes of Wrath,* but there is a lack of plausibility in Casy.	Preacher Jim *Casy states* several themes of *The Grapes of Wrath,* but *Casy lacks* plausibility.
Mark Twain had other talents besides his ability as a writer; public speaking was something else he did well.	Mark Twain was talented both *as a writer* and *as a public speaker.*
Twain was capable with words, but unfortunately acumen in business speculations was not one of his traits.	Twain had *great skill with words* but *little skill with business speculations.*

The left-hand sentences are wordy and roundabout. Those on the right, thanks to their balanced construction, are more concise and forceful.

Each time the writer polishes a working draft, he finds the techniques of coordination valuable. In one spot he connects skimpy sentences, in another he balances a pair of phrases, and so on—not overworking coordination, but using it wherever it can give his prose a greater fluency and force.

Practice

Use coordination to tighten up the following pieces of prose. Change wording wherever necessary and delete needless words. Each passage except the last can be converted into a single sentence.

For example, here is a passage in need of revision:

> Clyde has a tremendous capacity for hard work. He also has a managerial skill that would seem more appropriate in a chief executive for IBM. Lastly, he has an unwearying talent for lively writing. His writing is incisive too.

After revision this might be:

> Clyde has a tremendous capacity for hard work, a managerial skill that would seem more appropriate in a chief executive for IBM, and an unwearying talent for lively, incisive writing.

1. Last spring we decided the croquet set was beyond use. We invested in a rather fancy new one with hoops set in small wooden sockets. It also has mallets with rubber faces.

2. The croquet course is now exactly seventy-two feet long. We lined the wickets up with a string. The boy, however, is less fond of it now. We make him keep still while we are shooting.

3. Athleticism is not physical education. It is sports promotion. It is carried on for the monetary profit of the college through the entertainment of the public.

4. To be attractive to the female, man had to go in for somersaults. He had to go in for tilting with lances. He even began performing feats of parlor magic to win her attention. Man also had to bring her candy. He made tribute to her with flowers. He had to bring her the furs of animals.

5. In spite of all these "love displays" the male is constantly being turned down. Sometimes he is insulted. Sometimes he is thrown out of the house.

6. Road signs shout romance. It is crooned by transmitters. It is the subject of juke-box yowls.

7. Romance bulges on Cinemascope screens. TV sets flicker romance. Magazine covers contain gleams of it.

8. A whole galaxy of industries labors to lure him to her with perfumes. The lure may also be parasols. Sometimes it will be pendants. The same industries try to lure her to him with the checks on his shirt. Another lure is the monogram on his belt. Still another is the shaving lotion on his jaws.

9. The sand of the desert turns fertile fields into barren wastes. The encroaching sea has the same effect. Either one reduces whole populations to distress. Populations may even be reduced to starvation.

10. Euphemism is the tendency to call a spade "a certain garden implement." It is the tendency to call women's underwear "unmentionables."

11. The tendency towards euphemism is stronger in some eras than others. It is stronger in some people than others. Still, it always operates more or less in subjects that are touchy. The subjects may even be taboo. One of these subjects is death. Another is sex. Another is madness. There are others.

12. Thus we shrink from saying "He died last night." Instead we say "passed away." Perhaps we say "left us." We might say "joined his Maker." Another possibility is "went to his reward."

13. By looking at Wallace's mouth, one could tell whether he was plotting evil. One could also tell whether he had recently accomplished it.

14. In the world of soap opera a character's loss of the use of the legs may be temporary. On the other hand, it may be permanent.

15. The Lansings' large rooms are carpeted wall-to-wall in a neutral shade. The sofas are covered in a flowered muted chintz. The other alternative is beige brocade. The chairs are covered in the same material. The curtains drawn across the windows are of matching chintz.

16. The Lansings have comfort for their money. They have no fun, however. The observant guest cannot help but pity such spiritual constipation.

17. In some places, if individuals are caught in an incestuous act, they commit suicide. Otherwise they are killed by their relatives.

18. The breaking of this taboo is thought to endanger the very life of the society in some terrible way. The way, however, is indefinable. The death of the violators serves as a kind of appeasement.

19. College is the greatest place in the world for those who ought to go to college. It is the greatest place for those who go for the right reasons.

20. For those who ought not to go to college, it is a waste of time. It is also a waste for those who go for the wrong reasons. It is a waste of money, too.

21. (You will need at least four sentences for your revision of this passage.)

> Let us spell out the worst about this notorious mass-man. The worst about his mass-culture should also be noted. He has a meager idea of the abundant life, confusing quantity with quality. He also confuses size with greatness. Another confusion is that of comfort with culture. Lastly, he confuses gadgetry with genius. He has little appreciation of pure science. He appreciates the fine arts just as little. He has just as little capacity for the discipline that both require. Although he may stand in awe of them his real veneration goes to engineers. He reveres inventors, too. His veneration extends also to the manufacturers of True Romances. Similarly, he has reverence for those who manufacture Tin Pan Alley airs. He is frequently illiberal. He is suspicious of "radical" ideas. For "visionary" ideals he has only scorn. He exhibits hostility toward "aliens."

22

Tying Ideas Together: Subordination

Coordination makes ideas seem equal in importance. Consider the two coordinate ideas (joined by *and*) in the following sentence:

> The senator stood in front of the Capitol, *and* he spoke with a group of newspaper reporters.

That the senator talked with reporters seems no more and no less important than where he stood at the time. If the writer wished to emphasize one idea over the other, he would have to use, not coordination, but *subordination*. This means of linking ideas reflects their relative importance. It emphasizes the more important ideas and *subordinates* the others.

One means of subordination is the *dependent* or *subordinate clause*. It is dependent in that it cannot stand alone as a sentence. Therefore it is subordinate to an *independent clause*, which can stand on its own and express an idea of primary importance. In the following example the clause before the comma is dependent; the clause after, independent.

> As the senator stood in front of the Capitol, he spoke with a
> group of newspaper reporters.

Because the opening idea has been demoted to the rank of dependent clause, the second idea, still independent, stands out as the more important point. This form of the sentence, since it emphasizes the talk with reporters, would be appropriate in a paragraph about the senator's many talks with people during a typical day. In another context, however, the sentence might have to reverse its emphasis:

> As the senator spoke with a group of newspaper reporters,
> he stood in front of the Capitol.

This form could appear in a paragraph about the senator's ability to show up in many places each day. Now that his talk with reporters is relegated to a dependent clause, his appearing before the Capitol is the main point of the sentence.

So far we have looked at only one kind of dependent clause. A glance at other possibilities will show the flexibility of which the technique is capable.

> *While the senator stood in front of the Capitol,* he spoke with
> a group of newspaper reporters.
> *As soon as the senator stood in front of the Capitol,* he spoke
> with a group of newspaper reporters.
> *Now that the senator stood in front of the Capitol,* he spoke
> with a group of newspaper reporters.
> *As long as the senator stood in front of the Capitol,* he spoke
> with a group of newspaper reporters.
> *After the senator had stood in front of the Capitol,* he spoke
> with a group of newspaper reporters.
> *Whenever the senator stood in front of the Capitol,* he spoke
> with a group of newspaper reporters.

Because the senator stood in front of the Capitol, he spoke
with a group of newspaper reporters.

Although [or *though*] the senator stood in front of the Capitol, he spoke with a group of newspaper reporters.

An idea not quite important enough to warrant a dependent clause can sometimes be expressed in an *elliptical dependent clause,* which omits words and thereby becomes less prominent. The sentences on the left below contain fully worded dependent clauses; on the right the clauses are elliptical.

While the senator was standing in front of the Capitol, he spoke with a group of newspaper reporters.	*While standing in front of the Capitol,* the senator spoke with a group of newspaper reporters.
Whenever it was possible, he relied on people *that he knew well.*	*Whenever possible,* he relied on people *he knew well.*

A *phrase* subordinates an idea even further. The following sentences illustrate the many kinds of phrases from which the writer can choose. The independent clauses on the left are converted into phrases on the right.

The chemist worked late into the night, and *his eyes were growing weary,* and *his hands were becoming unsure.*	The chemist worked late into the night, *his eyes growing weary, his hands unsure.* [Absolute phrases]
He read a Superman comic book, and that was his only diversion during the long wait.	*Reading a Superman comic book* was his only diversion during the long wait. [Gerund phrase]
She made a mistake. *She set out on a long car trip,* yet *she did not know how to fix a flat tire.*	She made the mistake *of setting out on a long car trip without knowing how to fix a flat tire.* [Gerund phrases]
He was exhausted by the hours of grueling play, and he could no longer throw accurate passes.	*Exhausted by hours of grueling play,* he could no longer throw accurate passes. [Participial phrase]
The critics had panned the play, and it ended its run after the fourth night.	*Panned by the critics,* the play ended its run after the fourth night. [Participial phrase]
The novel is highly sentimental. *It could not please a discerning reader.*	This novel is too sentimental *to please a discerning reader.* [Infinitive phrase]

The desk was cluttered with books, papers, and old magazines, and *they could all have built a good-sized bonfire.*

The desk was cluttered with enough books, papers, and old magazines *to build a good-sized bonfire.*
[Infinitive phrase]

Albert Camus was famous both as a writer and as a leader of the French Resistance during World War II, and *he was a recipient of the Nobel Prize.*

Albert Camus, *a recipient of the Nobel Prize,* was famous both as a writer and as a leader of the French Resistance during World War II.
[Appositive phrase]

Hollywood is the center of American motion-picture production, and the town has been called "the dream factory."

Hollywood, *the center of American motion-picture production,* has been called "the dream factory."
[Appositive phrase]

He sold his phonograph, and *he received a hundred dollars for it.*

He sold his phonograph *for a hundred dollars.*
[Prepositional phrase]

Lincoln had studied formal rhetoric, and his study helped him now, *because he had to enter a series of debates,* and *the man he had to debate against was Douglas.*

Lincoln's study *of formal rhetoric* helped him now *in his debates against Douglas.*
[Prepositional phrases]

An idea not important enough to deserve a prepositional phrase can be expressed in just a word or two.

Happy to get news from her family, she opened the letter *with great speed.*

Happy to get news from her family, she opened the letter *quickly.*

It was a large house, a very large house, and it had twenty-one rooms and a veranda large enough to serve as an outdoor restaurant.

The spacious house [or *mansion*] had twenty-one rooms and a veranda large enough to serve as an outdoor restaurant.

In his tour of Europe, *a tour that lasted through the whole summer,* he used his Mercedes-Benz automobile, *which was a sedan model and a powerful car.*

In his *summer-long* tour of Europe he used his *powerful* Mercedes-Benz *sedan.*

There are exceptions to these principles; sometimes a phrase or a single word can be more emphatic than an independent clause. But because the principles generally hold true, subordination is an essential means of indicating the relative importance of ideas.

Subordination has other benefits as well. We can observe its several advantages by examining a passage that relies mostly on coordination and then a passage that uses subordination. Here is the inferior prose, a passage concerned with the character George Hurstwood, of Dreiser's novel *Sister Carrie:*

> Hurstwood has had no previous thought of stealing. He has been spending the evening in the bar and has been with some of the clientele. His mind has been upset, so he has been drinking, and his drinking has been somewhat greater than usual. Then the closing-up hour comes, and Hurstwood steps into his office and discovers something unusual. Another cashier has worked there in the daytime, and that cashier has been forgetful and has not locked the safe. This has not happened before. Hurstwood is about to lock the safe himself, but he glances into it and he is surprised, for he sees a great deal of money, and Fitzgerald and Moy usually didn't leave this much money there. The bills are in parcels, and Hurstwood picks them up and counts them, but he does this in a mechanical way. But then temptation strikes him, and only then does this happen, for the temptation is "floundering among a jumble of thoughts."

Now here is the second version, actually the original (by F. O. Matthiessen) from which the other was derived. This version, though it contains several coordinate structures, relies mainly on subordination.

> Hurstwood has had no previous thought of stealing. He has been spending the evening in the bar, drinking a little more than usual with some of the clientele because of his upset state of mind. When he steps into his office at the closing-up hour, he finds that the daytime cashier has forgotten to lock the safe, a thing that has not happened before. Glancing into

the safe before locking it himself, he is suprised to see far more money than he thought Fitzgerald and Moy usually left there. He picks up the parcels of bills and mechanically counts them. Only then, "floundering among a jumble of thoughts," does temptation strike him.

THEODORE DREISER

A comparison of these passages underscores the benefits of subordination. One benefit, as we have seen, is that subordination indicates the relative importance of ideas. The following sentence depends on coordination: "The bills are in parcels, and Hurstwood picks them up and counts them, but he does this in a mechanical way." *Part one, and part two, but part three*—so the sentence goes, each part seeming equally important with the others. But surely the fact that Hurstwood picks up the bills and counts them is more important than that the bills are parceled and the counting is mechanical. With subordination, the main idea gets the emphasis it deserves: *"He picks up* the parcels of bills and mechanically *counts* them." *He* (Hurstwood) is the subject of the sentence; *picks up* and *counts* are its verbs. The other two ideas are subordinated: *the bills are in parcels* is reduced to *parcels of; he does this in a mechanical way* is reduced to *mechanically*.

A second benefit of subordination is conciseness. The passage using coordination contains 162 words; the one with subordination, 112. Consider again the sentence about the money: "The bills are in parcels, and Hurstwood picks them up and counts them, but he does this in a mechanical way." This is a slow-moving twenty-one words. The version using subordination, with only eleven words, expresses the same ideas with twice the speed.

The sentence about money reveals still another advantage of subordination. Coordination provides too little variety of sentence structure; within that single sentence the repeated pattern of words becomes tiresome. But the techniques of subordination are so diverse that the writer skilled in using them can easily avoid a dulling sameness.

Practice

The following passages are composed entirely of short, simple sentences. Using both coordination and subordination, convert each passage into a single sentence. Change wording and word order if you wish, and eliminate needless words. Here is an example of the kind of passage you will be revising:

> We used to have an old croquet set. Its wooden balls were no longer round. They had been chewed by dogs. They were no rounder than eggs.

Here is a possible revision:

> We used to have an old croquet set whose wooden balls, having been chewed by dogs, were no rounder than eggs.
>
> E. B. WHITE

1. Grant set out to write the memoirs under handicaps. They were as serious as any that he had faced in the Civil War.
2. Grant was ill. He was suffering from cancer. It had struck him in the throat.
3. But he completed the first part of the manuscript. He did this by dictating it. Then it became impossible to use his voice. He wrote out the rest of the story.
4. He finished it in eleven months. He died about a week later. His death occurred on July 23, 1885.
5. The book sold three hundred thousand copies in the first two years after publication. It made $450,000 for Grant's family. The family had been impoverished.
6. The *Personal Memoirs* was a thick pair of volumes. It used to stand on the shelves of many homes. It was on the shelves of every pro-Union home. It was like a solid attestation of the victory of the Union forces.
   (Passages 1–6 are derived from sentences by Edmund Wilson.)

7. The side pockets of Wallace's jacket bulged. They went out over his pudgy haunches. They were like burro hampers.
8. They were filled with tools. They held screwdrivers, pliers, and files. They held wrenches and wire-cutters. They also held nail sets. I don't know what else they held.

9. There was even more than that. One pocket always contained a copy of *Popular Mechanics*. The copy was rolled up. The other held *Scientific American*. Or it might hold some other such magazine. It protruded from the top of the pocket.

10. His breast pocket contained a picket fence of things. Among these were drill bits and gimlets. There were also kitchen knives and other pointed instruments. In addition, there was another large collection. This included fountain pens and mechanical pencils.

11. He would walk. Then he would clink. He might also jangle. And he would peal.
   (Passages 7–11 are derived from sentences by Richard Rovere.)

12. Our nation's aquatic wildlife has been having difficulty. It has been finding our inland waters unbearable. This difficulty has been increasing.

13. Ten thousand ducks were recently destroyed on the Detroit River. These were scarce canvasback and redhead ducks. The destruction was caused by the release of sewage. The sewage had not been treated. This happened some months ago.

14. Dead fish have turned up in the Passaic River. They number in the thousands. Several northern New Jersey communities had been using the river. They had been drawing water from it. The water was used for drinking.

15. Fish can no longer survive in the Merrimack. At least, this is true in some parts of the Merrimack. This river is in New Hampshire. It was once famed for its fishing.

16. Many salmon runs are being disrupted. These take place in the Northwest. The salmon migrate up to the headwaters of streams. Their migration is relentless. Stretches of the streams are badly polluted. The fish perish.
   (Passages 12–16 are derived from sentences by Vance Packard.)

17. Students on our campus do care about grades. However, they are less concerned about learning. This is true of many of our students.

18. They are concerned about their grades. These will appear on their school record. However, they are not so much concerned about skills and knowledge. This is what the grades are meant to reflect.

19. My roommate is an instance of this. He openly admits that he works for grades. He admits that he does not work for anything he might learn.

20. He chose to major in English because the English department offers "snap" courses. At least it is his opinion that most of their courses are "snaps." These are courses that give high grades. They require little work.

21. He complains about what he has to read for English courses. His complaints are incessant. He calls the reading assignments "sludgy stuff." He never reads an unassigned book.

22. He does work on his papers for English. He works several hours each night on them. Still, he doesn't really care about what he is writing.

23. A paper comes back to him. He ignores the instructor's comments. These are written on the paper. Instead, he searches for the grade-mark. His search is anxious. He finds a *B*. Then he sighs with satisfaction. After that he tosses the paper away. It goes into the wastebasket.

(Items 24–31 come from a passage with this main idea: Clyde doesn't look like someone with great abilities.)

24. He is tall. He's about six-foot, four. He is loose. Sometimes he is limp.

25. He walks around the campus every afternoon. He is hunting down news. He chats with people. During this he never hurries.

26. He droops his head much of the time. He lets his belly hang out. He lets his feet slap the sidewalk. They are long feet. They are like so much loose leather.

27. His hair is cut in what might be called crew-style. It's rarely short, however.

28. He does get a crew-cut to begin with. Then, however, he lets it grow out. It grows out for ten or twelve weeks. Finally it becomes downright uncomfortable. It becomes uncomfortable around the ears and neck. Then he gets another crew-cut.

29. He wears glasses. They are round and colorless. His face is also round. It is colorless, too.

30. The face has three expressions. There are only those. One is a big, happy grin. A second is a lost-in-thought expression. Then the mouth is hanging open. The eyes hang open, too. The third ex-

pression is a serious, worried look. Then the mouth is pursed. The eyes are narrowed.

31. Most of the time he wears only one outfit. The only time he doesn't wear it is the Sundays when he attends chapel. The outfit includes a white shirt. It has long sleeves. It is not ironed. It is buttoned in some places. In most places, however, it hangs loose. The outfit also has khaki pants. These are loose. They are also baggy. Finally, the outfit includes brown loafers. These are loose, too. They are flappy.

Suffering from &

Grant suffered from cancer of the throat

[handwritten notes:]

I went —   — simple

I went + I saw John   — compound

When I went, I saw John — complex

I went + I saw John — how   { compound-complex
     did not look well   }   sentence.

subject + verb
~~begin~~   — loose

end —   — periodic

     balance

23

The End of the Sentence

Whenever possible, a sentence should end with important words. Thus the sentence will leave the reader with a strong final impression. And the words in the climactic position will receive the emphasis they deserve.

A sentence ending with a series, for example, generally should conclude with the most important item in the series.

> *Weak ending:* Even in his own lifetime Jonathan Swift was famous for his great satire *Gulliver's Travels*, his caustic writings on public issues, and his clever conversation.

Stronger: Even in his own lifetime Jonathan Swift was famous for his clever conversation, his caustic writings on public issues, and his great satire *Gulliver's Travels.*

Weak ending: The bombing killed over nine hundred people, destroyed property worth millions of dollars, and temporarily halted public transportation.

Stronger: The bombing temporarily halted public transportation, destroyed property worth millions of dollars, and killed over nine hundred people.

A *periodic sentence* ends with its main idea. The subordinate elements appear first, and the main idea—expressed in an independent clause—comes as a climax. Here are several examples (with the main ideas italicized):

In the prose of Addison and Steele, of Swift and Arbuthnot and Mandeville, *the . . . tradition of easy and polite writing persists.*

In the writing of such scholars as Richard Bentley and William Warburton *we often find ourselves floundering in ponderous sentences, and stunned by a learned and polysyllabic vocabulary.*

In view of the extent to which English prose was corrupted in the nineteenth century by the pompous phraseology of newspaper writers, *we have no right to assume that the journalist will always throw his influence on the side of easy and natural expression.*

JAMES R. SUTHERLAND, *On English Prose*

A prose style that overworks the periodic sentence and the series in climactic order will become monotonous; not every sentence should end with so strong a climax. But no sentence should end with trivia. Anticlimactic words should be shifted to an earlier point in the sentence or simply eliminated.

Weak endings	*Stronger*
Be sure that your sentences end with words that deserve the distinction you give them.	End with words that deserve distinction. BARRETT WENDELL, *English Composition*

The two writers have strikingly differed in their attitudes toward "the masses," as the Communists used to call them.

The two writers have strikingly differed in their attitudes toward what the Communists used to call "the masses."
EDMUND WILSON,
Europe Without Baedeker

In 1922, Emily Post brought out her *Etiquette*, which had sold two-thirds of a million by 1945 and even more than that.

In 1922, Emily Post brought out her *Etiquette*, which by 1945 had sold more than two-thirds of a million.
EDMUND WILSON, "Books of Etiquette and Emily Post," *Classics and Commercials*

Mrs. Post is not merely the author of a comprehensive textbook on manners: she is an imaginative writer of considerable ability, and the excitement of a novel is found in her book to some extent.

Mrs. Post is not merely the author of a comprehensive textbook on manners: she is a considerably imaginative writer, and her book has some of the excitement of a novel.
EDMUND WILSON, "Books of Etiquette and Emily Post," *Classics and Commercials*

Perhaps an occasional weak ending does no great harm. But if sentence after sentence fades away with insignificant words, the prose will seem flimsy:

Regardless of faith, color or condition, humans all around the earth last week were busily demonstrating that everybody loves a baby, thus showing that the old proposition has a good deal of truth in it even now. In America another baby was born every eleven seconds, as was shown by the flashing light atop the "U.S. population clock," which is located in Washington in the Commerce Department Building. A "world population clock" would have been flashing three times a second, if there were a clock of that kind. Enough little Chinese were being born to add another Canada to the world's population every year, and enough little Indians to add another New York City—the equivalents of Canada and New York City, that is. The world's population stood at 2.8 billion as

1960 began; it would be somewhere between 6 and 7 billion within 40 years, or so it seems from the reports of U.N. experts in this particular field.

Now here is the original passage from which the above was derived. The emphatic sentence endings strengthen the prose.

Regardless of faith, color or condition, humans all around the earth last week were busily demonstrating the truth of the proposition that everybody loves a baby. In Washington's Commerce Department Building, a light atop the "U.S. population clock" flashed every eleven seconds to mark the birth of another American. If a "world population clock" existed, it would have been flashing three times a second. Enough little Indians were being born to add the equivalent of another New York City to the world's population every year, and enough little Chinese to add another Canada. As 1960 began, the world's population stood at 2.8 billion; within 40 years, predicted U.N. experts, it would be somewhere between 6 and 7 billion.

"The Numbers Game," *Time*, Jan. 11, 1960

Practice

I. Revise these sentences to strengthen their endings. Wherever necessary, change wording and omit needless words.

1. He realized that the anatomy course would be expensive when he saw that he had to buy a dissecting kit, a microscope, two textbooks, and a lab apron.
2. The instructor announced that each student would dissect a human cadaver, a guinea pig, and a frog.
3. He grabbed his bags and ran for the plane as we all watched.
4. Now that the rioting prisoners had killed once, they might kill again, the warden stated.
5. He really hated all the boys on his floor, even though he usually played cards and exchanged pleasantries with them.
6. The tornado struck twenty minutes after the family had moved to the cellar to find protection there.

7. She rose from the table, hurled the ring at him, and walked out, not caring that other people in the restaurant were watching what she was doing.

8. The holocaust raged for hours and finally reduced three city blocks to ashy ruins, even though four fire companies had arrived when the blaze began, or shortly afterward.

9. That jaywalker would have been killed if Chico hadn't slammed on his brakes and swerved toward the curb at the same time.

10. The pedestrian began shouting abuse and threatening to throw a punch at Chico, even though Chico had actually saved the man's life through his skillful handling of the car—or so it seemed to Chico.

11. This time Chico stood his ground, despite the fact that he usually walked away from senseless arguments whenever he was able to do so.

12. Thorstein Veblen is now regarded as one of the great sociologists, even though many people who were personally acquainted with him thought him to be an eccentric egotist and not really anything more than that.

13. Veblen asserted that Americans judge people and possessions by judging how much money they are worth—or that this is our primary standard, at least.

14. Veblen claimed that we judge even tableware by "pecuniary canons of taste," which was his term for this way of evaluating things.

15. This is the reason why women do not cherish stainless steel dinnerware but prefer to own expensive silver—for with most American women such is the case.

II. For this exercise the sentence endings in a piece of professional writing (by Charles W. Ferguson) have been weakened. Rewrite the sentences to strengthen their endings.

The controlling principle of one who seeks to improve self-expression is that the writer should have not one style but an awareness of many, so that the one best suited to the subject at hand can be chosen for use. The best craftsmen follow this principle, one will find. In the heyday of *The American Mercury* and in his "Prejudices," H. L. Mencken showed himself a master of protest, dealing with Dr. Coolidge, the Bible Belt, the Sahara of the Bozart, mountebanks, and charlatans, and lashing out against many other things of that sort. In "The American Language" he showed an occasional flash of humor, but he respected the dignity of reader and subject and wrote with smooth regard for both, for the most part. He was a different Mencken from the earlier one. And his prose became properly benign, his style quiet, and his mood mellow when he wrote his reminiscent book, *Happy Days*, being a recounting of his childhood in the city of Baltimore, Maryland. There was no need to whambang in a book of that particular kind, it seems.

24

Weak Verbs and Strong Verbs

Inappropriate verbs can weaken sentences by making them wordy and awkward and sometimes by making them unclear.

The verb forms *it is, there is, there are,* and so on are occasionally desirable:

Today it is clear that Thomas Carlyle was not so profound a thinker as his contemporaries believed.

It is difficult to know whether that politician means his fiery statements or is trying to deceive his audiences.

But an inappropriate *it-is/there-is* construction will produce an ineffectual sentence.

Weak	Stronger
There was so much weakening of the company as a result of the strike that the company went bankrupt.	The strike so weakened the company that it went bankrupt.
It was the strike that made many new enemies for the union.	The strike made many new enemies for the union.
There are many politicians who remember thousands of their constituents by name.	Many politicians remember thousands of their constituents by name.
There have been offered two leading opposed interpretations of James's story *The Turn of the Screw*.	Leading critics offer two opposed interpretations of James's story *The Turn of the Screw*.

Verbs in the *passive voice* may also weaken sentences.

A verb is in the *active voice* when its subject performs an action:

The author crossed out two lines of dialogue.

Jon had switched off the television set.

In *passive voice*, the subject of the verb, instead of acting, receives the action:

Two lines of dialogue were crossed out by the author.

The television set had been switched off by Jon.

In passive voice the true actor is consigned to a prepositional phrase (*by the author / by Jon*) or omitted altogether:

Two lines of dialogue were crossed out.

The television set had been switched off.

Passive voice is appropriate, then, whenever the actor is unimportant. In the following passage, for instance, because the actors are less important than the person acted upon (Samuelson), the passive verbs are appropriate.

At five the next morning Samuelson *was awakened* by nurses and *prepared* for the operation. He *was given* no breakfast but only a cupful of medicine. He *was shot* full of drugs. At five-thirty his leg *was shaved* clean. Then he *was lifted* from his bed, *moved* over to a mobile cot, and *wheeled* away through long corridors, past staring faces. By this time, however, he *had been made* drowsy and complacent by the drugs, and was quite indifferent to the nurses and the faces and, finally, the doctor bending over him.

But most sentences require active voice. In most sentences the actor deserves the place of primary importance. He should appear as the subject of the sentence, not be tucked away in a prepositional phrase or eliminated altogether. The sentences on the left below, which are concerned with the Russian author Isaac Babel, should have made Babel their subject. By using passive voice and relegating Babel to unimportant positions, the sentences become awkward and unclear. The right-hand sentences restore naturalness and clarity.

Misuse of passive voice	*Active voice*
From his reading of the French writer De Maupassant much was learned by Babel.	Babel learned much from his reading of the French writer De Maupassant.
Indeed, one of his early stories was entitled *Guy de Maupassant,* and in it the reader was told about the awakening undergone by a young author while a volume of De Maupassant was being read.	Indeed, he entitled one of his early stories *Guy de Maupassant,* and in it he told of the awakening a young author underwent while reading a volume of De Maupassant.
A distinctive style was eventually fashioned by Babel, a style quite as spare and incisive as De Maupassant's but even more charged with emotion.	Babel eventually fashioned his own distinctive style, quite as spare and incisive as De Maupassant's but even more charged with emotion.
Scrupulous care was exercised in Babel's writing.	Babel exercised scrupulous care in his writing.

When his friend Paustovsky was allowed to read the work-in-progress of *Lybka the Cossack,* twenty-two drafts of it had already been written, but it was still not satisfactory to Babel.

When he allowed his friend Paustovsky to read the work-in-progress of *Lybka the Cossack,* Babel had already written twenty-two drafts of the story, but was still not satisfied with it.

Another verb form that needs watching might be called the *spread-out verb.* Extra words are crowded into the predicate —sometimes achieving greater fluency or expressiveness, but usually only wordiness.

The *idiomatic verb phrase,* for instance, can render sentences flabby and ineffectual:

> *With idiomatic verbs:* Because he *had taken to* Russell's book *The Problems of Philosophy,* the boy decided to *go through with* a sizable task. He would *study up on* everything Lord Russell *had put to paper.*

> *More concise:* Because he *had admired* Russell's book *The Problems of Philosophy,* the boy decided to *perform* a sizable task. He would *study* everything Lord Russell *had written.*

Another kind of spread-out verb begins with a *colorless verb* (particularly the verb *to be,* but also *do, get, give, have, make,* and others), then adds other words as complements. Though colorless verbs are a staple in our language, the needless use of them results in sentences like those on the left below.

Wordy	*More concise*
The committee *gave* the bill a brief *discussion,* then *moved* it *quickly* to the floor of the senate.	The committee *discussed* the bill briefly, then *hurried* it to the floor of the senate.
He *took a close look at* the contents of the test tube, then *made a shrugging motion.*	He *inspected* the contents of the test tube, then *shrugged.*
That evening *an abrupt change* in the weather *took place.*	That evening the weather *changed abruptly.*

As a well-trained anthropologist he knew that he must *make a determination as to* whether the savages *had an understanding of* how the seasons *undergo change.*	As a well-trained anthropologist he knew that he must *determine* whether the savages *understood* how the seasons *change.*
The testers *gave credence to the belief* that the "A-Test" *did not serve as an adequate indication of* intelligence.	The testers *doubted* whether the "A-Test" *measured* intelligence *accurately.*

Many writers persist in indiscriminately using not only spread-out verbs but passive verbs and *it-is/there-is* constructions. The prose that results from this practice is like the following:

> There is a crag on which the vulture rests in a sitting position, and there he is able to spend time waiting. The sun is seen as it comes up in a bound out of the sierra, and still the vulture stays put. He holds on in the same place until the sun-struck rocks and the hard earth begin to be hot and the thermal currents start to make a rising motion. When there is a strong enough upstream, the vulture makes a leap out from the cliff, works his way into the upstream by means of a twisting motion, and, without one laborious wingbeat, goes into a spiraling and soaring flight.
>
> By the time his station is reached, a half hour later and maybe more, there is a blazing heat coming down from the sun onto the plain. Every detail is made clear to the vulture's telescopic eye. And the updraft is steadily gaining in strength as the day goes on towards its zenith.

The skilled writer who found such prose in his working draft would spot the weak verbs and revise accordingly. His revision might resemble the original passage on which the above was based—John D. Stewart's depiction of how the vulture uses thermal currents to assist his flight:

> ... The vulture sits on a crag and waits. He sees the sun bound up out of the sierra, and still he waits. He waits until the sun-struck rocks and the hard earth heat up and the thermal currents begin to rise. When the upstream is strong

enough, he leaps out from the cliff, twists into it, and without one laborious wingbeat, spirals and soars.

By the time the vulture reaches his station, a half hour later and maybe more, the sun is blazing down on the plain and betraying every detail to his telescopic eye, and the updraft is strengthening as the day approaches its zenith. . . .

"Vulture Country," *Atlantic*, Aug., 1959

The forcefulness of this prose derives largely from the strength of its verbs.

Practice

I. Strengthen the weak verbs in the following sentences. (Probably only one sentence should be left as it is.) Eliminate needless words.

1. A game called *baseball* was observed by the king when a visit to the United States was made by him in 1954.
2. There were several reasons that he had for taking a year off from college.
3. It was soon realized by the editor that the novel he was in the process of reading was the work of a great writer.
4. His words were received by us with amazement.
5. There was such a large increase in the temperature of the water that illness began to make its appearance in all the fish.
6. Mr. Armstrong holds to the opinion that the president should have the right to perform any actions that would be suitable to an absolute dictator.
7. Mr. Puffle made up his mind to put up with his car's strange noises, since it was probable that he would not be able to put a stop to them even if he made the attempt.
8. There are several people in that district who are in opposition to the mayor's plan for reducing taxes.
9. A long vacation for Mr. Dyspepsia was recommended by Dr. Davis, because the doctor had the hope that the relaxation would have a soothing influence on the man's ulcers.
10. That an elaborate language is possessed by bees was proved by Karl von Frisch after they had been studied by him for more than thirty years.
11. When a store of honey has been found by a bee, directions

can be given by him to his fellow bees so that they will be able to find their way straight to it.

12. Immediately after Ketchum was hit on the head by the pitched ball, he dropped to the ground and lay there motionless, until finally he had to be carried off the field on a stretcher.

13. It was known among all the students that consideration was being given by the president of the college to the question of whether to turn in a resignation.

14. Mr. Mugwell has been made the recipient of the Larchboil Prize this year, for his novel about a shrewd woman whose fatherless children were supported by her through the practice of spiritualism.

II. Strengthen the weak verbs in this passage.

(1)It was the wish of Mary Ann Evans, a writer of fiction, to enter into marriage with George H. Lewes, the noted playwright and philosopher. (2)But Lewes was already involved in a marriage. (3)Even though there had been a separation from his wife, a divorce from her could not be got hold of by Lewes. (4)Miss Evans came to the decision that she would live with him anyway. (5)Victorian England was thrown into a rage by her conduct, and her name was made the subject of much notoriety. (6)When *Scenes of Clerical Life* was sent out by her to be submitted for publication, there was a refusal on the part of the publisher to allow her name to be put on the book. (7)The suggestion was put forth by the publisher that Miss Evans make use of a pen name. (8)The name of "George Eliot" was hit on by her as satisfactory.[1]

---

[1] This often-repeated account is largely false. Though Miss Evans did live with Lewes and arouse some Victorian indignation, her chief reason for using a pen name was probably that book reviewers of the time disparaged women writers.

25

Conciseness

Moving at half-speed, a motion-picture thriller about espionage would be slow-motion nonsense—laughable at first, then boring. Prose made sluggish by wordiness has the same effect. The remedy, conciseness, has been mentioned in several previous chapters, but it is so important a principle, and so easily violated, that it deserves a chapter of its own.

One means of achieving conciseness was discussed in the previous chapter: *convert weak verbs into strong ones.* Consider again two versions of a passage by John D. Stewart: first a version cluttered with weak verbs, then the original prose.

... *There is* a crag on which the vulture *rests in a sitting position*, and there he *is able to spend time waiting*. The sun *is seen* as it *comes up in a bound* out of the sierra, and still the vulture *stays put*. He *holds on in the same place* until the sun-struck rocks and the hard earth *begin to be hot* and the thermal currents *start to make a rising motion*. When *there is* a strong enough upstream, the vulture *makes a leap* out from the cliff, *works his way* into the upstream *by means of a twisting motion*, and, without one laborious wingbeat, *goes into a spiraling* and *soaring flight*.

... The vulture *sits* on a crag and *waits*. He *sees* the sun *bound up* out of the sierra, and still he *waits*. He waits until the sun-struck rocks and the hard earth *heat up* and the thermal currents *begin to rise*. When the upstream *is* strong enough, he *leaps* out from the cliff, *twists* into it, and without one laborious wingbeat, *spirals* and *soars*.

The version with weak verbs contains 112 words; Mr. Stewart's original, 64.

One variety of the *it-is/there-is* construction merits attention here. For example:

There is a distinct possibility that it will rain this afternoon.

This lengthy sort of opening can usually be replaced with a word or two:

It is obvious that ...	Obviously ...
It is certain that ...	Certainly ...
There is no doubt that ...	Undoubtedly ...
It is probably true that ...	Probably ...
There is a distinct possibility that ...	Possibly ...
There is a faint possibility that ...	Conceivably ...

Another cause of wordiness is *inadequate subordination*. An idea inadequately subordinated receives not only more emphasis than it deserves but more wordage. The two passages on the left below might appear in a working draft. On the right, subordination has reduced overweight clauses to phrases and phrases to single words.

Frank would punch out on the time clock. Then he would chat for a few minutes with one of the telephone operators. *She was a pretty girl who was posted at the check-out station.* (33 words)	*After punching out on the time clock,* Frank would chat for a few minutes with the *pretty* telephone operator *posted at the check-out station.* (23 words)
In 1933, *while he was in Miami, shortly after he had been elected President,* Roosevelt was nearly assassinated. *The attempt was made by a man named Giuseppe Zangara, who was an unemployed bricklayer.* (33 words)	In 1933, *in Miami, President-elect* Roosevelt was nearly assassinated *by an unemployed bricklayer, Giuseppe Zangara.* (15 words)

Perhaps the major cause of verboseness is *imprecision in wording.*

One result of imprecision is the overuse of *modifiers.* If the writer employs an inexact word, he is likely to add modifiers in an effort to convey his meaning. For example, he may add qualifiers (such as *very, exceedingly, somewhat,* and *extremely*).

Wordy	*Concise*
Morgan inspected the *somewhat bewildering* rows of dials on the instrument panel. He was *extremely surprised* to see that the fuel pressure had dropped *very noticeably.*	Morgan inspected the *puzzling* rows of dials on the instrument panel. He was *startled* to see that the fuel pressure had dropped *sharply.*

The use of vague or inexact verbs will lead to the overuse of adverbs.

Wordy	*Concise*
Cobbett *spoke strongly, with derision,* against the greed of the landed aristocracy.	Cobbett *censured* [or *derided*] the landed aristocracy for its greed.

And the writer who relies on vague nouns like *situation, aspect,* or *element* will use too many adjectives. He will refer to "*an un-*

fortunate aspect of the novel" instead of "*a flaw* in the novel," and will speak of *a grave and serious situation* when he could have called it *a tragedy, a catastrophe, a calamity, a crisis,* or whatever it was.

Imprecision in wording also causes *redundancy,* as in phrases like these:

important essentials	visible to the eye
present incumbent	handsome in appearance
green in color	look forward with anticipation
consensus of opinion	assembled together

The careful writer will detect redundancy even in less conspicuous forms:

> Civil strife between the two major political parties has slowed the country's progress in the advancement of agriculture and industry.

Strife between *the country's* political parties is necessarily *civil,* and *progress* is roughly the same as *advancement.* The revised sentence could be:

> Strife between the two major political parties has slowed the country's advancement in agriculture and industry.

Note the many redundancies in the following sentence:

> While the pilot was involved in the process of bringing the plane down to a safe landing on the runway, he concentrated on his task and thought only of that.

This could become:

> The pilot concentrated on landing the plane safely.

Of course, a writer is entitled to use repetition to achieve clarity, or to achieve special emphasis as Winston Churchill did when England entered World War II:

> We shall defend our Island, whatever the cost may be. . . . We shall fight on the beaches. We shall fight on the landing grounds. We shall fight in the fields and in the streets. We shall fight in the hills. We shall never surrender.

But if a writer is redundant for no good reason, if he writes *large in magnitude* or *engaged in the act of going to sleep,* he will show that while writing, he himself was partly asleep.

Another variety of imprecision is the *lengthy connective.* Some writers replace words like *if, because,* or *about* with connectives at least three or four words long.

Wordy	Concise
In the event that it rains, the game will be canceled, *owing to the fact that* there are no more open days in the season.	*If* it rains, the game will be canceled, *because* there are no more open days in the season.
During the time that Faulkner was writing *Sartoris,* he learned *a great deal with regard to the ways in which he could* give his characters the depth and complexity of real people.	*While* writing *Sartoris,* Faulkner learned *to* give his characters the depth and complexity of real people.

The connective phrase *point of view* often causes illogic as well as wordiness. The phrase is appropriate when the writer is speaking of a point from which somebody can view something:

> From Henry James's *point of view,* H. G. Wells seemed less a novelist than a mixture of journalist and reformer.

But in the following sentences the phrase produces wordy nonsense:

> The producers of "rock" music have been enormously successful *from the point of view* of making profit.
> *From the point of view* of personal privacy, we need laws against the new eavesdropping and wiretapping devices.

Neither *making profit* nor *personal privacy* can have a *point of view,* can see anything from anywhere. More logical and concise would be:

> The producers of "rock" music have made enormous profits.
> We need laws to guard our privacy against the new eavesdropping and wiretapping devices.

Another connective often used sloppily is *in terms of*. Jacques Barzun has berated educators for their "fantastic use and abuse" of the term:

> "In terms of" used to refer to things that had terms, like algebra. "Put the problem in terms of *a* and *b*." This makes sense. But in educational circles today "in terms of" means any connection between any two things. "We should grade students in terms of their effort"—that is, *for* or *according to* their effort.
>
> *Teacher in America*

Careless writers find other ways to be imprecise and wordy. Sir Ernest Gowers has mentioned their unnecessary and ludicrous use of *literally*. (The journalist who wrote that "M. Clemenceau literally exploded during the argument" obviously didn't know what *literally* means.[1]) And George Orwell has derided the *"not un- formation"* of which speechmakers are so fond: "It is *not un*likely that the bombing raids will *not* be *in*frequent." (Orwell suggested as a cure the memorization of this sentence: "A not unblack dog was chasing a not unsmall rabbit across a not ungreen field."[2]) But we need not dwell on all the abuses that critics have cited. The writer who strives for precision in wording will avoid most of them anyway. And if he also uses strong verbs and adequate subordination, he will eliminate most of the verbiage that could weaken his sentences.

Practice

I. The following passage can be made concise by means of subordination. Shorten the italicized clauses and phrases. Rearrange word order if you wish. (This padded prose is derived from an admirably concise passage by George Orwell.)

> It was in Burma, a morning *that was sodden, for it was during the time of the rains*. A light *that was sickly, and was like*

---

[1] Quoted by Sir Ernest in *Plain Words: Their ABC*.
[2] "Politics and the English Language," *Collected Essays, Journalism and Letters*, IV.

a yellow tinfoil, was slanting over the high walls into the yard *of the jail.* We were waiting outside the condemned cells, a row of sheds *that were fronted* with double bars, *and that were like cages for animals that were small.* Each cell measured about ten feet by ten and was quite bare within *except that there was a bed made out of a plank* and a pot *that was meant to contain water to be used for drinking purposes.* In some of them brown men, *who were entirely silent,* were sitting *in a squatting position* at the inner bars, *and their blankets were draped round them.* These were the men *who had been condemned, and they were due to be hanged,* an event which *would take place for each of them sometime within the next week or two.*

II. The following passages, derived from models of conciseness by professional authors, have been ruined by wordiness. The first passage contains roughly six hundred words; the second, five hundred; the third, two hundred. In each case the original was less than half as long.

Shorten the passages as much as you can without sacrificing their meaning.

1. (1)The kind of rat that is brown in color is as supple in its ability to change its shape as a piece of rubber is. (2)As a result, this kind of rat can squeeze its body in such a way, and make the body contort itself into such positions, that the rat is able to make its way through openings that are roughly only half as large in size as the rat itself is. (3)This kind of rat has jaws that are very capable, in addition to which he has incisor teeth that are long and curved in shape and are equipped with edges that are quite sharp enough for cutting. (4)It is capable of using its teeth to gnaw a notch in a wood plank made of oak, a shingle of the kind that is made from slate, or a brick that has been dried in the heat of the sun— a notch so considerable in size that it will be large enough to hold the body of the rat. (5)If the rat happens to be attracted by the sound that is caused by the running of water, it will gnaw with its teeth into the pipe—even if the pipe is made of lead. (6) Rats of all kinds are capable of an appreciable amount of vandalism, but the brown rat is the most ruthless sort of vandal of them all. (7)The brown rat is customarily capable

of destroying a great deal more than it actually has any real desire to use for consumption. (8)Instead of completely eating just a few selected potatoes from a sizable collection of potatoes, it will destroy dozens of them by taking just a bite or two out of each one of them. (9)The brown rat will render inedible all the apples that are in a store that sells groceries. (10)It will do the same to all the pears in the grocery. (11) And it will accomplish this within one single night by doing it all quite methodically and systematically. (12)If it wants to get hold of even a small quantity of material for nesting purposes, it will bring about the ruination of very large quantities of garments of clothing, rugs for floor-covering, upholstery, and books. (13)It will simply cut all these things up into a very ragged condition. (14)If the brown rat happens to be in a warehouse, it will on some occasions go completely and utterly out of control. (15)Within the space of just a few hours, rats gathered in a pack will rip open holes in hundreds of sacks that are being used for holding flour, grain of various kinds, coffee, and assorted other foodstuffs. (16)The pack will cause the contents to spill out, and the contents will be spoiled and made foul. (17)And in general there will be a mess that is very upsetting to anyone who sees it. (18)Now and then, every once in a while, when the brown rat is in markets that are used for the sale of live poultry, the rat seems to be taken hold of by a very strong desire for killing and for blood. (19)It happened that one night a burrow of these brown rats were in the part of the old Gansevort Market that was used for holding poultry. (20)The burrow of them bit into the throats of more than three hundred broiler-type chickens, and yet the rats actually ate not so much as a dozen of them for food. (21)This part of the market was finally abandoned, but before that took place, the rats had pretty nearly taken complete charge of it. (22)An appreciable number of rats made a habit of nesting in the desks used by the people who were employed at the market—to be specific, in the drawers contained in those desks. (23)If it happened that one of those desk drawers was pulled open by someone, the brown rats would make a leap to get out, and at the same time they would let out snarling noises.

2. (1)I have never had any great amount of patience with respect to those writers who make the reader put in an effort of some sort before the reader will be able to grasp what the writers have as their meaning. (2)You might have a look at the writings of some philosophers who are generally regarded as being great, and then you will see that there is a definite possibility that even the most subtle and sophisticated of reflections may be put into words that will be lucid to the reader. (3)Perhaps you may experience a certain measure of difficulty in reaching an understanding of the thought of Hume, and in the event that you have not been trained in the discipline of philosophy, there can be no doubt that the philosophical significance of his thought in its full implications will be beyond your grasp. (4)But nevertheless no person who has had any degree of education can be at a loss as he makes the attempt to arrive at an exact understanding of precisely what each sentence by Hume is intended to mean. (5)Only a very small number of people have been able to employ the English language in their writing with any more grace than that which is to be found in the writings of Berkeley.

(6)One thing that leads to the sort of obscurity I am referring to is that the person who is doing the writing—the writer himself—is not in possession of a thorough understanding of what it is that he truly means. (7)This sort of writer does have some sort of very indefinite impression as regards that which he has the desire of putting into words. (8)Perhaps, however, he is lacking in the necessary strength and power of mental perspicacity, or perhaps he is merely suffering from laziness. (9)In any case, the result is that he has not yet been able to form a clear idea in his mind of exactly what it is that he wishes to say. (10)Certainly, then, it is entirely understandable and quite natural that he should not be able to put forth an expression that is altogether precise. (11)For the idea that he has in his own mind is still highly uncertain and disarranged. (12)Among those writers who have difficulty from the point of view of making their thoughts clear, there are some who have a noticeable tendency to accept the supposition that their thoughts are not unimportant. (13)They believe that the thoughts have a significance that is definitely greater than might appear the first time one takes a look at them. (14)There is undeniably something in this belief that is flattering to the writer. (15)He thinks that his thoughts are so deeply profound in their meaning that they simply cannot be put into words that will be clear in terms of being read by all those people who like to read rather quickly and easily. (16)It is entirely natural that writers of this sort do not ever have it occur to them that the fault is not in the minds of those other people. (17) The fault is in their own minds, because their minds do not have the intellectual faculty for thinking with precision about ideas and reaching an exact understanding of them.

3.   (1)The kind of writing that has the most strength and vigor is that which avoids using unnecessary words and is written in such a way that it will be as concise as it possibly can be. (2)A sentence ought not to have any words that are not entirely necessary, and, for that matter, there should be no unnecessary sentences contained within a paragraph. (3) This is true for the very same reason that a drawing, if it is to be a good drawing, should have no lines that are not completely necessary, and a machine that is to be fully efficient should make use of no parts that are not absolutely necessary in terms of the actual working of the machine. (4)This is not to say that the goal of conciseness requires that the writer must invariably make all his sentences short, nor does this goal require that the writer must keep all detail out of his writing or treat what he is writing about only in the form of an outline. (5)But the ideal of conciseness does require that each and every word make a difference. (6)That is to say, every single word in the writer's prose should make some definite contribution to the prose. (7)In short, every word must tell.

26
Keeping Sentences Clear

OVERWEIGHT SENTENCES

If sentences are burdened with clause after clause and phrase after phrase, the result can be unreadable:

> Reference back to philosophic principles to expose erroneous assumptions and to establish common grounds for judgments of fact or value could not be justified easily by the record of its success in producing agreement. Philosophers have frequently expressed the expectation that philosophic disagreements would be resolved by applying scientific principles to a subject matter for the first time or that doctrinal disagreements in particular fields of inquiry or action would be re-

moved by discovering and expounding philosophic principles. Yet doctrinal differences seem to have persisted, after each such effort at resolution, translated into more inclusive and more obstinate philosophic oppositions, and the differences of philosophers have disappeared because they have been forgotten more frequently than because they have been resolved. Long before the formulation of such convictions in present-day varieties of pragmatisms and positivisms, the practical man, the artist, the scientist, and the theologian expressed impatience with philosophic considerations because they were impertinent to operations considered urgent, or incompatible with attitudes defended as realistic, or inadequate for ends assumed to be ultimate. The pragmatic impatience with theory and the positivistic exposure of "unreal" problems, however, even in their abbreviated expressions, are philosophies; and the dialectical consequences of principles are particularly apparent, though unexamined, in those minimal philosophies which are expressions of conviction concerning the subject of an inquiry or concerning the method by which the inquiry must be pursued. . . .

    RICHARD MCKEON, "The Philosophic Bases of Art and Criticism,"
Critics and Criticism, ed. R. S. Crane

This passage, which comes at the very beginning of an essay, gets the reader off to a discouraging start—partly because of the vague language, but mostly because of the length and complexity of the sentences.

    Not that sentences should never exceed, say, thirty-five words. Masters of prose style—such as Richard Hofstadter, Edmund Wilson, and George Bernard Shaw—employ longer sentences that are not only lucid but are pleasurable for their subtle twists and turns. Nevertheless, as the writer reviews his working draft, he should watch for sentences whose length and intricacy make them confusing. He can split them in two, delete words, and disentangle syntax—as the following passage does for the first three sentences quoted above.

    Philosophers have continually tried to find a set of basic principles, a common ground by which they could judge facts and values. But in this venture they have not been successful.

They have sought to resolve disagreements by applying scientific principles or by discovering irrefutable philosophical principles, yet their doctrinal differences have become larger and more obstinate. When philosophical differences have disappeared it has usually been because they have been forgotten, not because they have been resolved.

Are short sentences amateurish? Not necessarily. Though some reputable authors favor the long sentence, others rely mainly on short and medium-length sentences. Here speaks Bertrand Russell, for instance, winner of the Nobel Prize for literature:

> There are some simple maxims ... which I think might be commended to writers of expository prose. First: never use a long word if a short word will do. Second: if you want to make a statement with a great many qualifications, put some of the qualifications in separate sentences. Third: do not let the beginning of your sentence lead the reader to an expectation which is contradicted by the end. Take, say, such a sentence as the following, which might occur in a work on sociology: "Human beings are completely exempt from undesirable behaviour-patterns only when certain prerequisites, not satisfied except in a small percentage of actual cases, have, through some fortuitous concourse of favorable circumstances, whether congenital or environmental, chanced to combine in producing an individual in whom many factors deviate from the norm in a socially advantageous manner." Let us see if we can translate this sentence into English. I suggest the following: "All men are scoundrels, or at any rate almost all. The men who are not must have had unusual luck, both in their birth and in their upbringing." This is shorter and more intelligible, and says just the same thing. ...
>
> "How I Write," *Portraits from Memory*

Lord Russell's second and third admonitions about style would lead a writer to distrust long sentences. And Lord Russell follows the advice himself. The only long sentence in the above passage is the parody of sociological style, a sentence that stumbles and circles about in a manner likely to irritate the most patient of readers.

TROUBLE WITH MODIFIERS

Modifiers should be placed near the words they modify. The *misplaced modifier* is notorious for producing ridiculous sentences. For example:

> With her tail wagging excitedly, Aunt Sarah believed that the poodle was friendly.

Misplaced modifiers that are not so ludicrous are harder to spot. The writer of the sentence above might try this revision:

> With her tail wagging excitedly, the poodle seemed friendly to Aunt Sarah.

The sentence still does not express its intended meaning, which is that Aunt Sarah thought the poodle friendly in general, friendly to everyone. The form just given says that "the poodle seemed *friendly to Aunt Sarah*" without saying whether it seemed friendly in general. The phrase *to Aunt Sarah* is misplaced; it should be next to *seemed* rather than *friendly*:

> With her tail wagging excitedly, the poodle *seemed to Aunt Sarah* to be friendly.

Now the sentence is clear because the modifier adjoins the word it modifies. (The sentence is awkward in this form, however, and might well be revised for the sake of fluency: "Because the poodle was wagging her tail excitedly, Aunt Sarah believed her to be friendly.")

Here are further illustrations of the misplaced modifier:

> He happened to look toward the mountains and spot an airplane that was about to crash *while sitting in his backyard.*
>
> *Better:* Sitting in his backyard, he happened to look toward the mountains and spot an airplane that was about to crash.
>
> The librarian handed Gary a book across the desk *that was old and fragile.*
>
> *Better:* Reaching across the desk, the librarian handed Gary a book that was old and fragile.

> *Still getting his ticket,* the train he wanted to take began moving out of the station.
>
> *Better:* While he was still getting his ticket, the train he wanted to take began moving out of the station.

Not only phrases or clauses but also single-word modifiers can be guilty of misplacement. The unobtrusive word *only* can cause subtle changes in meaning when it is shifted from one place to another:

> *Only* he borrowed seven hundred dollars [*Only* modifies *he. He* borrowed the money, nobody else.]
>
> He *only* borrowed seven hundred dollars. [*Only* modifies *borrowed.* He *borrowed* the money. He didn't steal it or take it as a gift or take it in any other way but as a loan.]
>
> He borrowed *only* seven hundred dollars. [*Only* modifies *seven hundred dollars.* That was all he borrowed.]

The *dangling modifier* presents a slightly different problem. The word it is meant to modify has been omitted from the sentence. For example:

> *Entering it at three in the morning,* the vast railway station seemed strangely quiet.

The italicized modifier, a participial phrase, ought to modify a noun or pronoun, but the sentence contains none it can modify. The word it is intended to modify has to be added:

> Entering the vast railway station at three in the morning, *he* found it strangely quiet.

Here are further examples of the dangling modifier, with revisions:

> *Being known as an inveterate liar,* even his more credible stories were not believed.
>
> Because he was known as an inveterate liar, people would not believe even his more credible stories.
>
> *Guarded by two members of the opposing team,* his jump-shots still scored enough points to keep his own team in the lead.

Guarded by two members of the opposing team, he still scored enough points with his jump-shots to keep his own team in the lead.

While observing the highway traffic, it began to become congested.

While observing the highway traffic, he saw that it was becoming congested.

UNCLEAR REFERENCE OF PRONOUNS

A pronoun should refer clearly to its antecedent, the noun or nouns that the pronoun replaces. The following sentences contain pronouns whose reference is unclear.

When Gus hit the ball with his new bat, he broke *it*.

Although Sherwood Anderson had taught Hemingway a good deal about writing, *he* did a parody of *his* style, in the short work entitled *The Torrents of Spring*.

The italicized pronouns have several possible antecedents. Although some readers will know that a bat is more likely to break than a ball and that Hemingway, not Anderson, wrote *The Torrents of Spring*, even the knowledgeable reader may have to pause over those pronouns to determine their antecedents; and the reader who knows little about baseball or Hemingway will be quite mystified. One way to prevent uncertainty is to replace the unclear pronoun with the noun it stands for:

When Gus hit the ball with his new bat, he broke the bat.

Although Sherwood Anderson had taught Hemingway a good deal about writing, Hemingway did a parody of Anderson's style, in the short work entitled *The Torrents of Spring*.

Or the sentence may be reshaped entirely:

When Gus hit the ball, he broke his new bat.

Although Hemingway had learned a good deal about writing from Sherwood Anderson, he did a parody of Anderson's style, in the short work entitled *The Torrents of Spring*.

A pronoun used for *idea-reference* refers not merely to a noun or two, but to a phrase, a sentence, or even a group of sentences. The following sentence uses this sort of pronoun successfully. (The idea referred to is underlined once; the pronoun, twice.)

> In the mornings the clerk was always prompt, for he knew that this would please the boss.

But pronouns used for idea-reference sometimes result in fuzzy prose:

> John rose at five each morning to do calisthenics and spend an hour translating Plato's *Republic* from the Greek. *This* markedly influenced his later life.
>
> Arnold Bennett produced his novels quickly, aimed for popularity and sales, and wrote mostly about provincial characters, *which* limited the importance of his achievement.

In the first sentence the *this* could refer to the early rising, the calisthenics, the translating, Plato's *Republic*, or John's entire morning ritual. In the second sentence the *which* could refer to any of Bennett's practices or all of them. Revisions could be:

> John rose at five each morning to do calisthenics and spend an hour translating Plato's *Republic* from the Greek. His daily exposure to the ideas in the *Republic* markedly influenced his later life.
>
> Arnold Bennett produced his novels quickly, aimed for popularity and sales, and wrote mostly about provincial characters. All these practices limited the importance of his achievement.

Beyond these most obvious causes of obscurity there is a multitude of others, too many to be neatly classified and described. In the heat of writing his first draft, the writer need not be worried about all these problems and anxious that his every sentence be perfectly clear. After he has composed a working draft, he can coolly, almost impersonally, review his prose for lapses in clarity.

Practice

I.   Divide this sprawling sentence into shorter sentences to express the author's meaning more clearly. (Arrange the revision in chronological order, despite the author's confusing leap from the nineteenth century back to the eighteenth.)

> While the nineteenth century of the Christian Era saw the prairie Indian of North America turn one of the European intruder's weapons against its original owner by disputing with him the possession of the Plains with the aid of the imported horse, the eighteenth century had already seen the forest Indian turn the European musket to account in a warfare of sniping and ambuscades which, with the screening forest as the Indian's confederate, had proved more than a match for contemporary European battle-tactics, in which close formations, precise evolutions, and steady volleys courted destruction when unimaginatively employed against adversaries who had adapted the European musket to the conditions of the American forest.
>
> ARNOLD TOYNBEE, *A Study of History* (abridged edition, vol. II), quoted by Rudolf Flesch in *A New Way to Better English*

II. These sentences contain troublesome pronouns. Revise the sentences so that all antecedents will be unmistakably clear.

    1. Bainbridge first met Dusseldorf while he was a graduate student at the University of Bavaria.
    2. When the city editor assigned Hargis to make the interview, he complained that the reporters had been getting too many difficult assignments lately.
    3. The book he found in that second-hand bookstore, which was dirty and mildewed and wormeaten, turned out to be a valuable rarity.
    4. Fred met Howard at the cafeteria yesterday, but he made no mention of his plans for the future.
    5. Harold's father did not wish to attend the graduation ceremony, which would surely make him unhappy.
    6. As the fullback barged through the line of scrimmage, the opposing linebacker met him head-on, and after the pile-up was cleared away, it was discovered that he had broken his arm.

7. Mr. Blibbel refused to buy life insurance even though a salesman came to the house three times, which distressed Mrs. Blibbel.

8. This controversial book about the New Testament caused much disagreement—some of it angry—among leading religious figures, until finally the bishops of the church came together to do something about it.

9. Mr. Rogers spent the next two weeks alone in his room reading everything William Blake had written, which puzzled his family and friends.

10. The Saturday-night dance on the front lawn of the fraternity house attracted plenty of happy young people and caused plenty of noise for a while, but it was over by eleven o'clock. This was disturbing to the neighbors.

III. These sentences contain modifiers whose reference is unclear. Make necessary revisions.

1. After passing successfully for a first down, Grandmother cheered for our quarterback.

2. Developing an interest in writing poetry, his classmates began to regard Michael as an odd and possibly demented boy who might just as well be avoided.

3. His backhand was improving steadily while practicing under the guidance of the country-club professional.

4. The mother made an apple pie for the baking contest that was devoured by the boys before it had time to cool.

5. Sitting on a rare-book shelf in the library, Jonathan found the very book for which he had been searching.

6. The doctor who had responded to the announcement quickly gave orders to the nurses in attendance.

7. Senator Martin only had talked to his ghost-writers; he still had to speak with his economic advisors.

8. That day Jones was sporting a valuable watch on his well-tanned wrist, which was diamond-studded.

9. In amazement Mr. Thompson watched his car as it rolled down the hill without making any motion toward stopping it.

10. Knowing the full details of the story, Arthur seemed more understandable to her than when they had first met.

11. He wrote a novel about the childhood he had spent in Afghanistan with wild abandon.

12. While passing out the examination booklets, the students were warned by the instructor to organize their answers carefully in his condescending manner.

13. Bothered by the pain in his chest and saddened by the deaths of several people close to him, the work of thinking and writing nevertheless continued.

14. The policeman signaled to the driver who was careening from one side of the road to the other by flashing his headlights on and off.

15. Professor Stonewall urged his students before the end of their stay at college to read the novels of C. P. Snow as a preparation for the outside world.

16. She pondered the matter for several weeks, and then she answered the letter he had sent her with great reluctance.

17. To be sure of seeing the tennis matches, reservations are available at the local ticket agency.

18. Charles only wanted to meet the committee members who might be persuaded to vote against the bill, not those who strongly favored it.

19. The people's hero was carried around the stadium by a crowd of enthusiasts with eyes upraised and hands waving at the many admirers.

20. After discarding his elaborate ornamental style, the next style used was plain and direct.

21. While gazing up the face of the mountain, an avalanche was seen beginning way up at the top, and though still a small one he ran off to a safe distance.

22. To understand the development of modern poetry, the contribution made by Ezra Pound is essential knowledge for the student.

The Writer's Library

V

These pages recommend books the writer will find useful. Some are reference books; others contain further instruction in writing; others are valuable simply because their prose is worthy of emulation.

The writer's basic reference book is a *dictionary*—a good one. Be wary of advertisements such as this: "Special! *New American Webster's College Dictionary*. A Colossal Buy at $2.49!" Since none of the words in that title, not even *Webster's*, is controlled by copyright, hucksters use them freely to sell third-rate dictionaries. But the writer's dictionary should be first-rate—

accurate, thorough, able to answer most of his questions about words. Any of the following dictionaries will serve him well:

The American Heritage Dictionary of the English Language (American Heritage and Houghton Mifflin).

The Random House Dictionary of the English Language, College Edition (Random House).

Webster's New World Dictionary of the American Language, Second College Edition (World).

The writer will also need a *book of synonyms*. He may wish to use *Webster's New Dictionary of Synonyms* (G. and C. Merriam), whose synonymies are much more thorough than those in a college dictionary. Each synonymy offers more synonyms, tells more about distinctions between them, and quotes illustrative passages. Or he may prefer a *thesaurus*, which lists the synonyms without explaining distinctions. Writers who favor this kind of book argue that they can search it quickly for a few likely words and then, if necessary, consult the dictionary for fine distinctions. But anyone wanting a convenient book of synonyms should be warned that a thesaurus based on Peter Roget's quasi-philosophical scheme can keep him hunting ten minutes each time he needs a word. A thesaurus arranged "in dictionary form" (in alphabetical order) is easier to use. Either of these will be helpful:

The New American Roget's College Thesaurus in Dictionary Form, edited by Albert H. Morehead and others (Grosset and Dunlap. Paperback edition: New American Library).

The New Roget's Thesaurus in Dictionary Form, originally edited by C. S. O. Mawson, re-edited by Norman Lewis (Putnam). Available in a somewhat abridged paperback edition: *The New Pocket Roget's Thesaurus in Dictionary Form* (Washington Square Press).

The writer must also have an all-purpose *handbook*. This provides a fund of valuable information about composition, logic, grammar and usage, punctuation and mechanics, library research, and so on. There are many good handbooks available. Here are a few:

The Harper Handbook of College Composition,* George S. Wykoff
and Harry Shaw (Harper and Row).
The Prentice-Hall Handbook for Writers,* Glenn Leggett and others
(Prentice-Hall).
The Technique of Composition,* Kendall B. Taft and others (Holt,
Rinehart and Winston).

The writer may also profit by consulting a *guide to usage*
—if it is reliable. Some guides assume that *popular* usage is
good usage, that any wording accepted by the majority of Americans should be accepted by the writer. If "Winston tastes good
like a cigarette should" sounds right to most advertisers and
smokers, and if *like* as a conjunction satisfies television enter-
tainers and their mass audiences, then why should the writer resist it? So runs the argument. Thus one guidebook says this
about whether *like* should be used as a conjunction: "Some people believe that it is a grammatical mistake to use *like* in this
way. But they are a minority. . . . There is no reason why anyone
should take the trouble to learn when *like* is a conjunction and
when it is a preposition, unless he wants to." Other guidebooks
disagree. They insist that usage for written prose should depend
not on majority rule but on the example set by the best contemporary writers. If Dwight Macdonald and Richard Rovere and
Lewis Mumford refuse to use *like* as a conjunction, the rest of
us should follow their lead. One guidebook of this persuasion
says: "There is no point in discussing at length the pros and
cons of *like* as a conjunction, because in workmanlike modern
writing there is no such conjunction. Comparisons involving a
verb are introduced by *as* or *as if,* not by *like. I don't dance like
I once did* is not literate, any more than *He goes on like he was
crazy."* (Wilson Follett, *Modern American Usage*)

The books listed here recommend the forms of usage
found in the best current prose:

* Asterisks indicate textbooks. These are hard to obtain through regular
bookstores and ordinarily must be purchased from a college bookstore or
directly from the publisher. Textbooks are regularly revised and updated—
be sure to get the latest edition.

THEODORE M. BERNSTEIN, *The Careful Writer: A Modern Guide to English Usage* (Atheneum).

WILSON FOLLETT, *Modern American Usage* (Hill and Wang).

H. W. FOWLER, *A Dictionary of Modern English Usage,* second edition, revised by Sir Ernest Gowers (Oxford University Press). Some usages recommended here are more appropriate in England than in the United States.

This list is arranged in order of increasing difficulty. Anyone not accustomed to books of this sort might well begin with Mr. Bernstein's. Or he might begin with *The American Heritage Dictionary* (see reference on p. 252), whose articles on usage are based on the recommendations of approximately a hundred speakers and writers who "have demonstrated their sensitiveness to the language and their power to wield it effectively and beautifully."

These guides to usage, and the other books mentioned up to this point, are not meant to be read through but to be consulted for answers to particular questions. Now we turn to *books of instruction.* These offer courses of study that may be read profitably from beginning to end. They are written in an engaging style, and many of them keep the reader alert with questions to answer and exercises to perform. In addition to reviewing "first principles of the essay," the books listed here offer much instruction in advanced principles. Books in the first list discuss nearly all aspects of essay-writing.

CLEANTH BROOKS AND ROBERT PENN WARREN, *Modern Rhetoric, Shorter Edition** (Harcourt, Brace and World).

JOHN HALVERSON AND MASON COOLEY, *Principles of Writing** (Macmillan).

THOMAS S. KANE AND LEONARD J. PETERS, *A Practical Rhetoric of Expository Prose** (Oxford University Press).

PORTER G. PERRIN, *Writer's Guide and Index to English** (Scott, Foresman). The "Index to English" is a 400-page alphabetized handbook, so thorough that the writer who owns the text may have no need for a separate handbook.

RICHARD M. WEAVER, *A Rhetoric and Handbook** (Holt, Rinehart and Winston).

The following books concentrate mainly on prose style.

SIR ERNEST GOWERS, *Plain Words: Their ABC* (Knopf). Published in paperback as *The Complete Plain Words* (Penguin).

ROBERT GRAVES AND ALAN HODGE, *The Reader over Your Shoulder* (Macmillan). Offers valuable rules concerning "clear statement" and "the graces of prose," then analyzes carelessly written passages by such noted authors as George Bernard Shaw and T. S. Eliot.

DONALD HALL, editor, *The Modern Stylists: Writers on the Art of Writing* (The Free Press). Includes Orwell's superb essay "Politics and the English Language" and large portions of Fowler and Graves-and-Hodge.

LEO KIRSCHBAUM, *Clear Writing* (Meridian). Recommended especially for its chapters on style (Chapters 5–8) and for Chapter 10, "Seeing How Others Write."

WILFRED STONE AND J. G. BELL, *Prose Style: A Handbook for Writers** (McGraw-Hill).

PAUL C. WERMUTH, editor, *Modern Essays on Writing and Style** (Holt, Rinehart and Winston).

In addition to learning from books of instruction, the writer can learn directly from the *reading and analysis of good prose*. Merely by reading the prose for enjoyment, he will get some notion of what makes it good. By studying it closely, he can discover exactly how it achieves its effects. And the more he knows about how such prose is written, the better his own writing will be.

The following books offer lessons in the analysis of prose.

DONALD DAVIDSON, *Twenty Lessons in Reading and Writing Prose** (Scribner's).

THOMAS S. KANE AND LEONARD J. PETERS, *Writing Prose: Techniques and Purposes** (Oxford University Press).

CHARLES CHILD WALCUTT, *An Anatomy of Prose** (Macmillan).

Once the writer can analyze good prose and see what makes it good, he no longer needs to be prodded by an editor's questions and comments. He may then wish to examine, on his own, books whose prose is worthy of analysis, books such as those on the following list.

DANIEL J. BOORSTIN, *The Image: A Guide to Pseudo-Events in America* (1962). Concerning the modern "arts of self-deception": "how we hide reality from ourselves" and disguise it with "images."

RACHEL CARSON, *Silent Spring* (1962). A disturbing, influential study of the poisons being fed into our lands and waters.

GEORGE GAMOW, *The Creation of the Universe* (revised edition, 1961). Physical science in terms understandable to the layman.

ROBERT L. HEILBRONER, *The Worldly Philosophers: The Lives, Times and Ideas of the Great Economic Thinkers* (revised edition, 1961).

RICHARD HOFSTADTER, *Anti-Intellectualism in American Life* (1961). Historical study of the prejudices against intellect—in religion, politics, business, education, etc.

ANTHONY LEWIS, *Gideon's Trumpet* (1964). The story of how a convict's letter to the Supreme Court changed the course of the American system of justice.

DWIGHT MACDONALD, *Against the American Grain: Essays on the Effects of Mass Culture* (1962). Lively, witty essays, mainly arguing that mass culture debases literary talent—with Twain and Hemingway, among others, used as illustrations.

JOSEPH MITCHELL, *The Bottom of the Harbor* (1959) or *Old Mr. Flood* (1948). See pp. 310–311 of this text for a sample of the first book and p. 36 for a sample of the second.

GEORGE ORWELL, *The Orwell Reader*, ed. Richard Rovere (1956). One might begin with "A Hanging," "Such, Such Were the Joys," and the selections from *The Road to Wigan Pier* (passages from these appear in the present text on pp. 33, 102, and 192–194). "Politics and the English Language," a masterpiece, argues that clarity in the use of words is an essential weapon against the deterioration of the individual and society.

CLINTON ROSSITER, *The Political Thought of the American Revolution* (1963).

BERTRAND RUSSELL, *Basic Writings*, ed. Robert E. Egner and Lester E. Denonn (1961). A 700-page attempt to epitomize Lord Russell's contributions to many fields of study. Readers preferring shorter books on separate topics might try *Hu-*

man *Society in Ethics and Politics* (1954), which contains
the Nobel Prize address on "politically important desires,"
or *An Outline of Philosophy* (1927), which deals with basic
problems in the analysis of mind and matter.

PETER SCHRAG, *Village School Downtown: Boston Schools, Boston
Politics* (1967). Close study of a city school system plagued
by difficulties.

CHARLES E. SILBERMAN, *Crisis in Black and White* (1964). Analysis of
the social and psychological problems underlying America's
racial tensions.

ROBERT PENN WARREN, *Selected Essays* (1958). On literature: Faulkner,
Frost, Hemingway, etc.

EDMUND WILSON, *The Cold War and the Income Tax: A Protest*
(1963). A broadside against the Internal Revenue Service
and the federal expenditures on space exploration and the
military.

Often, writing is published that is a labor to read. An
author rushes his thoughts into manuscript, a publisher hurriedly
turns the manuscript into a book, and the reader is expected to
tolerate fuzzy thinking and fuzzy prose. But writers such as
those listed here insist on expressing themselves well. Edmund
Wilson, for example, writes about subjects as diverse as Karl
Marx and Gertrude Stein, Ernest Hemingway and Emily Post,
opera at the Metropolitan and burlesque at Minsky's, yet always
strives to achieve what Lionel Trilling has called a "bold lucidity
and simplicity."

Research and Documentation
VI

It can be enjoyable to muse upon controversial issues or discuss them with friends until late at night. Should Americans receive a guaranteed minimum income? Should Detroit be forced to produce cars that cause no air pollution? Should the United States experiment with devices for biological warfare? Should marijuana be legalized? To what extent should college students govern and educate themselves? But anyone deciding to write an essay on such a topic will probably have to admit that he needs to learn more about it. When the charm of late-night comradery no longer conceals the holes in his argument, he will realize that he must head for the library in search of informed opinions and hard facts.

Current controversies are not the only topics that may lead him to the library. Excellent student essays have been written on such topics as the evolution of early jazz, the embittered last years of Mark Twain, A. S. Neill's Summerhill and other schools governed by students, the effects of Navaho initiation rites on the adolescent mind, the question of whether Joseph Smith (founder of Mormonism) was a sincere enthusiast or a charlatan, and the question of whether Teddy Roosevelt and his Rough Riders were heroes or publicity-seekers.

Once the writer has chosen his topic, the next step is to gather the books and articles that can best help him understand it.

He might begin with encyclopedias. The *Britannica* or *Americana* may provide summary articles on his subject. Or he can consult more specialized sources:

The Catholic Encyclopedia (1907–1914), with two supplementary volumes (1922, 1951).

Dictionary of American Biography (1928–1937), with two supplements (1944, 1958).

Dictionary of American History (1942).

Dictionary of National Biography (1885–1900), with supplements (1901–1959). Biographies of British figures.

Dictionary of Philosophy and Psychology (1901–1905, revised 1918).

Encyclopedia of Educational Research (1960).

Encyclopedia of Philosophy (1967).

Encyclopaedia of Religion and Ethics (1908–1927).

Encyclopedia of the Arts (1946).

Encyclopaedia of the Social Sciences (1930–1935).

Grove's Dictionary of Music and Musicians (1954), with a supplement (1961).

Harper's Encyclopedia of Art (1937).

International Encyclopedia of the Social Sciences (1968).

The Jewish Encyclopedia (1901–1906).

Literary History of the United States (1963).

McGraw-Hill Encyclopedia of Science and Technology (1966).

New Catholic Encyclopedia (1967).

Universal Jewish Encyclopedia (1939–1943).

Constance M. Winchell's *Guide to Reference Books* lists other specialized sources.

Once these sources have given the writer an overview of his subject, he must find books and articles that provide a closer look. The library's card catalog will direct him to books. Indeed, it will probably list more than he can use. How can he tell which are the most reliable and the most likely to provide the material he needs? There are several ways he can find out. Bibliographies in the reference works mentioned above supply some basic titles. (The three-volume edition of *Literary History of the United States*, for instance, devotes one volume to bibliography.) He can find other bibliographies through Constance Winchell's *Guide to Reference Books* and the *Bibliographic Index*. He can also consult the *Book Review Digest*, which paraphrases reviews of books published since 1905. And in the card catalog he may find that a recent book on his subject contains a selective bibliography.

For articles, the chief resource is the *Reader's Guide to Periodical Literature*, which lists articles published in over a hundred popular magazines since 1900. Other guides are:

Essay and General Literature Index (1893–   ). A list of essays published in books of essays.

New York Times Index (1913–   ). A guide to recent history as it has been reported in the *Times*.

Poole's Index to Periodical Literature (1802–1906). A subject index of many nineteenth-century British and American periodicals.

Social Science and Humanities Index, known until 1965 as the *International Index to Periodical Literature* (1903–   ). A guide to scholarly articles.

Having gathered sufficient reading matter, the writer can prepare his *working bibliography*. He enters each book or article on a 3 x 5 or 4 x 6 index card. The card should record (1) the library call number to help him find the book or article when he needs it again, (2) the abbreviation he will later use on note cards referring to this source, and (3) the information he will need for his documentation and formal bibliography (see pp. 264–267).

HM   Kahler
136
K12t
            Kahler, Erich

            The <u>Tower</u> and <u>the</u> <u>Abyss</u>: An

            Inquiry <u>into</u> <u>the</u> Transformation

            <u>of</u> <u>the</u> Individual

            (New York, 1957)

With twenty or so cards like this, the writer is ready to start his reading and note-taking. The steps by which he prepares to write his essay have been discussed in Chapters 7, 8, and 14.

Documentation becomes a concern as soon as the writer begins his first draft. Wherever he writes something that will later require a note of acknowledgment, he should parenthetically record the source and page numbers, as do the italicized notations below.

> ... Second-rank leaders under Nazism were trained to suppress their personal opinions and emotions so that they could contribute all the more effectively to the greater strength and glory of the state (*Fromm, 257–260*). The result was a divided mentality similar to schizophrenia (*Kahler, 68–78*). "These men, after having done their gruesome work, after having watched, sometimes closely, the ordeal of their camp laborers ... after having directed and inspected excruciating experiments on humans, went home to their

families, parties, classes, delivered lectures, carried on their research ... without even the slightest sense of the flagrant contrast between the two aspects of their lives" (*Kahler*, 75).

Notice that the writer inserts an ellipsis (...) wherever he deletes words from a quotation. Notice also that quotations are not the only borrowings he must acknowledge. He indicates indebtedness whenever he relies on another writer's statement of fact or opinion, whether the statement is quoted or not.

In the final draft the writer shows his indebtedness formally, with *notes of acknowledgment*. He numbers the borrowings consecutively straight through the essay (not beginning with *1* on each page). If all notes appear at the end of the essay, he double-spaces the notes and puts triple-spaces between them. If the notes are inserted at the bottom of each page, he single-spaces them, with double-spaces in between. The notes can follow the forms given below.

A book by one author:

[1] Erich Kahler, *The Tower and the Abyss: An Inquiry into the Transformation of the Individual* (New York, 1957), pp. 68–78. [Indent the first line several spaces. Begin all subsequent lines at the margin.]

A book by several authors:

[2] Snell Putney and Gail J. Putney, *The Adjusted American: Normal Neuroses in the Individual and Society* (New York, 1966), p. 44. [List authors in the order given on the title page, not necessarily alphabetically. *New York:* the place of publication. *1966:* the date of publication of that particular edition. Standard abbreviations for *page* and *pages* are *p.* and *pp.*]

A book with a translator:

[3] Konrad Lorenz, *King Solomon's Ring: New Light on Animal Ways,* trans. Marjorie Kerr Wilson (New York, 1952), pp. 126–127. [The abbreviation *trans.* is standard for *translator* or *translated by.*]

A book with several volumes:

[4] Arnold Kettle, *An Introduction to the English Novel* (New York, 1960), II, 68. [The volume number is given in Roman numerals. After a volume number, no *p.* or *pp.* is necessary. Here, *68* is obviously the page number.]

An article by one person in a book edited by another:
  [5] Robert Paul Wolff, "The College as Rat Race," in *The Radical Papers*, ed. Irving Howe (New York, 1966), pp. 298–300. [The abbreviation *ed.* is standard for *editor* or *edited by*.]

An unsigned article from an encyclopedia:
  [6] "Lillie Langtry," *Encyclopedia Americana* (New York, 1967), XVI, 717.

A signed article from an encyclopedia:
  [7] Robert Ralph Bolgar, "Rhetoric," *Encyclopaedia Britannica* (Chicago, 1969), XIX, 258–259.

An unsigned article from a periodical:
  [8] "The Pill and Cancer," *Newsweek*, August 11, 1969, p. 59. [*Newsweek* supplied no volume number.]

Signed articles from periodicals:
  [9] Sara Davidson, "Rock Style: Defying the American Dream," *Harper's*, CCXXXIX (July, 1969), 54–55.
  [10] George Lichtheim, "The Future of Socialism," *Partisan Review*, XXX (Spring, 1963), 85–89.

After the first reference to a source, later notes can be much shorter, so long as they are clear:

  [11] Kahler, p. 75.
  [12] Kettle, II, 72.
  [13] "The Pill and Cancer," p. 59.

If the writer cites two or more works by the same person, each subsequent reference to the works should repeat the title, or an abbreviation of the title, so that the works will not be confused. Be thankful, however, that the abbreviations *ibid.* (in the same place), *op cit.* (in the work cited), and *idem* (the same) are passing out of fashion. They have been a nuisance to both writers and readers.

The *formal bibliography* given at the end of the essay is merely a summary of the sources cited in the notes of acknowledgment. The entries supply basically the same information as the notes, but in a somewhat different form. Notice the conventions followed in these samples.

Bolgar, Robert Ralph. "Rhetoric." *Encyclopaedia Britannica*. Chicago, 1969. XIX, 257–260. [The first line is even with the margin; later lines are indented several spaces. Most entries will be listed alphabetically under the author's last name; therefore the last name comes first.]

Davidson, Sara. "Rock Style: Defying the American Dream." *Harper's*, CCXXXIX (July, 1969), 53–62. [The page numbers in this entry, and in all entries for articles, list all pages contained in the article, even those not cited in notes of acknowledgment.]

Kahler, Erich. *The Tower and the Abyss: An Inquiry into the Transformation of the Individual*. New York, 1957.

Kettle, Arnold. *An Introduction to the English Novel*. 2 vols. New York, 1960. (First published in 1952–1953.) [The information in parentheses is not strictly necessary but may be useful to the reader. See the entry for Putney.]

Lichtheim, George. "The Future of Socialism." *Partisan Review*, XXX (Spring, 1963), 83–93. [The date of an article is in parentheses only when the volume number is supplied. Compare the entry for "The Pill and Cancer."]

"Lillie Langtry." *Encyclopedia Americana*. New York, 1967. XVI, 717–718. [Unsigned articles are listed alphabetically by title.]

Lorenz, Konrad. *King Solomon's Ring: New Light on Animal Ways*. Trans. Marjorie Kerr Wilson. New York, 1952.

"The Pill and Cancer." *Newsweek*, August 11, 1969, p. 59. [*Newsweek* supplied no volume number.]

Putney, Snell, and Gail J. Putney. *The Adjusted American: Normal Neuroses in the Individual and Society*. New York, 1966. (First published in 1964 with the title *Normal Neurosis*.)

Wolff, Robert Paul. "The College as Rat Race." In *The Radical Papers*, ed. Irving Howe. New York, 1966. Pages 296–306. [*Page* or *pages* must be written out, not abbreviated, when the first letter is capitalized.]

The forms offered here for notes of acknowledgment and for bibliography are largely derived from the *MLA Style Sheet*, compiled by William Riley Parker. For further information, obtain the *Style Sheet* (from the Modern Language Association, 60 Fifth Avenue, New York, N. Y. 10011) or consult a handbook of composition (such as one of those cited on p. 253).

The job of documenting sources is drudgery but still a necessity. We are all ignorant about most subjects, expert in few or none. When a writer approaches a subject new to him, he must depend to some extent on other writers who have already done much hard work at digging out facts and drawing conclusions. Although he may in the end uncover new facts and draw new conclusions, he must acknowledge his debt to the writers who helped him get started.

An ABC of Common Problems
VII

In commenting on your paragraphs and essays, instructors may use the symbols in this list to refer you to other sections of the text or to refer you to entries that deal with points of usage.

The entries on usage ignore many elementary points (for example, that a sentence ends with a period and a question with a question mark) and ignore many of the subtleties treated in dictionaries, handbooks, and guides to usage (see pp. 251–254). The forms of usage recommended follow the general practice of the best contemporary essayists and are appropriate in the formal, the high formal, and the middle informal styles—those you will use in most of your essays. (A discussion of levels of usage appears on pp. 161–165, 172–175.)

_____ General symbol for a weakness in style.

⊂⊃ General symbol for a mistake in mechanics, punctuation, grammar, usage, and the like.

Ab *Abbreviation* needed or misused.

1. In general, avoid using abbreviations: *Mon., Sept., Chas., Pres., Sec.,* and the like.

2. Some exceptions are: *etc., A.M., P.M., B.C., A.D.*

3. Abbreviations for certain Latin phrases are permissible, but for the sake of clarity should be replaced with unabbreviated English whenever possible: *ibid., op. cit., i.e.* (that is), *e.g.* (for example), *cf.* (compare), *viz.* (namely), and so forth.

4. Some organizations are so well known by their initials that the abbreviations cause readers no trouble: *TVA, YMCA, FBI, UN, DAR.*

5. Some abbreviations may be used with proper names: *Dr. Higgins; Mr. Oldham; John Farnham, M.D.; Capt. Graff.* (But the following use would be incorrect: *The Dr. and the Capt. were old friends.*)

Abs Too *abstract* or general. Be more specific. See pp. 7–9 (on the distinction between abstract-general wording and concrete-specific); 13–17, 21–24 (the need for specificity in the paragraph); 76–77 (the danger of too much abstractness and generality in the essay-idea); 190–194 (the need for specificity in prose style).

Ack Passage requires *acknowledgment* of source. See pp. 264–266.

Agr Mistake in *agreement*. A verb must agree in number with its subject. A pronoun must agree in number with its antecedent.

1. Interrupting phrases can cause mistakes in agreement:

This *company,* with all its skilled mechanics and electricians, *guarantee* quick repair of *their* appliances. [*Guarantee* should be *guarantees. Their* should be *its.*]

The *proposals*, even the plan for a newly constituted student government, *was* rejected. [*Was* should be *were*.]

Tom, along with hundreds of other graduating seniors, *have* received *their* papers for induction into the armed services. [*Have* should be *has*. *Their* should be *his*.]

2. Subjects joined by *and* usually require a plural verb:

The second vice-president and his assistant *are* helpless without their secretaries.

Occasionally, however, a compound subject may be regarded as singular:

Assault and battery *is* a serious charge.
Spaghetti and meatballs *has* made her fat.

3. A verb preceding the subject must still agree with it in number:

Here *come* the captain and his aide.
There *are* a copy of Aristotle's *Ethics* and a score of Bach's *Mass in B Minor* in the pack on Hardy's motorcycle.

4. Singular subjects joined by *or* or *nor* should be followed by singular verbs and pronouns:

When he pitched that day, neither his curve nor his knuckleball *was* working as well as *it* usually did.
Either Rosenberg or Gallatin *is* wrong and will soon have to admit *his* mistake.

When the subjects are all plural, the subsequent verbs and pronouns should be plural:

Neither the left-wingers nor the right-wingers *are* making *their* beliefs clear to the general public.

What happens when one subject is singular, another plural? Perhaps the sentence can be revised so that this problem will be avoided. Otherwise let verbs and pronouns agree with the nearer subject:

Neither the beautiful lawns and gardens nor the *house* itself *makes* this property worth the price.

Neither the house nor the beautiful *lawns* and *gardens make* this property worth the price.

5. If the subject differs in number from a predicate noun, the verb still agrees with the subject:

Their *consolation* in times of poverty and illness *was* their religious beliefs.
Their religious *beliefs were* their consolation in times of poverty and illness.

6. Collective nouns are singular in form but plural in meaning: *group, crowd, mob, team, committee*. Usually a collective noun takes singular verbs and pronouns:

The *mob was* dispersed before *it* reached the palace gates.
The *committee was* still undecided.

When a collective noun refers to the members of a group rather than the group as a unit, the noun may be followed by plural verbs and pronouns:

The *team were* still bickering among *themselves*.

If this construction seems awkward, revise in this way:

The members of the team were still bickering among themselves.

7. These pronouns should be regarded as singular: *each, either, neither, no one, anybody, anyone, everybody, everyone, somebody, someone*. Therefore:

Each insists that *his* plan is best.
Neither of these men *knows his* subject well enough to lecture on it.
Everybody in the room *has* had a chance to state *his* grievances.

When *any, each, every, either*, or *neither* serves as an adjective modifying a singular noun, the subsequent verbs and pronouns will be singular:

Every member of this group of malcontents *has* had a chance to state *his* grievances.

When *each* modifies a plural noun, the verbs and pronouns may be plural:

The members each *have* had a chance to state *their* grievances.

The pronoun *none* is sometimes singular, sometimes plural, as is made clear in Wilson Follett's *Modern American Usage*. When *none* means *no one* or *not a single one*, it should be regarded as singular. When it refers to more than one, it must be regarded as plural. Follett offers these examples:

Singular: None of us *is* entitled to cast the first stone.
Plural: None of the commentators *agree* on the meaning of this passage.

8. Constructions like *he is one of those who* can lead to mistakes:

He is one of those who *labors* on the mountainside farms for *his* living.

Labors and *his* are wrong. They should agree in number with *who*, which is plural because it refers to *those*. The following forms are correct:

He is one of those who *labor* on the mountainside farms for *their* living.
He was the most courageous of those who *have* lost *their* lives in this battle.

Ap *Apostrophe* needed or misused.
1. Use an apostrophe where letters or figures are omitted: *don't, they're, the Class of '57.*
2. An apostrophe can help form the plural of letters, figures, and words referred to as words:

Cross the *t*'s and dot the *i*'s.
If the *1920's* were the Jazz Age, the *1930's* were the Age of the Blues. (These apostrophes are not mandatory.)

3. An apostrophe is used in possessive nouns.
A singular noun adds *'s:*

Alice's car is worth a mere two hundred dollars in *today's* used-car market.

Occasionally, when a singular noun ends with *s* and contains several syllables, the added *'s* can sound awkward. You may wish to add only an apostrophe. Either of the following is correct:

The *princess's* elopement was a mistake.
The *princess'* elopement was a mistake.

A plural possessive generally adds only the apostrophe: *horses' illness, truck drivers' strike, ladies' impatience.* But if the plural form of the noun does not end in *s*, the possessive adds *'s*: *men's, women's, children's, sheep's, deer's.*
Joint possession is shown by an *'s* on the final noun:

Sam and Gus's bar is selling watered beer.

If the possessors own things separately, each noun should be in the possessive case:

Mike's, Joe's, and the *Johnsons'* overcoats were all left here last night after the party.

4. Indefinite pronouns use an apostrophe to show possession: *somebody's mistake, anyone's guess, no one's fault.* Personal pronouns, however, require no apostrophe: *theirs, ours, hers, its.* The contraction *it's* should not be confused with the possessive *its.*

Ar Unclear *arrangement* in a paragraph or a series of paragraphs. See pp. 30–36, 42–47 (arrangement in the paragraph); 110–111 (the short essay); 153 (the complex essay).

Bal *Balanced* construction needed. See pp. 202–203.

Ca Wrong *case* of noun or pronoun.

1. According to a longstanding rule, all predicate pronouns should be in the subjective case. That is, we should write

It is *I*. [not *me*]
That was *we* standing in the doorway. [not *us*]
This is *he*. [not *him*]
It was *she* who had read the book. [not *her*]
It was *they* who backed down at the last minute. [not *them*]

The last three usages present no problem: Use the predicate *he*, *she*, and *they*. The *I* and *we* are more troublesome. *It is I* and *That was we* have been giving way to the more colloquial *It is me* and *That was us*. In formal and high informal prose you should probably still use the predicate *I* and *we*—particularly in constructions like *It was I who played that role* and *That was we who rented the apartment*. But in writing less formal prose, you may let your own ear decide whether *I* is preferable to *me* or *we* to *us*.

2. In an elliptical clause beginning with *than* or *as*, use the same pronoun as you would if the clause were complete. This is wrong:

Sam has a better backhand than *me*.

The *me* is actually the subject of a clause whose verb is understood: *than I* [*have*] or *than I* [*do*]. The sentence should be:

Sam has a better backhand than *I*.

In the same way:

She has spent more on books this year than *he* [has].
I can type as quickly and accurately as *she* [can].
I like him more than *she* [does].
I like him more than [I like] *her*.

3. Objects of verbs and prepositions should be in the objective case:

The argument between *her* and *me* lasted till after midnight.
The problem for *him* and *us* was that we had all failed to
    buy tickets in advance.

The accountant advised *him, her,* and *me* to invest our money in government bonds.

That instructor ruined the semester for *us* students who were in his class.

On the other hand:

We students had a difficult semester. [Here *we* is attached to the subject *students.*]

4. The relative pronouns *who* and *whoever* (subjective) and *whom* and *whomever* (objective) can be troublesome. Their case depends on how they function in their own clauses. In *They don't know who is coming to the party,* the *who* is subject of the verb *is coming* in the clause *who is coming to the party.* But in *He did not know whom he ought to consult, whom* is the object of *consult* in the clause *whom he ought to consult.* This can be seen more easily if the words are shifted around: *he ought to consult whom.* In the following examples the clauses using words like *who* are italicized.

That jeweler downtown, *who has pawned her diamond to bet on the horses,* is supposedly her friend.

That jeweler downtown, *whom she regards as her friend,* has pawned her diamond to bet on the horses. [With reversed word order: *she regards whom as her friend.*]

Whoever tracks sand or mud into her swimming pool is never again allowed to use it.

Whomever you have in mind when you make those accusations, you are wrong. [With reversed word order: *you have whomever in mind.*]

Sometimes an intruding *I think, he knows, she believes,* or the like can be confusing. Someone may mistakenly write *She is the woman whom I believe distrusts all psychiatrists,* thinking that the pertinent clause is *whom I believe* (reversed: *I believe whom*). Actually, *I believe* is a parenthetical expression; it could be placed in parentheses with no loss to the sentence. The essential words of the clause in which *whom* appears are *whom distrusts all psychiatrists* and obviously should have been *who distrusts all psychiatrists.* In the following sentences, only the essential words of the subordinate clauses are italicized.

The student *who* the instructor believed *had the most likelihood of becoming a first-rate playwright* was our friend Malcolm.

Aaron Burr was a well-meaning man *who* I believe *thought he was working for the best interests of the United States.*

In questions the writer can sometimes substitute *who* for *whom* without offending the reader:

Who was that gift for?
Who was the discussion about?

5. H. W. Fowler, in *Modern English Usage,* stated that the following construction is always awkward and illogical:

You saying you are sorry alters the case.
Women having the vote reduces men's political power.

Saying is a noun, the subject of the verb *alters.* It is the *saying* of the apology, not the *you,* that "alters the case." Therefore the *you* must be made the possessive *your* to modify the noun *saying: Your saying you are sorry alters the case.* The same argument applies to the second sentence above. Not *women* themselves but their *having the vote* reduces men's power. Logically the sentence should be: *Women's having the vote reduces men's political power.* Theodore Bernstein, in *The Careful Writer,* offers another example supporting Fowler's argument: *I hate my best friend losing his job* seems to mean that the writer hates his friend; the sentence should be *I hate my best friend's losing his job.*

Though recent writers on usage tend to accept Fowler's argument, they point out exceptions to the rule. Mr. Bernstein cites a number of sentences in which the possessive would be awkward and would make little difference in meaning:

The eggs were shipped without *one being* broken. [Would *one's* really be better?]
We are mortified at the news of the *French taking* the town from the Portuguese. [*Frenchmen's?*]
[They had] no fear . . . of *bad becoming* worse. [*bad's?*]
He said that he was not writing his memoirs and that he strongly disapproved of *persons* active in public life *doing* so. [*persons'?*]

Cap *Capitalization* needed or misused.

1. Capitalize the first word of a sentence or a quoted sentence:

The child screamed, "Let's go home!"

2. Capitalize proper nouns: *Thomas Jefferson, Paul Dinkalacker, Montana, Peru, the Alps, Red China, the Washington Monument, Division Street, the Renaissance, Thanksgiving Day.*

3. Capitalize most words derived from proper nouns: *Christian, Buddhist, New Yorker, American, Faulknerian.* Some derivatives are not capitalized: *sixty watts, turkish towels, spartan, stoical, pasteurized, quixotic, malapropism.* When in doubt, check with a dictionary.

4. Capitalize a title when it is used as part of a proper name: *Senator Birdseye, General "Bullethead" Bowen, President Coolidge, President Jones, Dean Fisk, Professor Little, Uncle Charlie.*

5. When a title replaces a proper name, the title is sometimes capitalized, sometimes not, at the writer's discretion. The more important the person referred to, the more likely it would be that the writer would capitalize. *The President spoke* would be appropriate if the speaker was the President of the United States, possibly appropriate for the president of a college, probably inappropriate for the president of a club for rabbit hunters.

6. In the titles (or sub-titles) of books, magazines, essays, plays, poems, etc., the first and last words are capitalized and all other words except articles (*a, the*), conjunctions, and prepositions of fewer than six letters.

"At the San Francisco Airport" [a poem]
A Farewell to Arms [a novel]
The Wings of the Dove [a novel]
"Surrender Without Dishoner: A Way to End the War" [an article]

7. Other uses.
(a) Titles of kinship are capitalized when used as proper names; otherwise, not:

My sisters are going downtown with *Mother.*
They are going downtown with their *mother.*

(b) Points of the compass are capitalized when they refer to particular areas, not when they refer to directions:

He will soon be heading *west* again, but he hopes eventually to settle in the *East.*

(c) The name of a season is not capitalized unless you wish to give it special emphasis.
(d) The names of particular courses are capitalized; general areas of study are not.

He did excellent work in *Mathematics 112* and *Physics 256.*
He enjoys studying *mathematics* and *physics.*

Clar Paragraph-idea or essay-idea needs *clarification.* See pp. 13–17 (paragraph-idea); 89–92 (essay-idea).
Co *Coordination* needed or misused. See pp. 198–203 (uses of coordination); 206, 210–211 (misuses).
Col Wording too *colloquial* for this context. See pp. 163–165, 172–175.
Comp Faulty *comparison.*
1. Use the comparative form to compare two things, the superlative for more than two.

Which of the two houses is *more* expensive?
Which of the three is *most* expensive?

2. Avoid illogical comparisons of this kind:

Pat was more squeamish about the dissections than anyone
in her biology class.
Jacobus had a better batting average than anyone on his
team.

Pat, as a member of her biology class, is here said to be
more squeamish than herself. Jacobus's batting average,
strictly speaking, is said to be better than Jacobus's
batting average. These revisions would be more logical:

Pat was more squeamish about the dissections than anyone
else in her biology class.
Jacobus had the best batting average on his team.

3. Do not compare incomparables, such as *fatal, unique,
impossible, empty,* and *perfect.* If a gas tank is *empty,*
no other can be *more empty* or *most empty.* Something
perfect cannot be surpassed; nothing else can be *more*
or *most perfect.*

4. Be clear about what things are being compared. These
sentences are faulty:

The teachings of Freud have been more influential than
Otto Rank. [*teachings* compared with *Otto Rank*]
Despite his twenty years' work as a free-lance writer, his
yearly earnings are still less than his friend the plumber.
[*earnings* compared with *his friend the plumber*]

These versions are more logical:

The teachings of Freud have been more influential than the
teachings of Otto Rank [*or* than those of Otto Rank].
Despite his twenty years' work as a free-lance writer, his
yearly earnings are still less than those of his friend the
plumber.

Conc Inadequate *conclusion.* See pp. 118–120 (on the conclusion
of the short essay); 149–150 (the complex essay).

Cont Loss of *continuity*. See pp. 30–36, 42–48, 55–60 (continuity within the paragraph); 110–113 (the short essay); 153–155 (the complex essay).

D Mistake in *diction:* imprecise wording. See pp. 179–182.

Def Inadequate *defense* of a paragraph-idea. See pp. 21–24.

Div Improper *division* of a word.

1. If the last word in a line must be divided, it should be divided between syllables. When in doubt, consult a dictionary.

2. Place a hyphen at the dividing point.

3. Do not divide a word in such a way as to leave a single letter at the end of one line or the beginning of another.

4. Do not divide the last word on a page.

EI Unsatisfactory *essay-idea*. See pp. 73–77.

F Wording can be made more *forceful.*

FW Need for more *familiar wording*. See pp. 189–190, 191–194.

H *Hackneyed* wording or thought. See pp. 74–76 (triteness of thought); 165, 174 (hackneyed language).

Hy Mistake in *hyphenation.*

1. Hyphenate when dividing a word at the end of a line.

2. Hyphenate compound numbers from twenty-one to ninety-nine.

3. Hyphenate fractions used as modifiers:

He is two-thirds inspired, one-third insane.

4. Hyphenate when adding a prefix to a word beginning with a capital letter:

He is non-Communist but anti-American.

5. Hyphenate when a prefix ends with the same vowel as that with which the root word begins: *pre-election, anti-inflation, semi-independent, quasi-intellectual.* But check with a dictionary for the possibility of exceptions, such as *coordinate* and *cooperate.*

6. Hyphens are used in many adjectival compounds that precede nouns: *up-to-date thinking, day-to-day survival,*

twelve-foot planks, narrow-minded editorials. Some adjectival compounds, however, are run together rather than hyphenated. When in doubt, consult a dictionary (though dictionaries can disagree about hyphenation). *Webster's New World Dictionary* offers *clear-cut, cleareyed, clearheaded,* and *clear-sighted.*

7. Compound nouns are sometimes hyphenated, sometimes run together as one word, sometimes regarded as separate words. Consult a dictionary. *Standard College Dictionary* offers *tree-trimmer, treetop,* and *tree surgeon.*

Intro Inadequate *introduction.* See pp. 88–92, 97–104 (concerning the introduction of the short essay); 147–149 (the complex essay).

Intro AG *Introduction* lacks satisfactory *attention-getter.* See pp. 97–102.

Intro EI *Introduction* does not make the *essay-idea* sufficiently prominent. See pp. 88–92, 103–104.

It *Italics* needed or misused.

1. In manuscript, italics are indicated by underlining.

2. Italicize the titles of newspapers, magazines, books, plays, motion pictures, and musical compositions:

the *New York Times,* the *New Republic, Life,* West's novel *The Day of the Locust, A Streetcar Named Desire,* Bartok's *Second Piano Concerto.*

Short writings take quotation marks. See the entry for *Quot.*

3. Italicize foreign words and phrases unless they have been accepted as standard English. Consult a dictionary.

4. Use italics to indicate words, letters, or figures referred to as such:

The old rules governing *shall* and *will* are losing their authority.

That sentence sounds ridiculous: four words in a row begin with *th.*

5. Occasionally you may have to use italics for emphasis. Ideally, however, you should shape each sentence

so that its most important words will be emphasized without the help of italics.

K *Awkward.*

L Lack of *logic.*

M Unclear *modification.* See pp. 242–244.

NC *Not clear,* or not so clear as it should be.

NP *Nonparallel* construction. Coordinate elements must be similar in grammatical structure. In the following sentence they are not:

> As the examination period approached the end, the desperate student wrote *quickly* but *not taking much thought.*

Quickly, an adverb, is coordinated with *not taking much thought,* a participial construction. This mistake can be corrected in several ways. Here are two:

> As the examination period approached the end, the desperate student wrote *quickly* but *thoughtlessly.*
> As the examination period approached the end, the desperate student *wrote* quickly but *did* little thinking.

Here are other illustrations of this problem:

Nonparallel: During the vacation she spent much of her time *swimming, playing* tennis, and *at the dances.*
Better: During the vacation she spent much of her time *swimming, playing* tennis, and *dancing.*

Nonparallel: He lost all his money *by betting* large amounts in poker and *because he lacked caution* on the stock market.
Better: He lost all his money *by betting* large amounts in poker and *by gambling* recklessly on the stock market.
Or: He lost all his money by gambling recklessly *in poker* and *on the stock market.*

Nonparallel: John will either *play* the guitar tonight or *Ed will play.*
Better: Either *John will play* the guitar tonight or *Ed will play.*
Or: Either *John* or *Ed* will play the guitar tonight.

Nonparallel: Senator Thurston was the favorite of both *labor* and *of management.*

Better: Senator Thurston was the favorite of both *labor* and *management.*

Nu Mistake in writing of *numbers.*

1. A widely accepted rule is to write out numbers that can be expressed in one or two words but to use numerals otherwise: *twenty-seven, seven hundred, 187, 1,223, fifty-eight cents, $3.27.*

2. Numerals are generally used in dates, addresses, and chapter and page numbers.

3. Numerals should not be used at the beginning of a sentence. If you want to say *330 people attended the lecture,* either write the number out (*Three hundred and thirty people . . .*) or reverse the word order (*The lecture was attended by 330 people*).

4. When using numbers in a series, be consistent in writing them out or using numerals:

His grandmother is *eighty-eight,* his grandfather *ninety,* and his great-grandfather *one hundred and seven.* [Or use *88, 90,* and *107.*]

Om *Omission* of essential word, idea, or paragraph.

OP *Out of place:* an interruption that should be put elsewhere in the sentence, paragraph, or essay, or should be dropped altogether.

OS *Overweight sentence.* See pp. 239–241.

P (or ¶) Need for a new *paragraph.* The present overloaded paragraph should be divided into two (perhaps three) smaller ones. See p. 82.

PI (or ¶I) Faulty *paragraph-idea.* See pp. 21–22, 82.

Pn Mistake in *punctuation.*

1. Uses of the *comma.*

(a) To separate independent clauses joined by a conjunction:

Rick ignored the advice of friends and decided to gamble on speculative stocks, and now he has lost half his capital.

Maxwell had hoped to become a novelist, but he found that selling insurance paid better.

A short clause followed by *and* may require no comma:

He had won three hands and he already considered himself a master poker player.

(b) To separate words, phrases, or clauses in a series:

Robinson's Arthurian narratives are *Merlin, Lancelot,* and *Tristram.*

The highway went through the desert, into the fertile lands surrounding Los Angeles, and finally into the city itself.

(c) To separate coordinate adjectives: *the large, cold, unfriendly house / a shrewd, rascally politician / a vicious, irrational argument.* No comma is needed between adjectives that are not coordinate: *a heavy lead pipe / an old kitchen stove.* Noncoordinate adjectives can be spotted in two simple ways. First, if an *and* is inserted between them, the result sounds awkward: *a heavy and lead pipe.* Second, if the adjectives are reversed, the result is again awkward: *a kitchen old stove.*

(d) To follow introductory words, phrases, or clauses that ought to be separated from the rest of the sentence by a slight pause:

However, the sprinkling system did not stop the fire.
In short, we made a mistake.
After the fertilizer had been applied that spring, the weeds began to overrun the grass.
Having seen one film about the dangers of smoking, he did not wish to see another.

(e) To enclose parenthetical elements that interrupt the sentence:

This typewriter, oddly enough, types Gothic letters.
Professor Warren, as you know, wastes an hour a day keeping his pipe lit.
At this minute Senator Mulhare, together with his friends and parasites, is approaching the committee room.

(f) To separate a subordinate element at the end of a sentence when a pause is desirable:

Joseph Heller's *Catch–22* would have been better if it had been more concise, as the author himself has admitted.
Walter did not admire John, because John was often snobbish and arrogant.

Without the comma the sentence about Walter and John would seem to mean that Walter *did* admire John, but for other qualities than his snobbishness and arrogance.

(g) To separate nonrestrictive appositives and clauses from the rest of the sentence:

Reginald's newest play, *Night Sweat*, is his most vulgar.
This powder, which is highly narcotic and addictive, cannot be purchased without a doctor's prescription.
Mr. Macdonald, who handled the sale of the house, proved to be a reliable attorney.

These nonrestrictive elements are not necessary for identifying the nouns they refer to. Restrictive elements, however, are necessary and thus are not set off by commas:

Reginald's play *Night Sweat* is his most vulgar.
Any powder that is highly narcotic and addictive should not be available for purchase without a doctor's prescription.
The attorney who handled the sale of the house proved to be reliable.

(h) To avoid any lapse in clarity:

The operation would be delayed for all the doctors agreed that postponement would be safer. [A comma after *delayed* would prevent possible misreading.]
After all they had said and done only what they thought would be helpful. [Insert a comma after *after all*.]

2. Uses of the *semicolon*.

(a) To join independent clauses not joined by a coordinate conjunction:

He was delighted at the invitation; he had long wanted to meet the Davises.

(b) To join independent clauses when one or both are so complicated that a coordinate conjunction cannot do the job adequately by itself:

> Many of the readers who join book clubs and enjoy best sellers have learned to regard Robert Frost as a major poet and have put his *Complete Poems* on their shelves; but though the volume is widely owned, it is little read, like the Bible, and these people mostly accept Frost's greatness on faith or on the word of book reviewers and teachers of English.

(c) To join phrases in a series when the phrases contain commas:

> He is typical of our modern American mobility, having lived in Astoria, New York; Whiteville, North Carolina; Miami Beach, Florida; and South Orange, New Jersey— all before the age of ten.

3. Uses of the *colon*. The colon says, in effect, that something already mentioned will now be explained or amplified:

> I understood his meaning: he wanted me to leave.
>
> From the hospital bed Gertrude Stein addressed her friends: "What is the answer?" Getting no response, she laughed and said her last words: "In that case, what is the question?"
>
> Nelson Algren's *The Man with the Golden Arm* shows the sordid underside of life in Chicago: the purposeless existence of the petty thieves; the hopelessness of the Negroes; the stupor of the drunks; the powdered-and-rouged misery of the strippers; the ghoulishness of the drug peddlers; and the final despair of the drug takers, the convicts, and the insane.

4. Uses of the *dash*.

(a) To set off parenthetical elements too long or interruptive to be enclosed in commas:

> The day was so hot—it was the fourth hot day in a row— that Ray quit studying and spent the afternoon in an air-conditioned theater.

(b) To introduce the second part of a sentence when the second part helps explain the first:

All literature tends to be concerned with the question of reality—I mean quite simply the old opposition between reality and appearance, between what really is and what merely seems.
LIONEL TRILLING, "Manners, Morals and the Novel"

(c) To emphasize a final idea in the sentence:

She smiled and asked whether he got along well with the other prisoners, whether his health was improving, and whether he was learning a useful trade—but she didn't care at all.

Quot *Quotation* marks needed or misused.

1. Quotation marks enclose the titles of short pieces of writing:

T. S. Eliot's poem "The Hollow Men"
E. B. White's essay "The Future of Reading," from his book *The Second Tree from the Corner*

2. Quotation marks may enclose words referred to as words:

The slang word "hooker" means a prostitute.
The president's so-called "executive assistant" is a useless office boy.

3. Quotation marks should enclose direct quotations from dialogue or from another writer. Note the conventions of punctuation and capitalization shown in the following passages:

The chairman asked, "Is this the most important matter to be discussed?"
"Can we win?" he asked.
The mayor said only this: "Criminals must be treated as criminals!"
"Just because the air-conditioner is broken," the manager complained, "our customers are going elsewhere to shop."

Why did Huxley call his beliefs "the perennial philosophy"?
According to Fowler, a major enemy of good prose is the
"love of the long word"; "short words [he said] are
not only handier to use, but more powerful in effect."

A quotation within a quotation is enclosed in single
quotation marks.

One student remarked: "Gertrude Stein did not say, 'A rose
is a rose is a rose'; she usually said, 'A rose is a rose is
a rose is a rose,' and sometimes added more roses than
that."

4. If a quotation deserves special emphasis or occupies
ten lines or more, introduce it with a colon and indent it,
without enclosing it in quotation marks.

Ref Unclear *reference* of a pronoun. See pp. 244–245.

Rep Needless *repetition* of words or ideas. See pp. 232–233.

SF Unsatisfactory *sentence fragment.*

Sentence fragments can be clear and forceful:

Do professional writers work a set number of hours each
day? Yes. Generally eight or nine hours a day, just like
a laborer, salesman, or businessman. Doesn't the writer
wait for inspiration? No. What nonsense! If he waited
for "inspiration" or the so-called "right mood," he
would do little writing. Very little indeed.

This passage, however, is unusual in the number of
fragments it contains. In writing expository prose you
ordinarily will not utter so many exclamations or ask so
many questions that can take fragments as answers.
The overuse of fragments can result in a choppy, over-
excited style that sinks too near the level of cheap journalism.

Use fragments sparingly, then, and by all means
avoid the sort of fragment that serves no good rhetorical
purpose but merely reflects negligence or ignorance.

Poor: The new missile program will probably be voted
through now. Because three more senators have decided
to vote in favor of it.

Better: Because three more senators have decided to vote for the new missile program, it will probably be voted through.

Sk P (or Sk¶) *Skimpy paragraph.* See pp. 22–23, 82.

Sp Mistake in *spelling.*

Spec Be more *specific.* See pp. 7–9 (on the distinction between abstract-general wording and concrete-specific); 13–17, 21–24 (the need for specificity in the paragraph); 76–77 (the danger of too much abstractness and generality in the essay-idea); 190–194 (the need for specificity in prose style).

STS Need for a *subtopic sentence.* See pp. 34–36.

Sub *Subordination* needed or misused. See pp. 206–211.

Subj *Subjunctive* verb needed here.

1. Use the subjunctive to express a command, a statement of necessity, or a resolution:

The general ordered that the attack *begin.* [not *begins* or *began*]
It is necessary that the prisoner *be* searched. [not *is*]
He insisted that the meeting *come* to an end. [not *comes*]

2. Use the subjunctive when expressing a condition contrary to fact:

If Sabo *were* mayor he would make our traffic problems even worse. [not *was*]
If the judge *were* a more lenient man, the jail sentence might be only a year, but he is not lenient. [not *was*]
The newcomer drove through the maze of streets as if he *were* a longtime inhabitant of that city. [not *was*]

3. The subjunctive is used to express a wish:

I wish the day *were* over. [not *was*]
They wished he *were* a strong enough leader to unite the party. [not *was*]

T Mistake in verb *tense.*

1. Do not shift tense needlessly. The italicized verbs are incorrect.

He filled seven boxes with his old books, then drove to a bookstore in New Haven, but all he *gets* for all those books *is* three dollars. [*Gets* should be *got*. *Is* should be *was*.]

2. Use the present perfect tense to indicate action that began in the past and has continued into the present. The italicized verb is incorrect:

Now that we *are* sitting here for three hours, finally the train comes. [*Are* should be *have been*.]

3. When referring to two different times in the past, use the past perfect tense for the earlier of the two times. The italicized verbs are wrong:

Though he was now lead guitarist for the rock group *The Opportunists*, he *played* in traditional dance bands. [*Played* should be *had played*.]

When Mr. Simms testified before the investigating committee last fall, he revealed the price-fixing conspiracy of which he *was* formerly a part, a conspiracy that *cheated* customers of millions of dollars. [*Was* should be *had been*. *Cheated* should be *had cheated*.]

Ti Weak *title*. See pp. 123–125.

Top S Need for a *topic sentence* that stands out clearly. See pp. 30–34.

Trans Need for *transitions*. See pp. 55–60 (the use of transitions in the paragraph); 111–113 (the short essay); 153–155 (the complex essay).

Trans P (or Trans ¶) Need for a *transitional paragraph*. See pp. 153–155.

Us Error in *usage*. The following are some troublesome points not covered by other entries.

affect, effect. *Affect*, in its chief use, is a verb meaning *to influence*. *Effect*, as a verb, means *to bring about* or *accomplish*; as a noun it usually means *a result*. For other meanings, consult your dictionary.

among, between. *Between* customarily indicates relations between only two things or groups of things (*between*

two parked cars / between the leader and his warriors).
Among is used when more than two are involved
(*among the cars in the parking lot / among the warriors*). When you are doubtful about which is appropriate, *between* is the better bet.

as, like. *Like* can be a preposition, the first word in a
prepositional phrase:

He danced *like a savage.*
They frowned at each other *like longtime enemies.*

In the practice of the best writers, *like* is still not used
as a conjunction. *As* (or *as if*) is the appropriate conjunction. When *as* serves this function it will usually be
followed by a verb or an understood verb:

He danced *as if he were* a savage.
They frowned at each other *as if they were* longtime enemies.
He jogged for half an hour through Cherokee Park, *as he had*
on every morning for the past fifteen years.

Wilfred Stone and J. G. Bell, in *Prose Style* (see the reference on p. 255), point out that sentences such as the
following seem especially tempting to writers with a
craving to replace *as* with *like:*

He drives as his father did.
He runs as Nagurski used to.

Messrs. Stone and Bell suggest the happy compromise
of replacing *as* with *the way:*

He drives the way his father did.
He runs the way Nagurski used to.

can, may. *Can* expresses ability; *may* expresses permis-
sibility or possibility:

He can answer that question without any trouble.
With that go-ahead from the Finance Committee, the Senate
may now vote on the bill.
If the Senate passes the bill, however, the House may still
defeat it.

different from, different than. *Different from* is generally preferable:

His opinion of the governor's proposal is much different from mine.

The course in modern American poetry was different from what the students had expected.

Modern English Usage, however, states that *"different than* is sometimes preferred by good writers to the cumbersome *different from that which* etc."* For example:

He is using the word in quite a different sense from that in which he used it yesterday.

He is using the word in quite a different sense than he did yesterday.

When faced with such alternatives, you may use whichever you prefer.

disinterested, uninterested. *Disinterested* means *impartial, unbiased. Uninterested* means *indifferent.* A judge should be *disinterested* but not *uninterested.*

farther, further. *Farther* refers to physical distance (*farther from home / five miles farther*). *Further* refers to other kinds of distance (*to investigate further / to ponder the problem further*).

fewer, less. *Fewer* refers to number (*fewer troubles / fewer parties / fewer friends*). *Less* refers to quantity (*less trouble / less party-going / less friendship*).

if, whether. *Whether* is preferable in indirect questions and statements of doubt:

Uncle Roscoe asked whether Baby Joe could eat two dips of ice cream.

Mr. Koplin wondered whether the rain would weaken the foundation of his house.

imply, infer. *Infer* means *to deduce:*

After listening to Marcia's muddled story Howard reluctantly inferred that she was a liar.

Imply means *to suggest:*

When he implied that she was not telling the whole truth, she professed righteous indignation.

lend, loan. *Lend* is a verb, *loan* a noun. The banker *lends* money. The needy man asks for a *loan.*

lie, lay. *Lie* means *to recline. Lay* means *to put* (something) *down.* The principal parts of the verbs are

Lie	*Lay*
Present: He *lies* on the coach.	He *lays* the book down.
Past: He *lay* . . .	He *laid* . . .
Present participle: He is *lying* . . .	He is *laying* . . .
Past participle: He has *lain* . . .	He has *laid* . . .

reason is because, reason is that. Use *that,* not *because:*

The reason for his failing the course is that he has fallen in love again.

split infinitive. This form of expression is often awkward and can usually be avoided.

With split infinitive: The government wished *to actually destroy* freedom of the press.

Improved: The government wished *to destroy* freedom of the press.

With split infinitive: He wished *to more thoroughly understand* the "God-is-dead" theologians.

Improved: He wished *to understand* the "God-is-dead" theologians *more thoroughly.*

try and, try to. *Try to* is preferable. *Try and stop him* actually tells you to do two things: you should *try, and* you should *stop him. Try to stop him* makes better sense.

Wdy *Wordy.* See pp. 229–234.

WE *Weak ending,* to a sentence, a paragraph, or an essay. See pp. 47–48 (the paragraph); 118–120 (the short essay); 149–150 (the complex essay); 216–219 (the sentence).

WO *Word order* is awkward, unclear, or illogical.

WV *Weak verb.* See pp. 222–227.

Selected Answers and Aids

1. *The paragraph-idea*

   I.   1. c.

   II.   1. b.

   III. Many possible answers.

   IV. Many possible answers.

   V.   1. d., a., c., b.

   VI. 1. a., c., b.

   VII. If you have trouble answering, review exercise VI.

2. *Clarifying and defending the paragraph-idea*

   I.   1. Answers will vary. One possible clarification is this: Usually she is serenely quiet or talks softly and sensibly; but occasionally she bursts into a frenzy and gabbles nonstop for hours.

2–9. Many possible answers.

II. 1. The first sentence states the paragraph-idea. Sentences 2–7 offer clarification. The supporting evidence begins, "I will furnish some circumstantial evidence. . . ."

3. Building a solid defense

I. 1. Not satisfactory. This idea, which has served as the main idea for several long essays, certainly could not be dealt with in a single paragraph.

2. Satisfactory. See Joseph Mitchell's paragraph on p. 61.

II. 1. a. The first sentence states the paragraph-idea.

b. No.

c. The paragraph-idea can be defended in a paragraph. Compare the present version with the original by James Thurber on p. 40.

2. a. The final sentence states the paragraph-idea.

b. Yes. This paragraph appears in Frederick Lewis Allen's *The Big Change* (with slight differences in wording).

3. Compare this version with the original by Eric Goldman on pp. 36–37.

4. a. The opening sentence.

b. Yes. This paragraph was written by Vance Packard in his article "America the Beautiful—and Its Desecraters" (*Atlantic*, August, 1961).

5. Compare this version with the original by Frederick Lewis Allen on pp. 48–49.

6. b., c. This paragraph was written by a professional author— Vance Packard, in "The Ad and the Id" (*Harper's Bazaar*, August, 1957). Nevertheless it might be argued that the evidence is not convincing. What is your opinion?

4. Topic and subtopic sentences

I. 1. The first sentence is the topic sentence.

II. 1. *Topic sentence:* "The people of Soapland [the world of radio soap operas] are subject to a set of special ills." *First subtopic sentence:* "Temporary blindness, preceded by dizzy spells and headaches, is a common affliction of Soapland people."

5. Arranging the evidence

I. 1. The order is spatial, and may also be said to proceed topic by topic. First Holmes's body is described (his height and weight); then his face (the eyes, nose, and chin); then his hands.

6. *Transitions*

   I. The following analysis attempts to list *all* the words that might be considered markers.

      1. *In time; began* (Would you say that a verb may act as a transitional marker?)

      2. *Then; just before; in the summer of 1923*

  II. Answers will vary. All possibilities are listed, even some words that provide only faint echoes of words in previous sentences.

      2. *He; castoff clothes* (echoing *bum* from the first sentence); *he; flophouses* (again echoing *bum*); *cheapest rooms in cheap hotels* (and again)

      3. *he; slept; in doorways* (still echoing *bum*)

7. *The essay-idea*

   I. If you have difficulty rearranging these statements, review exercise VI on pp. 11–12.

  II. 1. The most likely are *b* and *e*. Possibly *c* could be handled in a short essay too, but the development would have to be superficial.

  III. 1. The idea is too general.

      2. One fault is that the statement lacks unity. A few changes in wording would make it coherent: "During his childhood Theodore Dreiser experienced dire poverty, yet several of his later novels focus on a wealthy man—Frank Cowperwood, a 'financier' and 'titan' of industry."

         The idea has the additional flaw of being too obvious to be worth an essay. Dreiser's early poverty could be established in a paragraph or two, and Cowperwood's wealth is obvious from the titles of the two books about him.

         A more interesting idea would be this: "Dreiser's childhood poverty caused him later to adulate Frank Cowperwood, the 'financier' and 'titan' of industry." But this cause-and-effect relationship would be difficult to prove.

8. *Planning the paragraph-ideas*

   I. 1. The paragraphs would tell about the three swindles.

      2. The paragraphs would explain how Butler satirized each of those religious beliefs. Perhaps each belief could be dealt with in a paragraph or two.

9. *The Introduction: presenting the essay-idea and its clarification*
In this practice session and the next, you are asked to analyze a number of introductions; but there is no single correct analysis for any of them. Although the analyses provided here are probably fairly sound, you may have good reasons for disagreeing with some of them.

I. 1. *Essay-idea.* Sentence 1.

Explanation of any vague or unfamiliar words. The word Mr. Hutchins has to explain is *athleticism* from sentence 1. His explanation occupies sentences 2, 3, and 4.

Restatement in more specific terms. In sentence 4 Mr. Hutchins explains that athleticism is "sports promotion . . . carried on for the monetary profit of the colleges through the entertainment of the public."

Rejection of wrong meanings. We are told that athleticism is *not* athletics (sentence 2) and *not* physical education (sentence 4).

10. *The Introduction: catching the reader's attention*

I. 1. *Provocative essay-idea.* Sentences 3, 4, and 5.

Rejection of widely accepted opinions. The popular view is presented in sentences 1 and 2, then contradicted in 3, 4, and 5.

Descriptive details. Sentence 2.

III. 1. First statement of *essay-idea:* Second part of sentence 2: "slavery . . . seems to be increasing."

Techniques of clarification:

Restatement in more specific terms. Sentence 3. And possibly a *rejection of wrong meanings* is found in sentence 2: "far from being a vanishing anachronism."

Techniques for attention-getting:

Provocative essay-idea. Sentence 2. Sentence 3 adds extra provocation by saying that some nations in which slave-owning is permitted are the protectorates of Western powers.

Rejection of widely accepted opinions. The popular view is stated in sentence 1, then contradicted in 2 and 3.

The occasion for writing. Sentence 1: debates in the United Nations.

Historical events. Sentences 2 and 3.

11. *Continuity*

I. If you have difficulty arranging these paragraph-ideas, review exercise II on pp. 51–53.

III. 1.
      I. London, shows, happy, population
     II. public, entertainment, the public

IV. 1. for, dragonflies, insect, pioneers (echoing *ancestors*), earliest forms

    2. trees (echoing *jungle*), that day, the club moss and the ground pines (possibly reminiscent of *jungle*), dragonfly

15. The introduction and the conclusion

If exercise I gives you trouble, review Chapters 9 and 10. If you find exercise II difficult, review Chapter 12.

16. Continuity

  I. If you find this exercise difficult, review exercise I on pp. 113–115.

 II. 1. *Section-idea coming before:* The basic urges of man do not vary from era to era.

    Section-idea coming after: The way the urges are expressed varies greatly from culture to culture and within the same culture from time to time and from class to class.

17. Extreme formality and extreme colloquialism

  I. 3. H. L. Mencken quotes this paragraph in his essay on Veblen, then offers these comments:

> Well, what have we here? What does this appalling salvo of rhetorical artillery signify? What was the sweating professor trying to say? Simply that in the course of time the worship of God is commonly corrupted by other enterprises, and that the church, ceasing to be a mere temple of adoration, becomes the headquarters of these other enterprises. More simply still, that men sometimes vary serving God by serving other men, which means, of course, serving themselves. This bald platitude, which must be obvious to any child who has ever been to a church bazaar, was here tortured, worried and run through rollers until it spread out to 241 words, of which fully 200 were unnecessary.
>
>   "Professor Veblen," *A Mencken Chrestomathy*

    Do you think that Mencken oversimplifies?

 II, III, and IV. Answers will vary.

  V. Here are Mr. Tate's original sentences—much more forceful than the vulgarized revisions of them.

1. Before the men of the Eleventh Corps could get to their
   (a)
feet, a horde of yelling demons, rising out of the earth, were
      (b)   (c)   (d)
upon them.

2. Far to the north and south the long, ragged gray lines
                                              (a)
moved forward like a machine.
      (b)   (c)

3. The lazy pickets of the Federals fired a few scattered
       (a)   (b)
shots, and fled.
               (c)

4. The Confederates came steadily on like a giant harvester,
                     (a)   (b)
cutting down the men trying to stand before them.
    (c)   (d)   (e)

5. At Talley's farm scattered [Federal] regiments lined up
                   (a)   (b)
behind breastworks to meet the onset.
                     (c)

6. In the reeling smoke the defenders looked out and saw
          (a)   (b)   (c)
the vast mass of the Confederates: they saw the flash of the
     (d)   (e)
rifles, the oncoming battle flags, the tanned faces, the blaz-
            (f)   (g)
ing eyes of their mysterious, terrible foes.
                             (h)

7. All their mounted officers tumbled like bags of meal to
   (a)   (b)   (c)
the ground.

8. The defenders fell back in panic.
       (a)   (b)   (c)

VI. Here is Mr. Thurber's original:

I passed all the other courses that I took at my University,
but I could never pass botany. This was because all botany
students had to spend several hours a week in a laboratory
looking through a microscope at plant cells, and I could
never see through a microscope. This used to enrage my instructor. He would wander around the laboratory pleased
with the progress all the students were making in drawing

the involved and, so I am told, interesting structure of flower cells, until he came to me. I would just be standing there. "I can't see anything," I would say. He would begin patiently enough, explaining how anybody can see through a microscope, but he would always end up in a fury, claiming that I could *too* see through a microscope but just pretended that I couldn't. . . .

"University Days," *My Life and Hard Times*

VIII. Here is a colloquialized rendition of the first few sentences:

You know, the critics of this great country of ours ought to pay some mind to this fellow Faulkner. His books are pretty tough going, but they're worth every minute of it. He's put out a lot of stuff and it's about a lot of different fascinating people and places. Sometimes he makes the tears come to your eyes, and other times he makes you come out with a belly-laugh right from the heels.

18. *The informal style*

I. 5. This is Mr. Warren's original, from "A Lesson Read in American Books," *New York Times Magazine*, Dec. 11, 1955.

II. 1. Middle informal
2. Middle informal
3. High informal, almost formal

19. *Choosing the right synonym*

I. 1. *Authoritarian* should be *authoritative*.
2. *Uninterested* should be *disinterested*. *Judicial* should be *judicious*.

II. Many possible answers.

III. 1. a. challenged
b. supernatural
3. a. notorious
b. a meager
j. manufacturers (Why not *creators* or *originators?*)
4. a. insignificant
b. a bitter

IV. I agree with Mr. Kirschbaum and offer the following evidence, much of which is derived from Mr. Kirschbaum's own analysis of the essay.

Sentence 1:

a stirring book. Hackneyed.

right. Vague. Are the people *right* in their beliefs about matters of fact, *right* in their political beliefs, morally *right*, or what?

Sentence 2:

proving. Inaccurate. One may *believe* that the people are "mostly right," and may offer evidence, even persuasive evidence, in favor of the belief, but I doubt that one can conclusively *prove* it.

Sentence 3:

quotes chapter and verse. Hackneyed and vague.

several light years ahead. Hackneyed and exaggerated.

Sentence 4:

buried in a cloud of dust. Hackneyed and exaggerated.

Sentence 8:

snowed . . . under. Hackneyed.

as much as he pleased. Exaggerated.

Sentence 11:

anyone. Exaggerated. Did *no one* expect a world state to be imminent?

Sentence 12:

very cheerful news. The *very* is unnecessary. Even the *cheerful* is dubious. By reading sentences 6–11 critically, one might easily draw conclusions that are not so cheerful: The people distrust new ideas and ignore warnings. Only after calamities are upon them do they begin to discard their traditional beliefs.

when all is said and done. Hackneyed.

Sentence 13:

sound biological sense. What is *biological sense?*

Sentence 14:

hurricane . . . which came down the street. Hackneyed and exaggerated.

would long since have become extinct. Vague and probably exaggerated.

Sentence 15:

somebody, somewhere, has stored up a little wisdom. This is so obvious that it is not worth stating—especially not in the last line of an essay.

20. *Familiar words and specific words*

I. Answers will vary.

II. 1. Answers will vary. One possibility is: A lady was jabbering to five or six children about the delights of owning a canary.

2–12. Answers will vary.

III. Answers will vary.

IV. 2. Here is one rendering of the first and second sentences into plain English:

> The typical confidence man or swindler steals from people by lying to them. He tricks them into believing that they will receive something valuable for whatever they give him.

21. *Tying ideas together: coordination*

Here are the original passages from which the chopped-up exercises were derived. Of course, your revisions may differ from the originals but still be satisfactory.

1. Last spring we decided the croquet set was beyond use, and invested in a rather fancy new one with hoops set in small wooden sockets, and mallets with rubber faces.

E. B. WHITE

2. The [croquet] course is now exactly seventy-two feet long and we lined the wickets up with a string; but the little boy is less fond of it now, for we make him keep still while we are shooting.

E. B. WHITE

3. Athleticism is not physical education but sports promotion, and it is carried on for the monetary profit of the college through the entertainment of the public.

ROBERT MAYNARD HUTCHINS

4. [To be attractive to the female,] . . . man had to go in for somersaults, tilting with lances, and performing feats of parlor magic to win her attention; he also had to bring her candy, flowers and the furs of animals.

JAMES THURBER, "Courtship Through the Ages,"
My World and Welcome to It

5. . . . In spite of all these "love displays" the male is constantly being turned down, insulted, or thrown out of the house.

JAMES THURBER, "Courtship Through the Ages,"
My World and Welcome to It

6. Road signs shout romance, transmitters croon it, juke-boxes yowl it.

FREDERIC MORTON

7. Romance bulges on Cinemascope screens, flickers from TV sets, gleams on magazine covers.

FREDERIC MORTON

8. A whole galaxy of industries labors to lure him to her with perfumes, parasols, pendants; her to him with the checks on his shirt, the monogram on his belt, the shaving lotion on his jaws.

FREDERIC MORTON

9. The sand of the desert or the encroaching sea turns fertile fields into barren wastes, and reduces whole populations to distress or starvation.

W. MACNEILE DIXON

10. [Euphemism] ... is the tendency to call a spade "a certain garden implement" or women's underwear "unmentionables."

PAUL ROBERTS

11. [The tendency toward euphemism] ... is stronger in some eras than others and in some people than others but it always operates more or less in subjects that are touchy or taboo: death, sex, madness, and so on.

PAUL ROBERTS

12. Thus we shrink from saying "He died last night" but say instead "passed away," "left us," "joined his Maker," "went to his reward."

PAUL ROBERTS

13. By looking at [Wallace's] ... mouth, one could tell whether he was plotting evil or had recently accomplished it.

RICHARD ROVERE

14. [In the world of soap opera a character's] loss of the use of the legs may be either temporary or permanent.

JAMES THURBER

15. [The Lansings'] large rooms are carpeted wall-to-wall in a neutral shade, the sofas and chairs are covered either in

flowered muted chintz or in beige brocade, and the curtains drawn across the windows are of matching chintz.

MARYA MANNES

16. The Lansings have comfort for their money but no fun, and the observant guest cannot help but pity such spiritual constipation.

MARYA MANNES

17. [In some places] if individuals are caught in an incestuous act, they either commit suicide or are killed by their relatives.

HORTENSE POWDERMAKER

18. The breaking of this taboo is thought to endanger the very life of the society in some terrible but indefinable way, and the death of the violators serves as a kind of appeasement.

HORTENSE POWDERMAKER

19. College is the greatest place in the world for those who ought to go to college and who go for the right reasons.

ROBERT MAYNARD HUTCHINS

20. For those who ought not to go to college or who go for the wrong reasons, college is a waste of time and money.

ROBERT MAYNARD HUTCHINS

21. Let us spell out the worst about this notorious mass-man and his mass-culture. He has a meager idea of the abundant life, confusing quantity with quality, size with greatness, comfort with culture, gadgetry with genius. He has as little appreciation of pure science as of the fine arts, and as little capacity for the discipline that both require; although he may stand in awe of them his real veneration goes to the engineers and inventors, the manufacturers of True Romances and Tin Pan Alley airs. He is frequently illiberal, suspicious of "radical" ideas, scornful of "visionary" ideals, hostile to "aliens". . . .

HERBERT J. MULLER, *The Uses of the Past*

23. *The end of the sentence*

I. Answers will vary. Here are some possibilities.

1. He realized that the anatomy course would be expensive when

he saw that he had to buy a lab apron, two textbooks, a dissecting kit, and a microscope. [In order of ascending cost.]

4. The warden stated that now that the rioting prisoners had killed once, they might kill again.

14. Veblen claimed that we judge even tableware by what he called "pecuniary canons of taste."

(Another possibility: Veblen claimed that we apply what he called "pecuniary canons of taste" even to tableware.)

24. *Weak verbs and strong verbs*

I. Answers will vary. Here are some possibilities.

1. When the king visited the United States in 1954, he observed a game called *baseball*.

2. He had several reasons for taking a year off from college. (Possibly you would prefer: He had several reasons for leaving college for a year.)

12. This sentence is probably satisfactory as it stands. True, the first and last clauses contain verbs in the passive voice: Ketchum *was hit*, and he *had to be carried*. But passive voice is suitable here. Because Ketchum is the center of interest in the sentence, we are entitled to make him the subject of those clauses even if we must employ passive voice to do so. Anyone who insisted on using active voice would have to write something like this: *Immediately after the pitch hit Ketchum on the head, he dropped to the ground and lay there motionless, until finally some men had to carry him off the field on a stretcher.* Isn't this inferior to the original? In this version, the pitch and "some men" snare some of the attention that should go to Ketchum.

25. *Conciseness*

II. Here are the originals.

1. (1, 2)The brown rat is as supple as rubber and it can squeeze and contort itself through openings half its size. (3) It has strong jaws and long, curved incisors with sharp cutting edges. (4)It can gnaw a notch big enough to accomodate its body in an oak plank, a slate shingle, or a sun-dried brick. (5)Attracted by the sound of running water, it will gnaw into lead pipe.... (6)All rats are vandals, but the brown is the most ruthless. (7)It destroys far more than it

actually consumes. (8)Instead of completely eating a few potatoes, it takes a bite out of dozens. (9, 10, 11)It will methodically ruin all the apples and pears in a grocery in a night. (12, 13)To get a small quantity of nesting material, it will cut great quantities of garments, rugs, upholstery, and books to tatters. (14)In warehouses, it sometimes goes berserk. (15, 16, 17)In a few hours a pack will rip holes in hundreds of sacks of flour, grain, coffee, and other foodstuffs, spilling and fouling the contents and making an overwhelming mess. (18)Now and then, in live-poultry markets, a lust for blood seems to take hold of the brown rat. (19, 20) One night, in the poultry part of old Gansevort Market . . . a burrow of them bit the throats of over three hundred broilers and ate less than a dozen. (21)Before this part of the market was abandoned . . . the rats practically had charge of it. (22)Some of them nested in the drawers of desks. (23) When the drawers were pulled open, they leaped out, snarling.

JOSEPH MITCHELL, "The Rats on the Waterfront,"
The Bottom of the Harbor

2.   (1)I have never had much patience with the writers who claim from the reader an effort to understand their meaning. (2)You have only to go to the great philosophers to see that it is possible to express with lucidity the most subtle reflections. (3,4)You may find it difficult to understand the thought of Hume, and if you have no philosophical training its implications will doubtless escape you; but no one with any education at all can fail to understand exactly what the meaning of each sentence is. (5)Few people have written English with more grace than Berkeley. . . .

(6)[One] cause of obscurity is that the writer is himself not quite sure of his meaning. (7, 8, 9, 10, 11)He has a vague impression of what he wants to say, but has not, either from lack of mental power or from laziness, exactly formulated it in his mind and it is natural enough that he should not find a precise expression for a confused idea. . . . (12, 13)Some writers who do not think clearly are inclined to suppose that their thoughts have a significance greater than at first sight appears. (14, 15, 16, 17)It is flattering to believe that they are too profound to be expressed so clearly that all who run may read, and very naturally it does not occur to such

writers that the fault is with their own minds which have
not the faculty of precise reflection. . . .

SOMERSET MAUGHAM, The Summing Up

(Possibly the phrase *very naturally* in the last sentence is wordy and even
illogical. Is the *very* needed?)

> 3. (1)Vigorous writing is concise. (2, 3)A sentence should
> contain no unnecessary words, a paragraph no unnecessary
> sentences, for the same reason that a drawing should have no
> unnecessary lines and a machine no unnecessary parts. (4,
> 5, 6, 7)This requires not that the writer make all his sen-
> tences short, or that he avoid all detail and treat his subjects
> only in outline, but that every word tell.

WILLIAM STRUNK, JR., and E. B. WHITE,
The Elements of Style

26. *Keeping sentences clear*

I. Answers will vary.

II. I cite the troublesome pronoun or two in each sentence, then offer
a revision. Obviously your own revisions may differ from these
and still be quite clear.

    1. *Troublesome pronoun: he* was a graduate student
Revision: Bainbridge first met Dusseldorf while Bainbridge was a
graduate student at the University of Bavaria.

    2. *Pronoun: he* complained
Revision: When the city editor assigned Hargis to make the
interview, Hargis complained that the reporters had been getting
too many difficult assignments lately.

III. 1. *Troublesome modifier:* After passing . . . first down
Possible revision: After our quarterback had passed successfully
for a first down, Grandmother cheered for him.

    2. *Modifier:* Developing an interest . . . poetry
Revision: Because Michael was developing an interest in writing poetry, his classmates began to regard him as an odd and
possibly demented boy who might just as well be avoided.

    3. *Modifier:* while practicing . . . professional
Revision: While practicing under the guidance of the country-
club professional, he was steadily improving his backhand.

    4. *Modifier:* that was devoured . . . time to cool
Revision: For the baking contest the mother made an apple pie
that was devoured by the boys before it had time to cool.

Index

2035 Orchard Lane
Merced, Ca. 95340

Include
Subordinate clause phrases

Darwin - Evolution